English Lexicology and Vocabulary Building for College Students

（2nd Edition）

大学实用英语词汇教程

（第2版）

主　编◎张莱湘
副主编◎毕晓宁　张晨花
编　者◎徐　斐　罗　勤

北京理工大学出版社
BEIJING INSTITUTE OF TECHNOLOGY PRESS

图书在版编目（CIP）数据

大学实用英语词汇教程／张莱湘主编．—2 版．—北京：北京理工大学出版社，2019.9（2022.7重印）

ISBN 978-7-5682-7580-4

Ⅰ．①大… Ⅱ．①张… Ⅲ．①英语-词汇-高等学校-教材 Ⅳ．①H313

中国版本图书馆 CIP 数据核字（2019）第 201162 号

出版发行／北京理工大学出版社有限责任公司
社　　址／北京市海淀区中关村南大街 5 号
邮　　编／100081
电　　话／（010）68914775（总编室）
　　　　　（010）82562903（教材售后服务热线）
　　　　　（010）68944723（其他图书服务热线）
网　　址／http://www.bitpress.com.cn
经　　销／全国各地新华书店
印　　刷／廊坊市印艺阁数字科技有限公司
开　　本／787 毫米×1092 毫米　1/16
印　　张／18
字　　数／423 千字
版　　次／2019 年 9 月第 2 版　2022 年 7 月第 2 次印刷
定　　价／68.00 元

责任编辑／梁铜华
文案编辑／梁铜华
责任校对／刘亚男
责任印制／李志强

图书出现印装质量问题，请拨打售后服务热线，本社负责调换

再版说明

WHAT IS NEW

本书是2013年北京理工大学出版社出版的《大学实用英语词汇教程》的再版。

该书的2013年第一版，是对几位有多年一线丰富教学经验的词汇课程老师的教学讲义的综合，主要由三大板块构成：词汇学理论、分类词根及主题分类词汇。该书在六年的教学实践检验过程中，也陆续收到了各种鼓舞编者的赞扬和切合实际的批评建议。因此，在充分吸纳了诸位语言学习者及教学从业者的宝贵意见后，再版时编者们对该书就以下几个方面做了相应调整。

1. 剔除大众非常熟知的词汇示例和一些过时的词义，突出词根板块词汇示例的实用性和指导性。

2. 替换部分过分依赖于语境或语义模糊的例句，便于读者全面了解词汇用法。

3. 增加常用词缀内容，有助于语言学习者活学活用。

4. 增加词汇搭配内容。因为编者在教学实践中发现，语言学习者通过练习或记忆的方式掌握了各种词汇，但是还不能恰当使用它们，因此增加了单词搭配（Collocation）章节。

由上可见，再版后的《大学实用英语词汇教程》各个知识板块结构比例更加合理，练习内容的实用性和指导性增强。当然，这一切都得益于各位教材使用者和教学从业者对本书的厚爱、中肯的建议和使用心得，是他们让这本书可以走得更远。寥寥数百字难以表达编者们的感谢之情，只愿再版后的书能为诸位带来更多实际的益处。

前言

PREFACE

词是语言表意的基本单位，脱离词汇，人们无法进行交流与沟通。为了让大学生全面了解英语词汇的演变和发展，以及词汇的内部结构特征，从而扩大词汇量，提高正确使用词汇的能力，我们编写了这本《大学实用英语词汇教程》。

本书体现了“理论为基础，自主趣味学”的理念，由三大板块构成：词汇学理论、分类词根和主题分类词汇。

第一部分以词汇学理论为基础，打破以往介绍词汇学理论只供英语专业学生学习的模式，在本书开始部分向非英语专业的大学生简要介绍英语词汇的基本概念、词汇发展的历史、词汇的构成方法、词汇的不同含义、词义关系、词义变化、词义和上下文的关系等内容，让学生的词汇学习有理论基础，且有文化内涵。

第二部分以分类方式介绍词根，把零散的词根分成“生命之旅”“敢作敢为”“听说睹写”“喜恶悲惧”“心灵世界”“自然宇宙”“战争之束”“法治社会”等八大领域，方便学生记忆。

第三部分围绕主题，特别设计在语境下介绍词汇的使用，提高学生正确使用词汇的能力。主题的选定考虑有趣、有用、有内涵三个原则，选取和学生日常生活相关的“Weather”“Health”“Character”“Crime”“At Home”“Money”“Arts”“Education”“Sports”等话题。借助一些图片，提高学生的兴趣，加深学生对词汇的记忆。

三大部分都设计了形式多样的练习题，使学生的词汇学习脱离了孤立的单词记忆，将学习词汇和巩固练习相结合，从而提高记忆效率。

本书突出实用性，通过向学生介绍词汇的历史、来源等，给学生提供分析词汇、了解词汇的新途径，使学生在英语学习过程中能利用学到的理论和方法来分析词汇，提高英语学习的乐趣和效率。编者坚信，本书对大学生全面提高词汇能力大有裨益。

本书在编写过程中得到北京理工大学外国语学院和北京理工大学出版社的大力支持，谨在此表示衷心的感谢。

由于水平有限，书中会存在疏漏和欠妥之处，欢迎读者和同行批评指正。

编　者

目 录
CONTENTS

Part I　Lexicology

Part II　Basic Roots and Words

Part III　Vocabulary in Context

Keys to Exercises

Appendixes

References

Part I Lexicology

Chapter One

Basic Concepts of Words and Vocabulary

Words are the building blocks of the English language, and in lexicology, basic concepts such as words and vocabulary need to be expounded before exploring word formation and word meaning.

1.1 The Definition of a Word

The definition of a word has always been controversial. Experts and linguists still do not agree on all aspects of a word.

In visual terms, a word can be defined as a meaningful group of letters. In terms of spoken language, a word is viewed as a sound or combination of sounds. In the eyes of semanticists, a word is a unit of meaning. To grammarians, a word is a free form that can function in a sentence.

To sum up, the definition of a word comprises the following points:

(1) A minimal free form of a language.

(2) A sound unity.

(3) A unit of meaning.

(4) A form that can function alone in a sentence.

A word is a minimal free form of a language that has a given sound and meaning and syntactic function.

1.2 Vocabulary

All the words in a language make up what is generally known as its vocabulary. It can refer to the total number of the words in a language, and it can stand for all the words used in a particular historical period. We can also use it to refer to all the words of a given dialect, a given book, a given discipline and the words possessed by an individual person. The general estimate of the present-day English vocabulary is over one million words.

1.3 Sound and Meaning

A word is a symbol that stands for something in the world. There is a symbolic connection between the sound and the referent, which is always arbitrary and conventional; there is no logical relationship between the two but people of the same speech community agree to the symbolic relationship. A dog is called a dog not because the sound and the three letters that make up the word just automatically suggest the animal in question. The same language may use the same sound to mean different things and different languages may use different sounds to refer to the same thing.

1.4 Sound and Form

The written form of a natural language is the written record of the oral form. Naturally the written form should agree with the oral form—The sound should be consistent with the form. This is fairly true of English in its earliest stage. In Old English, the speech of the time was represented very much more faithfully in writing than it is today. However, with the development of the language, discrepancies arose.

The internal reason for this is that the English alphabet was adopted from the Romans, which does not have a separate letter to represent each sound in the language so that some letters must do double duty or work together in combination.

Another reason is that the pronunciation has changed more rapidly than spelling over the years, and in some cases the two have drawn far apart.

The third reason is that some of the differences were created by the early scribes to make a line even or for easier recognition. The letters of some short vertical strokes such as *i*, *u*, *v*, *m*, *w*, *n* looked all alike. Consequently, their handwriting caused misunderstanding. To solve the problem in part, the letter *u* was changed into *o* when it came before *m*, *n*, *v*. This is how *sum*, *cum*, *wuman*, *wunder*, *munk* came to be written as *some*, *come*, *woman*, *wonder*, *monk*. Later, printing and dictionary helped to standardize and freeze the spelling of words.

Finally comes the borrowing, which is an important channel of enriching the English vocabulary. The large scale of borrowing words from different languages complicated the situation. Some borrowings stay in their former form and pronunciation; others have their pronunciation or spelling assimilated but not quite conforming to the rules of English language.

All in all, the written form of English is not a perfect representation of its spoken form.

1.5 The Classification of Words

Words may fall into the basic word stock and non-basic vocabulary by use frequency, into content words and functional words by notion, and into native words and borrowed words by origin.

1.5.1 Basic Word Stock and Non-basic Vocabulary

Basic Word Stock

The basic word stock is the foundation of the vocabulary accumulated over centuries and forms the common core of the language. Though words of the basic word stock constitute a small percentage of the English vocabulary, yet it is the most important part of it. These words have obvious characteristics.

1) All National Character

Words of the basic word stock denote the most common things and phenomena of the world around us, which are indispensable to all the people who speak the language.

They include words relating to:

Natural phenomena: rain, snow, fire, water, sun, moon, spring, wind, hill...

Human body and relations: head, foot, hand, face, father, mother, brother, sister, son, daughter...

Plants and animals: oak, pine, grass, pear, apple, tree, horse, cow, sheep, cat, dog, chicken...

Action, size, domain, and state: come, go, eat, hear, beat, carry, good, evil, old, young, hot, cold, heavy, white, black...

Numerals, pronouns, prepositions, and conjunctions: one, ten, hundred, I, you, your, who, in, out, under, and, but, till, as...

2) Stability

Words of the basic word stock have been in use for centuries. As they denote the commonest things necessary to life, they are likely to remain unchanged.

3) Productivity

Words of the basic word stock are mostly root words or monosyllabic words. They can each be used alone, and at the same time can form new words with other roots and affixes.

4) Polysemy

Words belonging to the basic word stock often have more than one meaning because most of them have undergone semantic changes in the course of use and thus become polysemous.

5) Collocability

Many words of the basic word stock enter quite a number of set expressions, idiomatic usages, proverbial sayings and the like.

Non-basic Words include the following categories:

(1) **Terminology** consists of the technical terms used in particular disciplines and academic areas (penicillin, algebra).

(2) **Jargon** refers to the specialized vocabularies by which members of particular arts, sciences, trades or professions communicate among themselves (paranoid for suspicious).

(3) **Slang** is a substandard language not acceptable in serious speech (buck for dollar). Slang is created by changing or extending the meaning of existing words though some slang words are new coinages altogether. Slang is colorful, blunt, expressive and impressive.

(4) **Argot** generally refers to the jargon of criminals (dip for pickpocket).

(5) **Dialectal Words** are the words used only by the speakers of the dialect in question (beauty for excellent in Australian English).

(6) **Archaisms** are the words or forms that were once in common use but are now restricted only to the specialized or limited use (thou for you, and quoth for said).

(7) **Neologisms** are the newly-created words or expressions, or words that have taken on new meanings (futurology, seckill).

1.5.2 Content Words and Functional Words

By notion, words can be grouped into content words and functional words.

Content words denote clear notions and thus are known as notional words. They include nouns, verbs, adjectives, adverbs and numerals, which denote objects, phenomena, actions, qualities, states, degrees, and quantities.

Functional words do not have the notions of their own. Therefore, they are also called empty words. As their chief function is to express the relation between notions, the relation between words as well as between sentences, they are known as form words. Pronouns, prepositions, conjunctions, auxiliaries and articles belong to this category.

However, functional words do far more work of expression in English on average than content words.

1.5.3 Native Words and Borrowed Words

Native Words

Native words are the words brought to Britain in the fifth century by the German tribes: the Angles, the Saxons, and the Jutes, thus known as Anglo-Saxon words. Native words are limited in number, but form the core of the English language.

Apart from the characteristics mentioned of the basic word stock, in contrast to borrowed words, native words have two other features:

(1) Neutral in style: They are not stylistically specific. Stylistically, native words are neither formal nor informal, whereas the words borrowed from French or Latin are literary and learned, thus appropriate in formal style.

(2) Frequent in use: Native words are most frequently used in everyday speech and writing.

Borrowed Words

Words taken over from foreign languages are known as borrowed words or loan words or borrowings in simple terms. It is estimated that English borrowings constitute 80 percent of the modern English vocabulary. The English language is noted for the remarkable complexity and heterogeneity of its vocabulary because of its extensive borrowings. Borrowed words are divided into 4 types.

(1) **Denizens** are borrowed words early in the past and now assimilated into English words such as *pork* (French) and *change* (French).

(2) **Aliens** are the borrowed words which have retained their original pronunciation and

spelling such as *blitz* (Greek) and *kowtow* (Chinese). These words are immediately recognizable as foreign in origin.

(3) **Translation-loans** are the words and expressions formed from the existing material in the English language but modeled on the patterns of another language such as *mother tongue* (Latin) and *long time no see* (Chinese).

(4) **Semantic-loans** are the native forms with borrowed meaning. The words of this category are not borrowed with reference to the form. But their meanings are borrowed such as *dream* and *pioneer*. *Dream* originally meant "joy" and "music," and borrowed from the Norse its modern meaning. *Pioneer* originally meant "explorer" and later borrowed the new meaning of "a member of the Young Pioneer" from Russian. In other words, English has borrowed a new meaning for an existing word in the language.

Quiz of Chapter One

I. Choose the best answer.

1. In Old English there was ________ agreement between sound and form.

   A. more B. little C. less D. gradual

2. Which of the following words is a functional word? ________.

   A. Often B. Never C. Although D. Desk

3. The term "vocabulary" is used in different ways because of all the following reasons EXCEPT that ________.

   A. it can refer to the common core of a language

   B. it can refer to the total number of the words in a language

   C. it can represent all the words used in a certain historical period

   D. it can stand for words in a given dialect or field

4. Which of the following characteristics of the basic word stock is the most significant? ________.

   A. Stability B. Collocability C. Productivity D. National character

5. The written form of English is a(an) ________ representation of the spoken form.

   A. selective B. adequate C. imperfect D. natural

6. Which of the following is NOT correct?

   A. A word is a meaningful group of letters.

   B. A word is a unit of meaning.

   C. A word is a sound or combination of sounds.

   D. A word is a form that cannot function alone in a sentence.

7. Words fall into the basic word stock and non-basic vocabulary by ________.

   A. use frequency B. notion C. productivity D. origin

8. The pronunciation has changed ________ spelling over the years.

   A. more slowly than B. as quickly as

C. more rapidly than　　　　　　　　　　D. not so quickly as

9. The differences between sound and form are due to the following EXCEPT ________.

A. the fact of more phonemes than letters in English

B. the stabilization of spelling by printing

C. the influence of the work of scribes

D. the innovations made by linguists

10. There are ________ functional words in the following sentence: *I like to see a movie.*

A. 2　　　　B. 3　　　　C. 4　　　　D. 5

II. Fill in the blanks.

1 The basic word stock forms the common ________ of the language.

2. The relationship between the sound and meaning is arbitrary or ________.

3. According to semanticists, a word is a unit of ________.

4. A word is a ________ form of a language that has a given sound and meaning and syntactic function.

Chapter Two
The Development of English Vocabulary

It is estimated that there are about 5, 000 languages all over the world, which can be grouped into about 300 language families, such as Sino-Tibetan Family, Indo-European Family and so on.

Chinese is a member in the Sino-Tibetan Family, while English is a member in the Indo-European Family, which hosts most languages of Europe, the Near East, and India. The branch of Indo-European (See Appendix One) that includes English is called the Germanic group.

The English people are of a mixed blood. The early inhabitants of the island we now call England were Celts or Britons. In 55 B.C. Britain was invaded by the Roman conqueror Julius Caesar. In 410 A.D. all the Roman troops returned to the Continent, thus ending the Roman occupation of Britain.

At the beginning of the fifth century Britain was invaded by the three tribes from Northern Europe: the Angles, Saxons and Jutes. These three tribes merged into one, and the three dialects they spoke naturally grew into a single language—the English language.

The history of the English language is divided into three periods:

(1) The Old English (450–1150).

(2) The Middle English (1150–1500).

(3) The Modern English (1500–present).

2.1 The Old English (450–1150)

The history of the English language begins with the conquest and settlement of what is now England by the Angles, Saxons, and Jutes from about 450 A.D. The language they spoke was Anglo-Saxon, which replaced the Celtic spoken by the former inhabitants Celts.

The OE (Old English) vocabulary, estimated at the size of 50, 000 to 60, 000 words, is almost purely Germanic. Although some 85% of it is no longer in use, those that survive all belong to the basic word stock of Modern English.

Owing to the Christianizing of Britain and the Vikings' invasions, the relatively few borrowings are mainly Latin and Scandinavian. Some 500 Latin words, many of which have to do with religious life (*candle*, *amen*, *apostle*, *altar*, etc.) appear in English writings. At least 900 everyday words of Scandinavian origin (*skill*, *skirt*, *egg*, *get*, *they*, *leg*, etc.) have survived in Modern Standard English.

2.2 The Middle English (1150-1500)

The Middle English period is from 1150 to 1500. The most important event to affect the history of English, the Norman Conquest (1066), took place at the end of the Old English period. The big changes that this invasion produced in the English society were accompanied by equal effects in the vocabulary of Middle English.

After their victory in 1066 at the Battle of Hastings under William the Conqueror, the Normans quickly assumed leadership and privilege in England. The Normans were originally Vikings—their name comes from North man (i.e., Norse). In a sense, the Norman Conquest can be seen as yet another Germanic invasion. But there was a difference this time. The Normans had earlier been given the control of a large piece of land along the northern coast of France—Normandy. As French subjects, they had adopted French culture. So the language they brought with them was not a Germanic language, but French.

The Norman French imposed a new political and cultural life on the land of Anglo-Saxon, and changed greatly the development of the English language. The Norman Conquest virtually introduced French-English bilingualism into England. The English were defeated, but not killed off, nor were they driven from their country. They were reduced to the status of an inferior people. Norman French became the polite speech. The Norman dialect of French became the language of the upper class, while English completely lost its scholarly and literary importance, and was used only by the peasants and people of the working class.

By the end of the 11th century, almost all of the people who held political or social power and many of those in powerful church positions were of Norman French origin. This resulted in a massive borrowing of French words into the English vocabulary.

By the end of the 13th century, English gradually came back into schools, law courts, and government and regained social status thanks to Wycliff's translation of the Bible and the writings of Chaucer.

Between 1250 and 1500, about 9,000 words of French origin (*state*, *power*, *prince*, *duke*, *pork*, *bacon*, *fry*, *coat*, *dress*, *mercy*, *peace*, etc.) poured into English. We can find those words relating to every aspect of human society.

2.3 Modern English (1500-present)

2.3.1 Early Modern English Period (1500-1700)

Modern English began with the establishment of printing in England. In the early period of Modern English, Europe saw a new upsurge of learning ancient Greek and Roman classics. This is known in history as the Renaissance.

Thanks to the Renaissance (early 14th C-1650), great numbers of Latin and Greek words were added to English. Latin and Greek were recognized as the languages of the Western world's great literary heritage and of great scholarship. Scholars translated literature from Latin and Greek into English, so over 10,000 Latin words (*focus*, *status*, *bonus*, *genius*, *criteria*, *species*, etc.) and Greek words (*democracy*, *logic*, *philosophy*, *astronomy*, *mathematics*, *alphabet*, *drama*, *grammar*, *poem*, *chaos*, *method*, *mystery*, etc.) entered the English language.

2.3.2 Late Modern English Period (1700-present)

This was a time of stabilizing and purifying the English language. Samuel Johnson edited *A Dictionary of the English Language* (*1755*), setting standards for using English words in spelling, meaning and usage.

In the mid-seventeenth century, England experienced Bourgeois Revolution followed by the Industrial Revolution and rose to be a great economic power. With the growth of colonization, British tentacles began stretching out to every corner of the globe, absorbing words from all major languages of the world.

The 19th and 20th centuries saw an unprecedented growth in the scientific vocabulary as a consequence of the industrial revolution and the scientific exploration and discovery. Since the beginning of the last century, especially, after World War II, the world has seen breathtaking advances in science and technology. Many new words have been created to express new ideas, yet more words are created by means of word formation.

2.4 Growth of Present-day English

Today, new words sweep in at a rate much faster than at any other historical period of time. New words are being invented or introduced every day to express new things and new changes in society, both material and intellectual. Meanwhile, they are coined and used to arouse public attention and interest. In time they gain acceptance and become part of the English vocabulary. Generally, there are three main sources of new words: the rapid development of modern science and technology; social, economic and political changes; and the influence of other cultures and languages.

2.4.1 Advance in Science and Technology

Since the end of World War II, tremendous new advances in all fields of science and technology have given rise to the creation in the English language of tens of thousands of new words. The great majority of these are technical terms known only to the specialists, but a certain number of them have become familiar to the public and passed into general use.

E.g. Words used in connection with the nuclear bomb: *chain reaction* (连锁反应), *radioactivity*(放射), *fall-out*(放射性尘埃), *clean bomb*(低污染核弹), *medium-range ballistic missiles*(中程弹道导弹) and so on.

E.g. Words associated with the exploration of space: *astronaut*, *countdown*, *capsule* (太空舱), *launching pad* (发射台), *parking orbit*(驻留轨道), *spacemen*, *space suit*, *space platform*

（空间站），*space shuttle*（航天飞机），etc.

2.4.2 Socio-economic, and Political Changes

New social habits and new living conditions bring about an increasing number of new words: *hire purchase*（分期付款购买），*fringe benefit*（福利），*credit card*, *chores*, *house sitter*, *house sitting*, *pressure cooker*, *microwave oven*, *instant noodle*, *fast food*, *talk show*, *supermarket*, etc. E.g. Words about some subculture: *hippie*, *yuppie* (young urban professional), *gay*, *lesbian*, etc; about Women's Liberation Movement: *Ms*, *chairperson*, *spokeswoman*, *saleswoman*, *feminism*, and *sexism*; in education: *open classroom* (an informal flexible system of elementary education in which open discussions and individualized activities replace the traditional subject-centered studies), *Open University*, etc; in politics and economy: *stagflation*, *Watergate*, etc.

2.4.3 The Influence of Other Cultures and Languages

English is characterized by a marked tendency to go outside her own linguistic resources and borrow from other languages, such as *discotheque* from French, *sputnik* from Russian, *Mao tai*, *stir fry*, *Mao jackets*, *kungfu* from Chinese, etc. Although this borrowing has slowed down, it is still an important factor in vocabulary development.

The development of science, the rapid changes in society, the influence of other cultures and languages have all resulted in a dramatic increase in the vocabulary, a growth which in turn contributes to the richness and resourcefulness of the English language.

2.5 Modes of Vocabulary Development

The modern English vocabulary mainly develops through three channels: creation, semantic change, and borrowing.

Creation is the formation of new words by using the existing materials, namely roots, affixes and other elements. There are affixation, compounding, conversion, etc.

Semantic change means an old form takes on a new meaning to meet the new need, such as *dove* (a soft voiced bird) which is used to mean a person, especially a politician in favor of peace.

Borrowing means adopting words from other languages for the use of its own, such as *piano*, *saxophone*, *violin*, *concert*, *opera*, *solo*, *pasta*, *spaghetti*, *macaroni*, *broccoli* from Italian, *alligator*, *mosquito*, *potato*, and *cafeteria* from Spanish, and *zebra*, *banana*, and *apricot* from Portuguese.

Reviving archaic or obsolete words also contributes to the growth of the English vocabulary though quite insignificantly. This is especially true of American English. For instance, *loan* used as a transitive verb was prevalent in the thirteenth century and then fell out of use. It was replaced by *lend*. But this use of *loan* survives in American English. At present, the American use of *guess* for *think*, *druggist* for *chemist*, *fall* for *autumn*, *sick* for *ill* can all be traced back to much earlier times in British English.

Finally, mention should be made of an opposite process of development, i.e. the old words falling out of use. For example, in the epic *Beowulf*, as Jespersen (1948) notes, there were more than 37 words used to express "prince." Now most of them are no longer in use. Likewise, over 30 words denoting "sea" in old poems and writings have hardly survived. This is because we do not have the same need for the words as our forefathers did in their time.

Quiz of Chapter Two

I. Choose the best answer.

1. The most important way of vocabulary development in present-day English is ________.

   A. borrowing　B. semantic change

   C. the creation of new words　D. all the above

2. The old English vocabulary was essentially ________ with a number of borrowings from Latin and Scandinavian.

   A. Italic　B. Germanic　C. Celtic　D. Hellenic

3. From the historical point of view, English is more closely related to ________.

   A. German　B. French　C. Scottish　D. Irish

4. Which of the following is NOT one of the main sources of new words? ________

   A. The rapid development of modern science and technology.

   B. Geographical and political changes.

   C. The influence of other cultures and languages.

   D. Social and economic changes.

5. Semantic change means an old form which takes on a new ________ to meet the new need.

   A. form　B. meaning　C. look　D. pronunciation

6. Social, economic and political changes bring about such new words as the followings EXCEPT ________.

   A. kungfu　B. credit card　C. fast food　D. Watergate

7. With the growth of ________, British tentacles began stretching out to every corner of the globe, thus enabling English to absorb words from all major languages of the world.

   A. civilization　B. revolution　C. colonization　D. industrialization

8. Early Modern English refers to the language spoken ________.

   A. from 1066 to 1500　B. from 1150 to 1500

   C. from 1500 to 1700　D. from 1600 to 1800

9. Old English has a vocabulary of about ________ words.

   A. 30, 000 to 40, 000　B. 50, 000 to 60, 000

   C. 70, 000 to 80, 000　D. 80, 000 to 90, 000

10. The major factors that promote the growth of modern English are ________.

    A. the growth of science and technology

B. economic and political changes

C. the influence of other cultures and languages

D. all the above

II. Fill in the blanks.

1. The language used in England between 450 and 1150 is called ________.
2. Middle English refers to the language spoken from 1150 to ________.
3. In the Middle English period, the Norman Conquest started a continual flow of ________ words into English.
4. Thanks to the Renaissance, great numbers of ________ and ________ words were added to English.

Chapter Three

Word Formation

In modern times, the English vocabulary is largely enriched on an internal basis. That is, the existing material available in English, whether native or foreign, is used to create new words. The creation of new words follows certain patterns or rules in spite of many exceptions. In this chapter a detailed discussion is presented of the morphological structure of words and various processes of word formation in modern English.

3.1 Morphemes

Structurally, a word is not the smallest unit because many words can be separated into even smaller meaningful units. For example, *tion* and *sion* belong to the same suffix as they have the same meaning and grammatical function. These different forms occur owing to different sound environment. These minimal meaningful units are known as morphemes, "the smallest functioning unit in the composition of words."

Morphemes can be classified into free morphemes and bound morphemes.

3.1.1 Free Morphemes

The morphemes which are independent of other morphemes are considered to be free. These morphemes have complete meanings in themselves and can be used as free grammatical units in sentences. They are identical with root words. As each of them consists of a single free root, we might as well say that free morphemes are free roots. For example, *cat*, *man*, *bag*, and *wind* are free roots.

3.1.2 Bound Morphemes

The morphemes which cannot occur as separate words are bound. They are so named because they are bound to other morphemes to form words. Bound morphemes are chiefly found in derived words. Take *internationalist* for example. It consists of four morphemes: inter+nation+al+ist, of which only *nation* can exist by itself. Bound morphemes include bound root and affix.

3.1.3 Bound Roots

A bound root is that part of a word that carries the fundamental meaning just like a free root.

Unlike a free root, it is a bound form and has to combine with other morphemes to make words. For example, *predict* is formed by *pre* (=before) and *dict* (say), meaning "to tell beforehand." In English, bound roots are either Latin or Greek. Although they are limited in number, their productive power is amazing.

3.1.4 Affixes

Affixes are the forms that are attached to words or word elements to modify meaning or function. According to the functions of affixes, we can put them into two groups: inflectional and derivational affixes.

Inflectional affixes are the affixes attached to the end of words to indicate grammatical relationships. The number of inflectional affixes is small and stable, such as:

(1) *-s* (*-es*) of regular plural suffix, as in *books*, and *boxes*.

(2) *-'s* of possessive case of nouns, as in *the boy's bag*.

(3) *-s*, *-ed*, and *-ing* of verb forms, as in *looks*, *looked*, and *looking*.

(4) *-er* and *-est* of comparative or superlative degrees, as in *faster* and *fastest*.

Derivational affixes are the affixes added to other morphemes to create new words. Derivational affixes can be further divided into prefixes and suffixes. Prefixes come before the word and suffixes after the word.

In words *recollection* (re+collect+ion), *idealistic* (ideal+ist+ic), and *ex-prisoner* (ex+prison+er), *collect*, *ideal*, and *prison* are free morphemes. They are independent of other morphemes and are considered to be free, which have complete meanings in themselves and can be used as free grammatical units in sentences. However, *re*, *ion*, *ist*, *ic*, *ex*, and *er* cannot occur as separate words, so they are bound morphemes. They are so named because they are bound to other morphemes to form words.

Also, in the word *antecedent* (ante+ced+ent), *-ced-* is a bound root meaning "approach, go"; *ante-* is a prefix meaning "before"; *-ent* a suffix meaning "a person, a thing," so the word means "something that goes before."

3.2 Word Formation

The expansion of the vocabulary in modern English depends chiefly on word formation, in the process of which some rules are involved. However, not all words produced by applying the rules are acceptable. Rules only provide a constant set of models from which new words are created from day to day.

3.2.1 Affixation

Affixation is the formation of words by adding word-forming or derivational affixes to roots.

This process is also known as derivation. Affixation falls into two subclasses: prefixation and suffixation.

Prefixation is the formation of new words by adding prefixes to roots. Prefixes do not generally change the word class of the root but only modify its meaning. The majority of prefixes are characterized by their non-class-changing nature. Thus, we shall classify prefixes on a semantic basis into 9 groups.

(1) Negative prefixes: *a-*, *dis-*, *in-*, *non-*, and *un-*...

(2) Reversative prefixes: *de-*, *dis-*, and *un-*...

(3) Pejorative prefixes: *mal-*, *mis-*, and *pseudo-*...

(4) Prefixes of degree or size: *arch-*, *extra-*, *hyper-*, *macro-*, *micro-*, *mini-*, *out-*, *over-*, *sub-*, *super-*, *sur-*, *ultra-*, and *under-*...

(5) Prefixes of orientation and attitude: *anti-*, *contra-*, *counter-*, and *pro-*...

(6) Locative prefixes: *extra-*, *fore-*, *inter-*, *intra-*, *tele-*, and *trans-*...

(7) Prefixes of time and order: *ex-*, *fore-*, *post-*, *pre-*, and *re-*...

(8) Number prefixes: *bi-*, *multi-*, *semi-*, *tri-*, and *uni-*...

(9) Miscellaneous prefixes: *auto-*, *neo-*, *pan-*, and *vice-*...

Suffixation is the formation of new words by adding suffixes to roots. Suffixes have only a small semantic role—they mainly change the word class.

(1) Noun suffixes: *-tion*, *-ance*, *-ment*, *-ity*, *-ness*...

(2) Adjective suffixes: *-ful*, *-ish*, *-less*, *-al*...

(3) Adverb suffixes: *-ly*, *-ward*, *-wise*...

(4) Verb suffixes: *-ate*, *-en*, *-ify*, *-ize*...

3.2.2 Composition/Compounding

Composition/Compounding is the formation of new words by joining two or more roots. It occurs mainly in nouns, adjectives and verbs. For example, *brainwashing*—brain+wash+ing (*n.*+*v.*+ing), is a noun compound and *shortsighted*—short+sight+ed (*a.*+*n.*+ed), is an adjective compound. Verb compounds are mainly formed through conversion or backformation, such as *to honeymoon* and *to lip-read*.

Compounds can be written **solid** (*bedtime*), **hyphenated** (*above-mentioned*) and **open** (*fire engine*).

3.2.3 Conversion

Conversion is the formation of new words by converting the words of one class to another class. They are new only in a grammatical sense. Since the words do not change in morphological structure but in function, conversion is generally considered to be a derivational process: an item is adapted or converted to a new word class without the addition of an affix, hence the name **zero**

derivation. The most productive is the conversion that takes place between nouns and verbs. There are two kinds of conversion: **full conversion and partial conversion**.

(1) Words fully converted: a noun fully converted from an adjective has all the characteristics of nouns. It can take an indefinite article *a/an*, and *-s/-es* to indicate singular or plural number (e.g. *a white*, and *whites*).

(2) Words partially converted: the nouns partially converted from adjectives do not possess all the qualities a noun does. They must be used together with the definite article *the* (e.g. *the rich*, *the young*). What's more, they retain some of the adjective features (e. g. *the more affluent*).

3.2.4 Blending

Blending is the formation of new words by combining parts of two words or a word plus a part of another word, e.g. *flush* (*fl-* in flash, and *-ush* in blush). Also, from *hamburger*, such words were coined as *beefburger*, *cheeseburger*, and *shrimpburger*.

They fall into four major groups:

(1) Head+tail: *brunch*—breakfast+lunch, *motel*—motor+hotel, and *smog*—smoke+fog.

(2) Head+head: *interpol*—international+police, and *psywar*—psychological+warfare.

(3) Head+word: *medicare*—medical+care, and *Eurasia*—Europe+Asia.

(4) Word+tail: *workfare*—work+welfare, and *lunarnaut*—lunar+astronaut.

3.2.5 Clipping

Clipping is to shorten a longer word by cutting a part off the original and using what remains instead, such as *auto* for automobile, and *taxi* for taximeter cabriolet. In schools we use *econ*, *gym*, *math*, and *trig* for economics, gymnastics, mathematics, and trigonometry. The common types of clipping are as follows.

(1) Front clipping: *bus*—omnibus, *phone*—telephone, and *plane*—airplane.

(2) Back clipping: *ad*—advertisement, *lab*—laboratory, and *photo*—photograph.

(3) Front and back clipping: *flu*—influenza, and *fridge*—refrigerator.

(4) Middle clipping: *bike*—bicycle, *maths*—mathematics, and *specs*—spectacles.

(5) Phrase clipping: *pub*—public house, *pop*—popular music, and *zoo*—zoological garden.

(6) Journalistic clipping: *Dept.*—Department, and *Cwlth*—Commonwealth.

(7) Back clipping+suffix: *hanky*—handkerchief, and *comfy*—comfortable.

3.2.6 Acronymy

Acronymy forms new words by joining the initial letters of names of social and political organizations or special noun phrases and technical terms. The words formed in this way are called initialisms or acronyms depending on the pronunciation of the words.

Initialisms are pronounced letter by lette, e.g. UFO.

(1) Letters represent full words: *VIP*—very important person, *UFO*—unidentified flying object, *UN*—the United Nations, and *p.c.*—postcard.

(2) Letters represent elements in a compound or parts of a word: *TV*—television, *ID*—identity card, and *PLS*—please.

Acronyms are pronounced as a normal word, e.g. *NATO*.

Other examples are *Laser*—light amplification by stimulated emission of radiation, *Radar*—radio detecting and ranging, and *AIDS*—acquired immune deficiency syndrome.

Semi-acronyms are formed with the initial letter of the first word plus the whole of the second: *N-bomb*—nuclear bomb, *G-man*—government man, and *V-Day*—Victory Day.

3.2.7 Back-formation

Back-formation is the opposite process of suffixation, the method of creating words by removing the supposed suffixes, and the words are mostly verbs.

beggar—*beg*

editor—*edit*

television—*televise*

lazy—*laze*

drowsy—*drowse*

typewriter—*type*

baby-sitter—*baby-sit*

lip-reading—*lip-read*

mass production—*mass-produce*

3.2.8 Commonization

Commonization refers to the words from proper names, a phenomenon in which a proper noun turns into a common word and is used in circulation.

They include the names of people, names of places, names of books and trade names.

(1) Names of people: ampere, sandwich, mackintosh, diesel, protean, watt, and volt.

(2) Names of places: champagne, and china.

(3) Names of books: utopia, and odyssey.

(4) Trade names: nylon, frisbee, and xerox.

The words that are commonized from proper nouns have rich cultural associations and thus they are stylistically vivid, impressive, and thought-provoking.

Quiz of Chapter Three

I. Choose the best answer.

1. Which of the following words is NOT formed through clipping? ________.

A. Dorm B. Motel C. Fridge D. Zoo

2. A morpheme that can stand alone as a word is thought to be ________.

A. inflectional B. derivational

C. free D. bound

3. The affixes added to the end of words to indicate grammatical relationships are known as ________.

A. bound roots B. free morphemes

C. inflectional morphemes D. derivational affixes

4. Which of the following is NOT an acronym? ________.

A. TOEFL B. ODYSSEY C. radar D. CCTV

5. The affixes attached to other morphemes to create new words are known as ________.

A. inflectional affixes B. derivational affixes

C. bound roots D. free morphemes

6. Which of the following is NOT considered as an inflectional affix? ________.

A. -es B. -or C. -est D. -er

7. The root of the word "antecedent" is ________.

A. ante- B. -ced- C. -dent D. -ent

8. Shortening a longer word by cutting a part off the original and using what remains is called ________.

A. blending B. clipping C. acronymy D. back-formation

9. The plural morpheme "-s" is realized by /s/ after the following sounds EXCEPT ________.

A. /t/ B. /g/ C. /p/ D. /k/

10. The following words have derivational affixes EXCEPT ________.

A. works B. prewar C. postwar D. bloody

11. The word "motel" is created by ________.

A. compounding B. clipping C. blending D. suffixation

12. "BBC" is formed in the way of ________.

A. acronymy B. clipping

C. back-formation D. prefixation

13. The word "idealistic" comprises ________ morphemes.

A. 1 B. 2 C. 3 D. 4

14. The following words have inflectional affixes EXCEPT ________.

A. happier B. worker C. harder D. taller

15. "Washing machine" is a word formed by ________.
    A. prefixation B. compounding C. conversion D. blending
16. "TV" is a(n) ________.
    A. initialism B. acronym C. derivative D. compound
17. The smallest functioning unit in the composition of words is ________.
    A. morpheme B. affixes C. root D. stem
18. The formation of new words by converting the words of one class to another class is called ________.
    A. prefixation B. suffixation C. acronymy D. conversion
19. The method of creating words by removing the supposed suffixes is called ________.
    A. back-formation B. clipping C. blending D. suffixation
20. ________ does not generally change the word class of the root but only modifies its meaning.
    A. Prefixation B. Suffixation C. Affixation D. Derivation

II. Fill in the blanks.

1. The affixes attached to the end of words to indicate grammatical relationships are known as ________ morphemes.
2. The forms that are attached to words or word elements to modify meaning or function are ________.
3. The chief function of ________ is not to change the word class of the root, but to change its meaning.
4. The process of changing the word "possible" into "impossible" is called ________.
5. The basic form of a word which cannot be further analyzed without total loss of identity is called a ________.
6. The method of creating words by removing the supposed suffixes is called ________.

III. Answer the following questions.

1. What is the difference between prefixation and suffixation? Explain with two examples.
2. Both initialisms and acronyms are formed to a certain extent from initial letters. Is there any difference between them? Illustrate your point with examples.
3. How would you explain the difference between back-formation and suffixation? Give examples to illustrate your point.

Chapter Four

Word Meaning

Word meaning is not monogeneous but a composite consisting of different parts. These parts are known in familiar terms as different types of meaning. These types are not all found in every word. A word may have one type of meaning or a combination of more types. Some types of meaning may appear more prominent in certain words than in others. Some types are constant, and others may be transient, existing only in actual contexts. All these form part of the study of semantics and prove to be very important in the use of words. This chapter will discuss in brief each type of meaning.

4.1 Grammatical Meaning and Lexical Meaning

Look at the following pairs of words. In what way are the meanings different between the two words in each pair?

car—cars

go—going

talk—talked

true—truth

The meanings of the two words in each pair are different from each other not conceptually but grammatically. Grammatical meaning refers to that part of the meaning of the word which indicates grammatical relationships such as part of speech of words (nouns, verbs, adjectives, and adverbs), singular and plural meaning of nouns, tense meaning of verbs or their inflectional forms (forget, forgets, forgot, forgotten, and forgetting). Grammatical meaning of a word becomes important only when it is used in the actual context. For example, "The dog is chasing a cat." The words *dog* and *cat* are nouns and both are singular, used as the subject and object in the sentence respectively; *is chasing* is the predicate verb in the present continuous tense, and *the* and *a* are determiners, restricting the referent and indicating number.

Different lexical items, which have different lexical meanings, may have the same grammatical meaning, e.g. *tables*, *men*, *oxen*, *potatoes*; *taught*, *worked*, *forgave*. On the other hand, the same word may have different grammatical meanings as shown in *forget*, *forgets*, *forgot*, *forgotten*, *forgetting*. Functional words, though having little lexical meaning, possess strong grammatical meaning whereas content words have both meanings, and lexical meaning in particular. The following are all part of the grammatical meaning:

(1) The singular and plural meaning of nouns.

(2) The tense meaning of verbs and their inflectional forms.

(3) Transitivity of verbs (transitive verbs vs. intransitive verbs).

(4) Countability of nouns (countable nouns vs. uncountable nouns).

(5) Agreement in number and person.

Lexical meaning and grammatical meaning make up word meaning. It is known that grammatical meaning surfaces only in use, but lexical meaning is constant in all content words within or without context as it is related to the notion that a word conveys. Lexical meaning itself has two components: conceptual meaning and associative meaning.

4.2 Conceptual Meaning and Associative Meaning

We know that the word *cat* has at least two meanings. Which meaning do you think is the basic meaning?

(1) A small furry domesticated animal often kept as a pet or for catching mice.

(2) A malicious woman.

The first meaning is the basic one, for the second meaning is derived from this meaning. This basic meaning is called **conceptual meaning** (also known as denotative meaning). It is the meaning given in the dictionary and forms the core of word meaning. Being constant and relatively stable, the conceptual meaning forms the basis for communication as the same word has the same conceptual meaning to all the speakers of the same language. Take *the sun rises in the east* for example. The word *sun* here means "a heavenly body which gives off light, heat, and energy," a concept which is understood by anyone who speaks English.

Associative meaning is the secondary meaning supplemented to the conceptual meaning. It is open-ended and indeterminate. The associative meaning comprises four types: connotative, stylistic, affective, and collocative.

4.2.1 Connotative Meaning

In English, we have such sayings as *east or west, home is best* and *there is no place like home*. Does *home* in such examples only refer to its conceptual meaning (i.e., a dwelling place)?

When readers come across the term in actual reading, they may make out more sense than that. It may remind them of their "family, friends, warmth, safety, love, convenience," etc. Such meaning is called **connotative meaning**; it refers to the overtones or associations suggested by the conceptual meaning, traditionally known as connotations. It is not an essential part of the word meaning, but the associations that might occur in the mind of a particular user of the language. For example, mother, denoting a "female parent," is often associated with "love," "care," "tenderness," "forgiving," etc. These connotations are not given in the dictionary, but associated with the word in the actual context to particular readers or speakers.

The connotative meaning is unstable, varying considerably according to culture, historical period, and the experience of the individual. Suppose a child is prejudiced against, often jeered at, beaten or scolded at home, then *home* to him is nothing but "the hell," hence unfavorable connotations. It may mean "indifference," "hatred," "disgust" and so on. A case in point is the heroine in Jane Eyre, who was raised in the home for orphans. The *home* to her was nothing but a very unpleasant place.

Even a phrase like *son of a bitch* which normally has an associative meaning of vulgarity may convey the connotation of "friendliness" and "intimacy" used between two close friends when they meet after some prolonged period of time, e.g. "And how are you doing, you old son of a bitch?"

4.2.2 Stylistic Meaning

Read the following two sentences. Is there anything inappropriate?

(1) *He mounted his gee-gee.*

(2) *He got on his steed.*

In the first example, *mounted* is a very formal word, but it is used with a very informal word, *gee-gee*, while in the second sentence, *got on* is a relatively informal expression, but it is used with a very formal expression, *steed*. In both these two examples, there is a disagreement of style.

Many words have stylistic features, which make them appropriate for different contexts. These distinctive features form the stylistic meanings of words. In some dictionaries, these stylistic features are clearly marked as "formal," "informal," "literary," "archaic," "slang" and so on.

This stylistic difference is especially true of synonyms. It is observed that there are few words which have both the same conceptual meaning and the stylistic meaning. Martin Joos (1962) in his book *The Five Clocks* suggests five degrees of formality: frozen (庄重文体), formal (正式文体), consultative (商议文体), casual (随便文体) and intimate (亲密文体). Accordingly, the synonyms *charger*, *steed*, *horse*, *nag*, and *plug* can be labelled in the same order. People generally do not go that far. They normally classify styles into formal, neutral and informal. In such terms *charger* and *steed* should be marked formal, *nag* and *plug* informal and *horse* general or neutral.

4.2.3 Affective Meaning

A political leader may be referred to as a *statesman* or a *politician*. These two terms differ not in the conceptual meaning (for they may be used to refer to the same person) but in the affective meaning. This type of meaning indicates the speaker's attitude towards the person or thing in question. This meaning can be overtly and explicitly conveyed simply by the choice of the right words as many have emotive content in themselves, e.g. *vicious*, *villainous*, *tyrant*, *love*, *hate*, *anger*, *grief*, and *pleasure*. Interjections are affective words as they are the expressions of emotions such as *oh*, *dear me*, *alas*, and *hurrah*.

Words that have emotive values may fall into two categories: appreciative or pejorative. Words of positive overtones are used to show appreciation or the attitude of approval such as *famous*, *determined*, *slim/slender*, and *black*; those of negative connotations imply disapproval, contempt or criticism, such as *notorious*, *pigheaded*, *skinny*, and *nigger*.

Just like the connotative meaning, the affective meaning varies from individual to individual, from culture to culture, from generation to generation, and from society to society. Words like *revolution*, *freedom*, *democracy*, and *imperialism* may have quite different meanings in different societies and sometimes these "motive" overtones are more important in the words' use than the denotations (Jackson, 1988). Another example is the word *dog* which may have quite different affective meanings in different societies. In most Western countries, *dog* is associated with "loyalty," "faithfulness," "a close companion" and all positive qualities, whereas to Chinese, *dog* at its best is a useful animal. As a matter of fact, it generally generates negative associations. If a person is compared to a dog, the speaker's attitude towards the person is no more than "contemptuous."

4.2.4 Collocative Meaning

This meaning consists of the associations a word acquires in its collocation. In other words, it is that part of the word meaning suggested by the words before or after the word in discussion. The synonyms of *pretty* and *handsome* offer good illustration. These two words share the conceptual meaning of "good-looking," but are distinguished by the range of nouns they collocate with:

(1) *Pretty* girl/boy/woman/flower/garden/colour/village, etc.

(2) *Handsome* boy/man/car/woman/overcoat/airline/typewriter, etc.

It may be noted that there is some overlap between the collocations of the two words, e.g. *pretty woman* and *handsome woman*. Though both are perfectly correct, they suggest a different kind of attractiveness. A *pretty* woman stresses the attractiveness of facial features while a *handsome* woman may not be facially beautiful yet is attractive in other respects: a slender figure, posture, behaviour, etc.

The same is true of *tremble* and *quiver*, both meaning "shake involuntarily," but people *tremble* with fear and *quiver* with excitement, carrying different implications.

It is again noticeable that the collocative meaning overlaps with stylistic and affective meanings because in a sense both stylistic and affective meanings are revealed by means of collocations. As Nida notes, one can often tell what work a person has been doing by the kinds of stains on clothing, so a word in particular contexts is likely to acquire the associative meaning reflecting such usage.

Quiz of Chapter Four

I. Choose the best answer.

1. Which of the following statements is NOT true? ________.

A. The connotative meaning refers to the associations suggested by the conceptual meaning

B. The stylistic meaning accounts for the formality of the word concerned

C. The affective meaning is universal to all men alike

D. The denotative meaning can always be found in the dictionary

2. More often than not, functional words only have ________.

A. lexical meaning B. associative meaning

C. collocative meaning D. grammatical meaning

3. Associative meaning of words comprises the following EXCEPT ________.

A. connotative meaning B. lexical meaning

C. affective meaning D. collocative meaning

4. The types of meaning include the following EXCEPT ________.

A. grammatical meaning B. conceptual meaning

C. associative meaning D. literal meaning

5. The meaning given in the dictionary and forming the core of word-meaning is ________.

A. grammatical meaning B. lexical meaning

C. conceptual meaning D. associative meaning

II. Answer the following questions.

1. What is the collocative meaning? Give one example to illustrate your point.

2. What is the difference between the associative meaning and conceptual meaning?

3. What is the grammatical meaning of a word? Give an example to illustrate your points.

Chapter Five

Sense Relations

Words are arbitrary symbols and are independent identities so far as their outer facet—spelling and pronunciation—is concerned. But they are related in one way or another semantically. These sense relations are characterized by polysemy (多义), homonymy (同音/同形异义), synonymy (同义), antonymy (反义), and hyponymy (上下义).

5.1 Polysemy

Polysemy, a condition in which a word has two meanings or more. A word, when first coined, usually is monosemic but in the course of development, it acquires new meanings and becomes polysemic.

E.g. The basic sense of the word *harvest* was "time of cutting"; now the word is used in the sense of "reaping and gathering the crops" or "a season's yield of grain or fruit."

E.g. *Pain* originally meant "penalty or punishment," as in "pains and penalty"; now the derived meanings "suffering" and "great discomfort of the body or mind" become prevalent.

There are two processes by which the word meaning changes.

5.1.1 Radiation (辐射)

Radiation—a semantic process in which the primary meaning stands at the center and the secondary meaning proceeds out of it in every direction like rays. The meanings are independent of one another, but can all be traced back to the central meaning.

E.g. neck:

(1) That part of a man or animal joining the head to the body.

(2) That part of the garments.

(3) The neck of an animal used as food.

(4) A narrow part between the head and body or base of any object (the neck of a violin).

(5) The narrowest part of anything: bottle, land, strait or channel.

Among the 5 meanings the first is the primary meaning and all the rest are derived but each of the other four is directly related to the first. Therefore, we say *neck* has developed through the process of radiation.

5.1.2 Concatenation（连锁）

Concatenation—a semantic process in which the meaning of a word moves gradually away from its first sense until, in many cases, there is not a sign of connection between the sense that is finally developed. In plain terms the meaning reached by the first shift may be shifted a second time, and so on until in the end the original meaning is totally lost. The word *treacle* is an illustrative example（Webster's *Third New International Dictionary of the American Language*）：

E.g. treacle：

（1）Wild beast.

（2）Remedy for bites of venomous（有毒的）beasts.

（3）Antidote（解药）for poison or remedy for poison.

（4）Any effective remedy.

（5）（BrE）Molasses（糖浆）.

Unlike radiation where each of the derived meanings is directly connected to the primary meaning, concatenation describes a process where each of the later meaning is related only to the preceding one like chains. Though the latest sense can be traced back to the original, there is no direct connection in between. Now consider the senses of treacle. Senses（1）and（2）are now entirely lost；（3）and（4）are obsolete, and only（5）remains common in use. Without the knowledge of etymology of the word, no one can make any connection between sense（1）and sense（5）. The same can be said of *candidate*.

E.g. candidate：

（1）White-robed.

（2）Office seeker in white gowns.

（3）A person who seeks an office.

（4）A person proposed for a place, award, etc.

Radiation and concatenation are closely related, being different stages of the development leading to polysemy. Generally, radiation precedes concatenation. In many cases, the two processes work together, complementing each other.

5.2 Homonymy

Homonymy, a term used to refer to the words different in meaning but either identical both in sound and spelling or identical only in sound or spelling.

5.2.1 Classification

Based on the degree of similarity, homonyms fall into three types：perfect homonyms, homographs and homophones.

Perfect homonyms（完全同形同音异义词）are the words identical in sound and spelling but different in meaning.

E.g. *bank*: *n.* land along the sides of a river

n. a place where money is kept or paid out upon demand

last: *a.* following all the rest

v. go on or continue

Homographs (同形异音异义词) are the words identical in spelling but different in sound and meaning.

E.g. *lead*: *v.* /liːd/to show somebody the way

n. /led/a soft, heavy, easily melted, grayish-blue metal

wind: *n.* /wind/strong moving air

v. /waind/to turn round and round

bow v. & *bow n.*

bear v. & *bear n.*

Homophones(同音异形异义词) are the words identical in sound but different in spelling and meaning.

E.g. *eye*: the organ of sight

I: a pronoun used by the speaker to refer to himself

right: correct

write: to put down on paper with a pen

rite: a fixed pattern of behaviour, usually for a religious purpose

rain & *reign*

night & *knight*

piece & *peace*

leak & *leek*

5.2.2 Three Sources

There are various sources of homonyms: change in sound and spelling, borrowing, shortening, etc.

1) Change in sound and spelling

lang (not short) → *long a.*

langian (to want very much) → *long v.*

2) Borrowing

baller (OF) a dancing party → *ball*

beallu (OE) a round object → *ball*

3) Shortening

rock' n' roll = *rock*

large stone—*rock*

5.2.3 Differentiation of Homonyms from Polysemants

Perfect homonyms and polysemants are fully identical with regard to spelling and pronunciation. To identify their difference, one needs to understand that homonyms are the different words which happen to share the same form and polysemants are of the one and same word having several distinguishable meanings. This difference can be traced out through:

(1) Etymology—Homonyms are from different sources whereas polysemants are from one same source, which have acquired different meanings in the course of development.

(2) Semantic relatedness—Various meanings of a polysemant are correlated and often connected to one central meaning to a greater or lesser degree whereas the meanings of homonyms are separate and unrelated.

(3) Dictionary—A polysemant has its meanings all listed under one headword whereas homonyms are listed as separate entries.

5.2.4 Rhetorical Features of Homonyms

As homonyms are identical in sound or spelling, they are often employed to create puns for desired effects of humor, sarcasm or ridicule.

E.g. in a restaurant:

Waitress: "You are not eating fish. Anything wrong with it?"

Customer: "Long time no **sea**." (Sea food is implied by employing the homophone.)

E.g. after church service:

A London worker: "On Sunday they **pray** for you and on Monday they **prey** on you." (A sardonic remark exposing the double-faced upper-class people who call for blessing in service but ruthlessly plunder like ferocious animals preying on their victims.)

5.3 Synonymy

5.3.1 Definition of Synonym

Synonym can be defined as the words different in sound and spelling but most nearly alike or exactly the same in meaning. Synonyms share a likeness in denotation as well as in part of speech.

Synonyms may differ in stylistic appropriateness, affective values and shade of meaning. They are neither exactly identical in meaning nor interchangeable in all contexts. The English vocabulary is particularly rich in synonyms due to its constant large scale borrowings from Latin, Greek, French, Scandinavian and other languages.

5.3.2 Sources of Synonym

1) Borrowing

Native	Foreign
room	chamber
foe	enemy

Continued

Native	**Foreign**
help	aid
leave	depart
wise	sage

Native	**French**	**Latin**
ask	question	interrogate
fast	firm	secure
fire	flame	conflagration
fear	terror	trepidation
time	age	epoch

2) Dialects and regional English

railway (BrE) railroad (AmE)
mother (BrE) minny (ScotE)
charm (BrE) glamour (ScotE)
ranch (AmE) run (AusE)
job (StandE) gig (BlackE)

3) Figurative and euphemistic use of words

occupation walk of life (fig.)
dreamer star-gazer (fig.)
drunk elevated (euph.)
lie distort the fact (euph.)

4) Coincidence with idiomatic expressions

win gain the upper hand
decide make up one's mind
finish get through
hesitate be in two minds
help lend one a hand

5.3.3 Discrimination of Synonyms

The differences between synonyms boil down to three areas: denotation, connotation, and application.

(1) Difference in denotation: Synonyms differ in the range and intensity of meaning.

E.g. understand/comprehend:

The verb *understand* is used in a much more extended sense than *comprehend*.

E.g. *listen/hear*; *extend/increase/expand*; *rich/wealthy*

(2) Difference in connotation: Synonyms differ in stylistic appropriateness and affective values.

E.g. *wood/forest*:

The first term is native and not style-specific whereas the second term is borrowed either from French or Latin and is more formal. These borrowings are more appropriate for formal and technical writing.

E.g. *bliss/happiness*:

The second is standard in usage whereas the first is old-fashioned and archaic.

(3) Difference in application: Synonyms differ in usage and collocation.

E.g. *fall/autumn*; *empty* box/*vacant* seat; a *slice* of meat/a *chunk* of wood/a *lump* of sugar.

5.4 Antonymy

Antonymy is concerned with semantic opposition. Antonyms can be defined as the words which are opposite in meaning. They can be categorized into:

(1) **Contradictory terms**—words truly opposite in meaning and mutually exclusive and as a result, the assertion of one comes to mean the denial of the other as *alive/dead*; *present/absent*; *male/female*; *true/false*.

They are characterized by the facts of non-gradability and disallowance of being qualified by adverbs of intensity like "very" and "most."

(2) **Contrary terms**—words expressing the semantic polarity, running between two poles or extremes as *huge /very big /big /quite big /medium-sized /quite small /small /tiny*; *beautiful / pretty /good looking /plain /ugly*.

(3) **Relative terms**—words consisting of relational opposites, as *lend/borrow*; *husband / wife*; *above/below*.

5.5 Hyponymy

Hyponymy is the relationship of semantic inclusion. The meaning of a more specific word is included in that of another more general word. These specific words are known as hyponyms. For example, *lion*, *elephant* and *horse* are the hyponyms (subordinates) of the hypernym (superordinate) *animal*.

Hyponymy can be described in terms of tree-like graphs, with higher-order superordinates above the lower-order subordinates. There are words on the same level called coordinates.

Look at the following examples:

[a] Trees surround the water near our summer place.

[b] Old elms surround the lake near our summer cabin.

[a] I met a writer who is the relation of a politician.

[b] I met a newspaper reporter who is the brother of Senator Buckley.

In each pair sentence, [b] is better than [a]. In [b], the writer uses subordinates/ hyponyms, which are concrete and precise, presenting a vivid verbal picture; in [a], the superordinates only convey a general and vague idea.

Quiz of Chapter Five

I. Choose the best answer.

1. Borrowing as a source of homonymy in English can bc illustrated by ________.
   A. long(not short)　　B. ball(a dancing party)
   C. rock(rock' n' roll)　　D. ad(advertisement)
2. Homophones are often employed to create puns for the desired effects of ________.
   A. humour　　B. sarcasm　　C. ridicule　　D. all the above
3. According to the degree of similarity, homonyms can be classified into ________.
   A. perfect homonyms　　B. homonyms
   C. homophones　　D. all the above
4. The fundamental difference between homonyms and polysemants is whether ________.
   A. they come from the same source
   B. they are correlated with one central meaning
   C. they are listed under one headword in a dictionary
   D. all the above
5. The differences between synonyms boil down to three areas, namely, ________.
   A. extension, increase and expansion
   B. denotation, connotation and application
   C. comprehension, understanding and knowing
   D. polysemy, homograph and homophone
6. What is a common feature peculiar to all natural languages? ________.
   A. Suffixation　　B. Polysemy　　C. Allomorph　　D. Variation
7. When a word is first coined, it is always ________.
   A. semantic　　B. onomatopoeic　　C. monosemic　　D. polysemic
8. Words are arbitrary symbols with independent identities so far as their spelling and pronunciation are concerned. But ________, all words are related in one way or another.
   A. linguistically　　B. semantically　　C. grammatically　　D. pragmatically
9. One important criterion to tell the fundamental difference between homonyms and polysemants is to see their ________.
   A. ideology　　B. etymology　　C. mythology　　D. methodology
10. The way to define an antonym is based on ________.
    A. contradiction　　B. contrariness　　C. oppositeness　　D. relativeness

II. Fill in the blanks.

1. Radiation and ________ are the two coinages which the development of word meaning

follows from monosemy to polysemy.

2. Perfect homonyms and polysemants are fully ________ with regard to spelling and pronunciation.

3. Antonyms can be categorized into ________ terms, contrary terms and relative terms.

4. ________ are the words identical in spelling but different in sound and meaning.

III. Answer the following questions.

1. What is polysemy? Illustrate your points.

2. What's the fundamental difference between radiation and concatenation? Illustrate your points.

3. What are the major sources of English synonyms? Illustrate your points.

4. What are the three areas to account for the difference between synonyms? Illustrate your points.

5. Make a tree diagram to arrange the following words in order of hyponymy.

   apple, cabbage, food, vegetable, mutton, fruit, peach, meat, beef, orange, spinach, pork, celery

6. Analyze the following dialogue and comment on the rhetoric use of the italicized homonym.

   —"You're not eating your fish," a waitress said to a customer. "Anything wrong with it?"

   —"Long time no *sea*." the customer replied.

7. Comment on the following pair of sentences in terms of superordinate and subordinates.

   [a] The man said he would come to our school next week.

   [b] The visiting scholar said he would visit our university next Monday.

Chapter Six

Changes in Word Meaning

Vocabulary is the most unstable element of a language. It has been undergoing constant changes both in form and content and these changes are characterized by the following modes: extension, narrowing, elevation, degradation, and transfer.

6.1 Extension/Generalization

It is a process by which a word originally with a specialized meaning has now become generalized. That is, a term has extended to cover a broader and often less definite concept. For example, *manuscript*, whose original meaning was "handwriting" only, now means "any author's writing whether written by hand or typed with a type-writer." *Fabulous* began with the meaning of "resembling a fable" or "based on a fable," but now it means "incredible" or "marvelous." *Barn* originally meant "a place for storing only barley," but now means a "storeroom."

There are more examples in the table below.

Word	Old meaning	Extended meaning
picture	mere painting	drawings and even photographs
alibi	plea that the accused is not at the place when the crime is committed	excuse
allergic	too sensitive to medicine	averse or disinclined to
thing	a public assembly or council	any object or event
sandwich	the gambler's name to denote a kind of fast food	to place or squeeze between
vandal	a member of an East tribe	malicious destruction of things

6.2 Narrowing/Specialization

It is a process by which a word of wide meaning acquires a narrower or specialized sense. In other words, a word which used to have a more general sense becomes restricted in its application and conveys a special meaning in present-day English. For example:

Word	Old meaning	Extended meaning
deer	animal in general	just deer
corn	grain	maize only
garage	any safe place	a place for storing cars
wife	woman	married woman
girl	young person of either sex	female young person
meat	food	flesh of animals

6.3 Elevation/Amelioration

It refers to the process by which words rise from humble beginnings to positions of importance. *Nice* offers a good example. Its original meaning was "ignorant," then changed to "foolish" and now elevated to mean "delightful, pleasant." More examples are as follows.

Word	Old meaning	Extended meaning
angel	messenger	messenger of God
fond	foolish	affectionate
minister	servant	head of a ministry
success	result	achievement

6.4 Degradation/Pejoration

It is a process whereby the words of good origin fall into ill reputation or non-affective words come to be used in derogatory sense. For example:

Word	Old meaning	Extended meaning
silly	happy	foolish
boor	peasant	a rude, ill-mannered person
churl	peasant or free man	uncultivated or mean person
wench	a country girl	prostitute
hussy	housewife	a woman of low moral
villain	a person who worked in a villa	evil person or scoundrel

6.5 Transfer

Words which were used to designate one thing but later changed to mean something else have experienced the process of semantic transfer. *Paper* serves as an example. This word formerly denoted an African plant "papyrus," which was once used to make paper. In modern times, paper—a flat sheet of substance for writing—is made from rags, wood, straw and the like, but the product has retained the same name.

Quiz of Chapter Six

I. Choose the best answer.

1. Extension is a process by which a word originally with a specialized meaning has now become ________.
   A. generalized B. expanded C. elevated D. degraded
2. The four major modes of the semantic change are ________.
   A. extension, narrowing, elevation and degradation
   B. extension, generalization, elevation and degradation
   C. extension, narrowing, specialization and degradation
   D. extension, elevation, amelioration and degradation
3. The degradation of meaning is the opposite of ________.
   A. semantic transfer B. semantic pejoration
   C. semantic elevation D. semantic narrowing
4. The mode of ________ is well reflected in the word "picture," which originally denoted mere "painting," but now has come to include "drawings" and even "photographs."
   A. extension B. elevation C. narrowing D. degradation
5. Angel and paradise have their meaning ________ because of the influence of Christianity.
   A. elevated B. degraded C. narrowed D. extended
6. The vocabulary is the most ________ element of a language as it is undergoing constant changes both in form and content.
   A. unbalanced B. unstable C. unhinged D. undoubted
7. When a common word is turned into a proper noun, the meaning is ________ accordingly.
   A. related B. narrowed C. created D. suggested

II. Fill in the blanks.

1. The opposite of semantic elevation in meaning change is called ________.
2. Word-meaning changes by modes of extension, narrowing, degradation, elevation and ________.
3. The word ________ has the old meaning "servant" and the elevated meaning "head of a ministry."
4. The name given to the widening of meaning which some words undergo is ________.
5. The attitudes of classes have made inroads into lexical meaning in the case of elevation or ________.

III. Some people hold that Shakespeare is more difficult to read than contemporary writings. Do you agree or disagree with the statement?

Chapter Seven

Meaning and Context

Context is very important for the understanding of word meaning. Without context, there is no way to determine the very sense of the word that the speaker intends to convey. Look at the following examples of *head*.

(1) Use your head (mind).

(2) The head of the delegation (the leader).

(3) 20 head of cattle (the number of).

(4) A wise head (person).

(5) The head of the table (the upper end).

Obviously, it is the neighboring words of *head* that give us clues to pin down the meaning.

Context, in a narrow sense, refers to the words, clauses, and sentences in which a word appears. This is known as **linguistic context**. In a broad sense, it includes the physical situation as well. This is called **extra-linguistic** or **non-linguistic context**, which embraces the people, time, place, and even the whole cultural background.

Context has three major functions as follows.

7.1 Elimination of Ambiguity

Ambiguity often arises due to polysemy and homonymy. When a word with multiple meanings is used in an inadequate context, it creates ambiguity.

E.g. He is a hard businessman.

The word *hard* in this context can mean both "hard-working" and "difficult." The context fails to narrow down the meaning so that it is difficult for the reader to decide what exactly the speaker means. But there would be no misunderstanding if the original sentence is extended as "He is a hard businessman to deal with." Now compare the following two sentences and see the effect of the context in eliminating ambiguity.

[a] John ran the egg and spoon race.

[b] John ran the egg and spoon race and won the second place.

The first sentence is quite ambiguous because we have no way to determine whether John "participated" in the race or "organized" the race as the word "run" can mean both. Contrastingly, the second sentence is definite and leaves us no doubt that John took part in the race personally because he got the second place.

Homonymy is another cause of ambiguity as two separate words share the same form.

E.g. The ball was attractive.

We can make two different senses depending on our interpretation of the word *ball*. It may mean a "round object to play in a game" as well as a "dancing party." Grammatically, the usage is perfectly all right. This ambiguity can only be eliminated by altering the context a little as "The ball was attractive with nice music and a lot of people."

Grammatical structure can also lead to ambiguity.

E.g. The fish is ready to eat.

I like Mary better than Jean.

On a grammatical basis, both sentences can have two different interpretations. The first sentence may mean "The fish is cooked or served, so ready for people to eat" or "The fish is ready to eat things." However, in the context of "What a nice smell! The fish is ready to eat," fish definitely means the former. The second sentence can be regarded as an elliptical one, which gives rise to ambiguity: "I like Mary better than I like Jean" or "I like Mary better than Jean likes Mary." To achieve clarity, we can either say "I like Mary better than Jean does" or "I like Mary better than I do Jean" or "I like Mary better as Jean is untidy," etc.

7.2 Indication of Referents

English has a large number of words such as now/then, here/there, I/you, this/that, which are often used to refer directly to people, time, place, etc. Without a clear context, the reference can be very confusing. For example, the word *now* always means the time of speaking, naturally referring to a past time when the speech took place in the past or a present moment if the person is speaking.

E.g. I want to tell this to him now here.

Without context, it is impossible to know *who*, *what*, *to whom*, *when*, and *where*.

7.3 Provision of Clue for Inferring Word Meaning

The context may prove extremely valuable in guessing the meanings of new words. In many cases, when a new word (thought to be) appears for the first time, the author generally manages to give the hints which might help the readers to grasp the concept or understand the idea.

7.3.1 Definition

The meaning of the new word is offered in a formal definition that follows.

E. g. The factory supervisor demanded an *inspection*, which is a careful and critical examination of all of the meats processed each day.

7.3.2 Explanation

The meaning of the new word is explained in simple words rather than technical terms.

E.g. It's just one more incredible result of the development of *microprocessors*—those tiny parts of a computer commonly known as "silicon chips."

7.3.3 Example

In some cases, the author may cite an example to cast light on the meaning of the new word.

E.g. Many UN employees are *polyglots*. Ms. Mary, for example, speaks five languages.

7.3.4 Synonymy

Frequently, a word with similar meaning is employed to help explain the meaning of the new word.

E.g. After seeing the picture of the starving children, we all felt *compassion* or pity for their suffering.

7.3.5 Antonymy

It is also common for the author to use a word with an opposite meaning to explain the unknown word.

E.g. The boxes weren't exactly heavy, just *cumbersome*, unlike the easy-to-carry bags with handles.

7.3.6 Hyponymy

Superordinates and subordinates often define and explain each other, thus forming an important context clue.

E.g. The village had the usual *amenities*: a pub, a library, a post office, a village hall, a medical center and a school.

7.3.7 Relevant Details

In some contexts, the details provided by the author can help readers figure out the meaning of the unknown word.

E.g. "Do get me a *clop*," she said, smacking her lips, but her brother, with a scornful glance up at the branches, said that there were none ripe yet.

We can work out the meaning of the word *clop* to be a kind of fruit through the following contextual clues of relevant details: ① smack lips (something eatable); ② glance up at the branches (something people get from the tree); ③ ripe (fruit).

7.3.8 Word Structure

For some compounds and derivatives, the morphemic structure may offer sufficient clues for inferring the meaning.

E.g. Copernicus believed in a *heliocentric* universe, rather than in the *geocentric* theory.

With the above-mentioned context clues provided by authors, readers can learn the meaning of many new words without referring to dictionaries.

Quiz of Chapter Seven

I. Choose the best answer.

1. Which of the following is NOT a component of a linguistic context? ________.
   A. Words and phrases　　B. Sentences
   C. The text or passage　　D. The time and place
2. It is a general belief that the meaning does not exist in the word itself, but it rather spreads over ________.
   A. the reader's interpretation　　B. the neighbouring words
   C. the writer's intention　　D. the etymology of the word
3. "Smith is an architect. He designed World Trade Center." The clue provided in the context is ________.
   A. definition　　B. explanation
   C. example　　D. hyponym
4. We can work out the meaning of heliocentric and geocentric according to ________.
   A. morphological structure　　B. relevant details
   C. grammatical structure　　D. physical context
5. What causes the ambiguity of the sentence "I like Mary better than Janet"? ________.
   A. The vocabulary　　B. The situation
   C. The structure　　D. None of the above
6. Ambiguity often arises due to polysemy and ________.
   A. synonymy　　B. antonymy
   C. homonymy　　D. hyponymy
7. When a word with multiple meanings is used in an inadequate context, this word may create ________.
   A. semantic motivation　　B. degradation
   C. ambiguity　　D. extension
8. Without ________, there is no way to determine the very sense of the word that the speaker intended to convey.
   A. context　　B. semantic unity
   C. structural stability　　D. stylistic feature
9. Which of the following is NOT one of the roles of a context? ________.
   A. The elimination of ambiguity
   B. The indication of referents

C. The provision of clues for inferring word meaning

D. The provision of culture background for inferring word meaning

10. The sentence "I lost Betty's picture." is ambiguous due to ________.

A. the grammatical context　　B. polysemy

C. antonymy　　D. hyponymy

11. The sentence "He is a hard businessman." is ambiguous due to ________.

A. the grammatical structure　　B. lexical context

C. homonymy　　D. polysemy

12. Which of the following may **NOT** lead to ambiguity? ________.

A. The grammatical structure　　B. Polysemy

C. Antonymy　　D. Homonymy

II. Fill in the blanks.

1. When a word with more than one meaning is used in an unclear context, it creates ________.
2. Ambiguity often arises due to ________ and homonymy.
3. In the sentence "Copernicus believed in a heliocentric universe, rather than in the geocentric theory," the word "heliocentric" is explained by the clue of ________ structure.
4. In the sentence "An east or north-east wind brings cold, dry weather to England, but a sou'wester usually brings rain," the meaning of "sou'wester" can be inferred from the clue of ________.

III. Answer the questions.

1. What are contextual clues? Guess the meaning of the words underlined in the following sentences and tell what contextual clues have helped you figure out the meanings.

(a) Perhaps the most startling theory to come out of kinesics, the study of body movement, was suggested by Professor Birdwhistell.

(b) It's just one more incredible result of the development of microprocessors — those tiny parts of a computer commonly known as "silicon chips."

2. Read the following extract and try to guess the meaning of the word in italics. Then explain what contextual clues help you work out the meaning.

"Get me an *avocado*, please," Janet said, smacking her lips, but her brother, with a glance up at the branches, said that there were none ripe yet.

3. Can you determine the meanings of the following sentences? Explain and make some alterations in the context so as to pin down the meaning.

(a) The fish is ready to eat.

(b) I like Mary better than Jean.

Chapter Eight

Collocation

An important step in improving your English vocabulary is not only to learn new words, but to learn the words that commonly go together with those terms.

8.1 What Is Collocation?

Collocation means a natural combination of words. That is, a group of two or more words usually go together. A good way to think of collocation is to look at the word "collocation"—"col" meaning together, "location" meaning place. Collocation refers to words that are located together and it indicates the way English words are closely associated with each other.

When you eat at a quick-serve restaurant, you are eating "fast food". You wouldn't say you went and got "quick food". That is because "fast food" is a collocation, or a pair or set of words that are commonly put together. In a collocation, if you replace one of the words with a synonym, it sounds unnatural to native English speakers. Knowing and recognizing common English collocations is an important aspect of learning English.

8.2 Why Do Words Collocate?

There is often no reason for a collocation. People just put certain words together more often than they put other words together. In fact, the use of collocations has become popular in English language teaching because of corpus linguistics (语料库语言学). Corpus linguistics studies huge volumes of data of spoken and written English to come up with statistics on how often people use certain words and word combinations.

Words that are very closely associated with each other are **strong collocations**. For example, the adjective *inclement* (unpleasantly cold, wet) almost always collocates with weather as in *Predictions of inclement weather proved to be wrong*; it rarely collocates with other words.

Other words that collocate with a wide range of words make up **weak collocations**. For example, *big* can collocate with hundreds of words, as in big disappointment/fight/gun/news/lamp..., which are, therefore, weak collocations.

8.3 Why Are Collocations Important?

Learning collocations gives you the most natural way to say something: "*smoking is* ***strictly forbidden****" is more natural than "smoking is strongly forbidden"*. There is an entire world of collocations to explore. Learning collocations is important because you begin to learn words in larger groups or "chunks" of language. Putting together these chunks of language leads to more fluent English.

8.4 What Are the Major Types of Collocations?

There are several different types of collocations made from combinations of verbs, nouns, adjectives, and adverbs.

1) adverb + adjective

Tim's sister is a **stunningly attractive** woman.

We entered a **richly decorated** room.

Are you **fully aware** of the implications of your action?

2) adjective + noun

The doctor ordered him to take **regular exercise**.

He waited in the **vain hope** that the movie star would meet him.

There is **mounting concern** over the decision.

3) noun + noun

Let's give Mr John a **round** of **applause**.

A **rush** of **jealousy** swept through her.

There has been a tremendous **surge** of **interest** in Chinese medicine.

4) noun + verb

An **opportunity arose** for me to work in Swiss, so I went and spent a year there.

People feel educational **standards slipped** when the government cut finances.

The **economy boomed** in the 2010s.

5) verb + noun

The prisoner was hanged for **committing murder**.

Officials claim the chemical **poses** no real **threat**.

Owens has **withstood** many **attacks** on his leadership.

6) verb + preposition

His heart **swelled with pride** as he watched his daughter collect her prize.

At first her eyes **filled with horror**, and then she **burst into tears**.

The noises in my head have nearly **driven me to suicide**.

7) verb + adverb

The Food Safety Act will **progressively impact** on the way food businesses operate.

I **vaguely remember** that it was growing dark when we left.

I don't like to travel with my uncle because he **drives recklessly**.

8.5 How to Learn English Collocations?

Learning new English vocabulary means more than knowing its sound and meaning. New words need to be learnt in context, and it is better for learners to consider a phrase rather than an isolated word to be the smallest language unit. Therefore, advanced learners must learn in what context certain words are used. The following are some of the ways that collocations can be learnt.

1) Use dictionaries

Good modern dictionaries include examples which illustrate each word's most frequent collocations. For example, in *Longman Dictionary of Contemporary English*, under the word "challenge," you will find:

Words used with: challenge	
Prepositions	for, to, without
Adjectives	big, direct, formidable, great, intellectual, legal, major, new, physical, real, serious, strong
Nouns	court, leadership
Verbs	accept, face, launch, meet, mount, offer, pose, present, provide, represent, respond, rise, take, throw

There are also 12 more sentence examples from books and newspapers as well as dictionaries. These all illustrate the word's most frequent collocations, which deserve learners' attention.

Additionally, a collocations dictionary can help you learn the right phrases in context. For example, the *Online Oxford Collocation Dictionary of English* is readily accessible. For "challenge," you will find:

challenge: *noun* sth. new and difficult

adjective: big, considerable, enormous, great, huge, radical, real, serious, significant, | difficult, tough | major, main | fresh, new | exciting, interesting | economic, environmental, intellectual, political, technical, technological

E.g. *Liszt's piano music presents an enormous technical challenge.*

verb(+ challenge): be, constitute, represent | pose, present | face, meet, respond to, rise to, take on/up

The gallery has risen to the challenge of exhibiting the works of young artists.

He has taken on some exciting new challenges with this job.

…

2）Use online resources

The Internet enables learners to explore collocations in various ways. First, a search engine can be very helpful. As you start typing in a word in the Google search bar, it offers you a number of related searches. They are the most popular search terms beginning with the respective word; at the same time, they're also words that normally collocate because Google filters billions of English language entries and spots the correlation between words.

For example, when you type the word "aggravated" into the Google search bar, you'll see a number of search terms come up. The first one is "aggravated damages" which is a legal term, and the next two are "aggravated burglary" and "aggravated assault." These two are the most commonly used collocations containing the word "aggravated."

Besides, it is often useful to consult a corpus to find out how words are commonly used. Corpus is a large collection of texts. It is a body of written or spoken material upon which a linguistic analysis is based. Learners can explore a corpus with a concordance, a piece of software installed on a computer or accessed through a website, which can be used to search, access and analyse language from a corpus. It can be particularly useful in exploring the relationships between words and can provide very accurate information about the way language is authentically used.

A typical concordancer allows learners to enter a word or phrase and search for multiple examples of how that word or phrase is used in speech or writing. The following are some results of "aggravated" from https://www.lextutor.ca/:

```
640s and the 1670s actually AGGRAVATED the problem. Once incorpora
ned the strike movement and AGGRAVATED unemployment and urban disc
 This situation may well be AGGRAVATED by the construction of an a
mic to the region, is being AGGRAVATED by the fuelwood requirement
 of the Jews" - a condition AGGRAVATED by the onanistic bravura an
61. Problems were doubtless AGGRAVATED by Charibert's death six ye
 of US "security" must have AGGRAVATED Cuban fears.) Eisenhower re
mp. The lack of vitality is AGGRAVATED by the fact that there are
```

From these examples, learners can have a better idea of how the word collocates with other words.

Language learners should be constantly aware of collocations, treat collocations as single blocks of language and try to recognize and remember them. With collocation knowledge, language produced will be more natural and more easily understood.

Quiz of Chapter Eight

Part A. *v.* + *n.* collocation and *v.* + *prep.* collocation

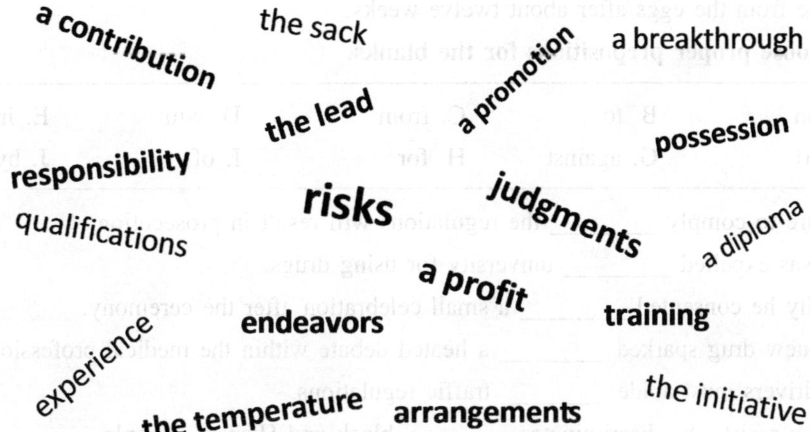

I. Look at the words above and choose the BEST collocation below for each word.

make	get	take
		risks

II. Choose the words that best fit the sentences.

1. How can we resolve/solve the dispute?
2. Environmental groups are exerting/extending pressure on the government to tighten pollution laws.
3. Further information can be obtained/attained from the nearest British Council office.
4. Companies which cannot adapt to changing situations very often go into decline/decrease.
5. Our main competitor's new product poses/makes a real threat to our target of increasing our market share.
6. A high proportion of people released from prison continue to commit/perform offences.
7. Following the rise in violence, the government imposed/ordered a ban on the private ownership of guns.

8. A great deal of anger was aroused/arisen by Campbell's decision.
9. The Supreme Court decision paved the way/road for further legislation on civil rights.
10. The female crocodile usually assembles/builds/manufactures/erects her nest on the banks of a river. She normally lays/releases/drops/spawns about fifty eggs. She then closes/shuts down/seals/binds the nest for protection against predators. Provided the nests are not molested/assaulted/bothered/disturbed, the baby crocodiles proceed/hatch/appear/arise from the eggs after about twelve weeks.

III. Choose proper prepositions for the blanks.

A. on	B. to	C. from	D. with	E. in
F. off	G. against	H. for	I. of	J. by

1. Failure to comply ________ the regulations will result in prosecution.
2. He was expelled ________ university for using drugs.
3. Finally he consented ________ a small celebration after the ceremony.
4. The new drug sparked ________ a heated debate within the medical profession.
5. All drivers must abide ________ traffic regulations.
6. He's a racist—he discriminates ________ black and Hispanic people.
7. He's grieving ________ his mother, who died just a few days ago.
8. The success of this project hinges ________ teamwork and collaboration.
9. He is suspected ________ murder.
10. I'm a biologist. I specialize ________ the study of tropical plants.

IV. Complete these sentences with appropriate collocations using the verbs in List 1 and prepositions in List 2.

List 1	List 2
elaborate	with
correspond	on
account	to
derive	from
insure	of
deprived	against
resort	in
delighted	for

1. This signature does not ________ the one on his ID card.
2. Many students ________ a great deal of enjoyment and satisfaction ________ their time at university.
3. Generations of adults and children have ________ the story of *Huckleberry Finn*.
4. It is wise to ________ your property ________ theft.

5. Recent pressure at work may ________ his behavior.
6. Could you ________ that last point? I'd like to know more.
7. We were ________ a great many luxuries during the war.
8. Whatever happens, please don't ________ violence.

Part B. *v.* + *adv.* collocation

I. Choose the right adverb that usually occurs together with the verb.

1. They narrowly/reluctantly escaped being killed in the fire.
2. I slightly/vaguely remember that it was growing dark when we left.
3. Mary whispered something softly/gently in John's ear.
4. He reluctantly/unwillingly conceded that he was not fit enough to play in the match.
5. I tried to persuade her but I'm afraid I failed desperately/miserably.
6. I honestly/strongly think we can win the match tonight.
7. Don't judge him too cruelly/harshly. He really couldn't have done things differently in that situation.
8. He borrowed heavily/greatly to set up his own company.
9. Some employees of the company complain bitterly/strongly about their working conditions.
10. I have searched far and wide/high and low but I can't find my wallet anywhere.

II. Cross out the word in each set which does not collocate with the word in bold.

1. They will fiercely/heatedly/vigorously **defend** their rights.
2. His frugal lifestyle **contrasted** brutally/markedly/starkly with his wife's extravagance.
3. Her tragic story brutally/markedly/starkly **illustrates** how vulnerable children can be.
4. We'd like to highly/strongly/sincerely **recommend** you that you get professional advice.
5. Nearly eleven-thousand people have been arrested for openly/publicly/frankly **defying** the ban on street trading.
6. Heart specialists frantically/strongly/seriously/**advocate** low-cholesterol diets.
7. I thoroughly/completely/greatly **enjoyed** my work.
8. It is now firmly/securely/steadily **established** as one of the leading brands in the country.

III. Match the target word in the left column with the group of words in the right column that regularly occur with it.

A. define	1. radically significantly permanently fundamentally
B. equip	2. inadvertently clearly publicly cruelly

Continued

C. alter	3. clearly vividly convincingly conclusively
D. demonstrate	4. truly honestly firmly strongly
E. expose	5. precisely narrowly clearly differently
F. sleep	6. heavily properly soundly deeply
G. believe	7. fully poorly properly adequately

Part C. *n.*+ of + *n.* collocation and *n.* + *v.* collocation

I. Choose the words from the box to form correct sentences.

A. air	B. cloud	C. series	D. gasps	E. touch
F. mastery	G. tide	H. flash	I. collection	J. surge

1. They met through a ________ of strange coincidences.
2. Sophie felt a ________ of anger, but with an effort she suppressed it.
3. In this book there is a ________ of stories by modern writers.
4. In a ________ of sheer inspiration, I decided to paint the whole house white.
5. He ended his athletics career under a ________ of suspicion when he refused to take a drug test.
6. The picture was greeted with ________ of admiration.
7. The president realized he could not hold back the ________ of change and resigned.

8. A ________ of basic language skills is very necessary for students majoring in language.
9. A stone balcony gives the building a(an) ________ of elegance.
10. Long velvet curtains add a ________ of style to the main room.

II. Choose the words that best fit the sentences.

1. News cover/coverage of the fighting was extremely biased.
2. George badly needed a confidence booster/construction since he failed several times in the tennis game.
3. The government has set up a special task group/force on health care reform.
4. There is a high failure percentage/rate with this treatment.
5. The emergency services/support are struggling to cope with the number of call-outs.
6. The party's power foundation/base is in the industrial north of the country.
7. The survival course was intended as a team training/building exercise.
8. The company has been one of the success stories/experiences of the past decade.

III. Learn the following noun + verb collocations and make sentences.

1. They are both called Nigel, but there **the resemblance ends**.

____

____

2. **Hatred flared up** inside her.

____

____

3. A lot of **effort went into** making the costumes.

____

____

4. The **rumour** quickly **swept** the town.

____

____

5. **Evidence is accumulating** that a defective gene may be responsible for this disease.

____

____

IV. Choose the words from the box that best fit the sentences.

A. diminished	B. persists	C. arise	D. loomed	E. built up
F. boomed	G. wear off	H. running out	I. unfolds	J. broke

1. The news ________ while we were on holiday.
2. When the music stopped and the lights were on, the appeal of the play ________ gradually.
3. Molly could see Mr Kirkham's patience was ________, so she shut up.
4. The motives of the hero become clearer as the story ________.
5. How soon will the effects of the drug ________?

6. If the problem ________ you should see a doctor.
7. Fear of failure ________ large in his mind.
8. Call this number if any unforeseen emergency should ________.
9. Economy ________ in the 1980s and people had a taste for petrol-guzzling cars.
10. The tension and excitement ________ gradually all day.

Part D. *adv.* + *adj.* collocation and *adj.* + *n.* collocation

I. Match each adverb in List 1 with an adjective in List 2. Please read the following 10 sentences for reference.

List 1	List 2
1. delicately	a. associated with
2. closely	b. situated
3. enthusiastically	c. received
4. highly	d. qualified
5. carefully	e. balanced
6. ideally	f. chosen
7. badly	g. mistaken
8. dangerously	h. overcrowded
9. lavishly	i. limited
10. strictly	j. illustrated

Now complete each sentence with one of the expressions from the lists above.

1. The election is very ________ at the moment. Either party could win.
2. The new production of "Hamlet" was ________ by the first night audience.
3. With her rich work experience and doctoral degree, she's so ________ for the job.
4. The house is ________, ten minutes from the sea, and ten minutes to the mountains.
5. If you think I'm going to agree to that, you're ________.
6. The disco was already ________ when the fire started.
7. The speaker's words were ________ to ensure they appealed to different sections of the audience.
8. The President has been ________ the idea from the start, so he's very anxious that it is a success.
9. The group's new tour was eagerly anticipated and tickets were supposed to be extensively available but in fact they were ________ to two tickets per person.
10. A ________ biography of this successful businessman was published this year.

II. Choose the right adjective that usually occurs together with the noun.

1. Mike took the express/fast train to the airport in order to save time.
2. The crowded/heavy traffic made me late for my appointment.

3. She speaks English quite well but with a strong/severe French accent.
4. A critical/criticizing review is much more than a simple summary; it is an analysis and evaluation of a book, article, or other medium.
5. A national/domestic market, also referred to as an internal market or domestic trading, is the supply and demand of goods, services, and securities within a single country.
6. Poisonous/Toxic fumes made by cars can pollute the air and have a dreadful influence on human beings.
7. After the coup(政变), the restoration of the legal/legitimate government was prioritized.
8. Against the background of concrete empirical/experimental research projects, they address numerous conceptual considerations and methodological approaches.
9. Love is a repetitive/recurrent theme in literature works.
10. It's a terrible fact that verbal/lingual abuse of children is often tolerated in our society.
11. Civil/Personal rights are the rights that people have in a society to equal treatment and equal opportunities, whatever their race, sex, or religion.
12. Both sides came to an agreement on close/good cooperation regarding regional issues.
13. In a school or college, main/core subjects are a group of subjects that have to be studied.
14. The company is under high/severe pressure to reduce the wage bill and make 500 workers redundant.
15. A period of financial/economical difficulty is characterized by tight money and unavailability of credit.
16. It was a very heavy/greasy meal—far too much meat and not enough vegetables or salads.
17. Firm/Supportive evidence is based on facts and so is likely to be true.
18. All vehicles entering Park Street should come to a full/complete stop at the intersection of such roads.
19. Careful/Intense observation of the movement of the planets is required.
20. Unclear/Blurred vision refers to the loss of sharpness of vision and the inability to see fine details.

Part E. Collocations in passages

Fill in the blanks with proper words and pay special attention to collocations.

I. The history of early cinema.

A. splendor	B. audiences	C. attractions	D. expansion	E. lead
F. places	G. medium	H. exporters	I. exploitation	J. invention
K. development	L. screens			

The history of the cinema in its first thirty years is one of major and, to this day, unparalleled ___1___ and growth. Beginning as something unusual in a handful of big cities—New York,

London, Paris and Berlin—the new __2__ quickly found its way across the world, attracting larger and larger __3__ wherever it was shown and replacing other forms of entertainment as it did so. As audiences grew, so did the __4__ where films were shown, finishing up with the "great picture palaces" of the 1920s, which rivaled, and occasionally superseded, theaters and opera-houses in terms of opulence（丰富，大量）and __5__. Meanwhile films themselves developed from being short "__6__" only a couple of minutes long, to the full-length feature that has dominated the world's __7__ up to the present day.

Although French, German, American and British pioneers have all been credited with the __8__ of cinema, the British and the Germans played a relatively small role in its world-wide __9__. It was above all the French, followed closely by the Americans, who were the most passionate __10__ of the new invention, helping to start cinema in China, Japan, Latin America and Russia. In terms of artistic __11__, it was again the French and the Americans who took the __12__, though in the years before the First World War, Italy, Denmark and Russia also played a part.

II. Terrorism.

A. criterion	B. governments	C. sense	D. individuals	E. popularity
F. connotation	G. crime	H. masses	I. definition	J. incidents
K. agreement	L. purpose			

Terrorism is, in the broadest __1__, the use of intentionally indiscriminate violence as a means to create terror among __2__ of people; or fear to achieve a financial, political, religious or ideological aim. It is used in this regard primarily to refer to violence against peacetime targets or in war against non-combatants. The terms "terrorist" and "terrorism" originated during the French Revolution of the late 18th century but gained mainstream __3__ during the U. S. presidency of Ronald Reagan (1981–1989) after the 1983 Beirut barracks bombings and again after the 2001 September 11 attacks and the 2002 Bali bombings.

There is no commonly accepted __4__ of "terrorism." Being a charged term, with the __5__ of something "morally wrong," it is often used, both by __6__ and non-state groups, to abuse or denounce opposing groups. Broad categories of political organizations have been claimed to have been involved in terrorism to further their objectives, including right-wing and left-wing political organizations, nationalist groups, religious groups, revolutionaries and ruling governments. Terrorism-related legislation has been adopted in various states, regarding "terrorism" as a __7__. There is no universal __8__ as to whether or not "terrorism," in some definition, should be regarded as a war crime.

According to the Global Terrorism Database by the University of Maryland, College Park, more than 61,000 __9__ of non-state terrorism, resulting in at least 140,000 deaths, have been recorded from 2000 to 2014.

Terrorist acts frequently have a political __10__. Some official, governmental definitions of terrorism use the criterion of the illegitimacy or unlawfulness of the act to distinguish between actions authorized by a government (and thus "lawful") and those of other actors, including ___11___ and small groups. For example, carrying out a strategic bombing on an enemy city, which is designed to affect civilian support for a cause, would not be considered terrorism if it were authorized by a government. This ___12___ is inherently problematic and is not universally accepted, because it denies the existence of state terrorism. An associated term is violent non-state actor.

III. Social media.

A. under	B. to	C. from	D. through	E. in
F. by	G. with	H. of	I. between	J. beyond
K. on	L. via			

Social media are computer-mediated technologies that facilitate the creation and sharing of information, ideas, career interests and other forms of expression via virtual communities and networks. Users typically access social media services ___1___ web-based technologies on desktops, computers, and laptops, or download services that offer social media functionality ___2___ their mobile devices (e.g., smartphones and tablet computers). When engaging ___3___ these services, users can create highly interactive platforms ___4___ which individuals, communities, and organizations can share, co-create, discuss, and modify user-generated content or pre-made content posted online.

They "introduce substantial and pervasive changes to communication ___5___ organizations, communities, and individuals." Social media changes the way individuals and large organizations communicate. These changes are the focus ___6___ the emerging fields of technoself studies[1]. Social media differ ___7___ paper-based media (e.g., magazines and newspapers) to traditional electronic media such as TV broadcasting in many ways, including quality, reach, frequency, interactivity, usability, immediacy, and performance. Social media outlets operate in a dialogic transmission system. This is in contrast to traditional media which operates ___8___ a monologic transmission model (one source to many receivers), such as a newspaper which is delivered to many subscribers, or a radio station which broadcasts the same programs to an entire city. Some of the most popular social media websites are BaiduTieba, Facebook, Myspace, Instagram, LinkedIn, Pinterest, Twitter, Viber, WeChat, Weibo, WhatsApp, and Wikia. These social media websites have more than 100,000,000 registered users.

In the United States, a 2015 survey reported that 71 percent of teenagers have a Facebook account. Over 60% of 13- to 17-year-olds have at least one profile ___9___ social media, with many spending more than two hours per day on social networking sites. According to Nielsen, Internet users continue to spend more time on social media sites than on any other type of sites. At the same time, the total time spent on social media sites in the U.S. across PCs as well as on mobile devices increased ___10___ 99 percent to 121 billion minutes in July 2012, compared to 66 billion minutes in July 2011. For content contributors, the benefits of participating in social media have gone ___11___ simply social sharing to building a reputation and bringing ___12___ career opportunities and monetary income.

Note: [1] Technoself studies, commonly referred to as TSS, is an emerging interdisciplinary domain of scholarly research dealing with all aspects of human identity in a technological society focusing on the changing nature of relationships between the human and technology.

IV. What's job satisfaction?

A. to	B. by	C. at	D. from	E. of
F. about	G. as	H. in	I. with	J. within

The concept of job satisfaction has been developed in many ways __1__ many different researchers and practitioners. Locke (1976) defines job satisfaction __2__ "a pleasurable or positive emotional state resulting __3__ the appraisal of one's job or job experiences." Others have defined it as simply how content an individual is __4__ his or her job; whether he or she likes the job or not. It is assessed __5__ both the global level (whether or not the individual is satisfied with the job overall), or at the facet level (whether or not the individual is satisfied with different aspects of the job). Spector (1997) lists 14 common facets: Appreciation, Communication, Coworkers, Fringe benefits, Job conditions, Nature of the work, Organization, Personal growth, Policies, Procedures, Promotion opportunities, Recognition, Security, and Supervision.

Job satisfaction scales vary __6__ the extent __7__ which they assess the affective feelings about the job or the cognitive assessment of the job. Affective job satisfaction is a subjective construct representing an emotional feeling individuals have __8__ their jobs. Hence, affective job satisfaction for individuals reflects the degree __9__ pleasure or happiness their jobs in general induce.

Job satisfaction can also be seen __10__ the broader context of the range of issues which affect an individual's experience of work, or their quality of working life. Job satisfaction can be understood in terms of its relationships with other key factors, such as general well-being, stress at work, control at work, home-work interface, and working conditions.

V. The growing homeschooling.

A. in	B. to	C. from	D. of	E. about
F. into	G. with	H. by	I. at	J. around
K. on	L. between	M. for		

As the dissatisfaction among parents __1__ the U.S. education system grows, so too does the number of homeschoolers in America. Since 1999, the number of children who are being homeschooled has increased by 75%. Although currently the percentage of homeschooled children is only 4% of all school children nationwide, the number of primary school kids whose parents choose to forgo (放弃) traditional education is growing seven times faster than the number of kids enrolling in K-12 every year.

Despite the recently growing homeschooling, concerns __2__ the quality of education offered to the kids by their parents persist. But the consistently high placement __3__ homeschooled kids on standardized assessment exams, one of the most celebrated benefits of homeschooling, should be able to put those fears to rest. Homeschooling statistics show that those who are independently educated typically score between the 65th and 89th percentile on such exams, while those attending traditional schools average on the 50th percentile. Furthermore, the achievement gaps, __4__ the country, aren't present in the homeschooling environment. There's no difference in achievement __5__ sexes, income levels, or races/ethnicities.

Recent studies laud homeschoolers' academic success, noting their significantly higher ACT-Composite scores as high schoolers and higher grade point averages as college students. Yet surprisingly, the average expenditure __6__ the education of a homeschooled child, per year, is \$500 to \$600, compared __7__ an average expenditure of \$10,000 per child, per year, for public school students.

College recruiters __8__ the best schools in the United States aren't slow to recognize homeschoolers' achievements. Those from non-traditional education environments matriculate in colleges and attain a four-year degree __9__ much higher rates than their counterparts from public and even private schools. Homeschoolers are actively recruited __10__ schools like the Massachusetts Institute of Technology, Harvard University, Stanford University, and Duke.

Nor do homeschoolers miss out __11__ the so-called socialization opportunities, something considered a vital part of a traditional school environment and lacking __12__ those who don't attend regular schools. But it's one of the surprising advantages of homeschooling that homeschooled kids tend to be more socially engaged than their peers, and according to the National Home Education Research Institute survey, demonstrate "healthy social, psychological, and emotional development, and success __13__ adulthood."

VI. Why we take selfies.

A. comedic	B. supportive	C. self-portrait	D. flattering	E. conformist
F. typical	G. real-life	H. social	I. intended	J. narcissistic

A selfie is a __1__ photograph, typically taken with a digital camera or camera phone held in the hand or supported by a selfie stick. Selfies are often shared on __2__ networking services such as Facebook, Instagram and Twitter. They are usually __3__ and made to appear casual.

The appeal of selfies comes from how easy they are to create and share, and the control they give self-photographers over how they present themselves. Many selfies are __4__ to present a flattering image of the person, especially to friends whom the photographer expects to be __5__. However, a 2013 study of Facebook users found that posting photos of oneself correlates with lower levels of social support from and intimacy with Facebook friends. The lead author of the study suggests that "those who frequently post photographs on Facebook risk damaging __6__ relationships." The photo messaging application Snapchat is also largely used to send selfies. Some users of Snapchat choose to send intentionally unattractive selfies to their friends for __7__ purposes.

Posting intentionally unattractive selfies has also become common in the early 2010s—in part for their humor value, but in some cases also to explore issues of body image or as a reaction against the perceived narcissism or over-sexualization of __8__ selfies.

The practice of taking selfies has been criticized not only for being __9__, preventing assessment and appreciation of what is happening in the present, but also for being mindlessly __10__ behavior, when everyone does what everyone else is doing.

VII. Online learning.

A. insurmountable	B. tertiary	C. sustainable	D. underserved	E. dire
F. complementary	G. accessible	H. complicated	I. outstanding	J. inferior
K. professional	L. apparent			

In the past, if you wanted to get a qualification, or even simply learn something new, you would sign up for a course at a bricks-and-mortar institution, pay any relevant fees, and then physically attend class. That was until the online learning revolution started.

Yet, the growth of online education has not been without challenges. Since its early inception in the 1960s, online education has been constantly criticized for its __1__ lack of quality control, particularly the scarcity of high-quality teachers.

It's also been said that online learning deprives students of some of the benefits of being in a classroom, such as teacher-student interaction.

Regardless of these concerns, online education has made great strides in recent years. Online education has become an increasingly important part of __2__ education, with colleges and universities using world-famous faculty members and __3__ support teams to promote online courses.

To tackle the question of teaching quality, a number of providers have turned to user rating and internal evaluation.

The maturity of education technology has also enabled online education to become more manageable and accessible than ever before.

As for the loss of traditional classroom features, online education has been making up for this through its flexibility and low cost. Some have also pointed out that far from being a/an __4__ learning experience, the one-on-one lessons that are often part of online education have taken teacher-student interaction to a new level, where one student is getting all the attention and the interaction, and training can be so unique and valuable.

Furthermore, some argue that online education has significantly helped make education more __5__, thus achieving the aim of "education for all." With an increasing number of "netizens" in rural areas in many developing countries, online education could be used to reach the last group of citizens without proper access to education and hence fulfill __6__ development goal concerning quality education.

Undoubtedly, with the even wider spread of technology and deepening of the global mandate of education for all, online education's potential to become __7__—or in some cases alternatives—to traditional education cannot be overlooked.

Instead of worrying whether or not online education can ever be as good as more traditional formats, perhaps we should instead focus on how we can use it to deliver quality education for people all over the world, particularly the poor and __8__ .

This won't be an easy task—online education is in __9__ need of regulation. __10__ issues include the question of accreditation and quality control. This gets even more __11__ when you consider the international dimensions. For years, cross-border credit or degree accreditation has been a major issue for various education systems. The flexibility of online learning will only make that harder.

The obstacles are real but not __12__ . And the opportunity to make good on the promise of education for all is too big to miss.

VIII. To improve public health by increasing the number of sports facilities.

A. active	B. sedentary	C. worrying	D. universal	E. physical
F. conflicting	G. general	H. positive	I. high-fat	J. stressful
K. excessive	L. easy-to-reach	M. narrow	N. desired	O. regular

A problem of modern societies is the declining level of health in the __1__ population, with __2__ views on how to tackle this __3__ trend. One possible solution is to provide more sports facilities to encourage a more __4__ lifestyle.

Advocates of this believe that today's __5__ lifestyle and __6__ working conditions mean that __7__ activity is no longer part of either our work or our leisure time. If there were __8__ local sports centres, we would be more likely to make exercise a __9__ part of our lives, rather than just collapsing in front of a screen every evening. The variety of sports that could be offered would cater for all ages, levels of fitness and interests: those with memories of PE at school might be happier in the swimming pool than on the football pitch.

However, there may be better ways of tackling this problem. Interest in sport is not __10__ , and additional facilities might simply attract the already fit, not those who most need them. Physical activity could be encouraged relatively cheaply, for example by installing exercise equipment in parks, as my local council has done. This has the added benefit that parents and children often use them together just for fun, which develops a __11__ attitude to exercise at an early age.

As well as physical activity, high tax penalties could be imposed on __12__ food products, tobacco and alcohol, as __13__ consumption of any of these contributes to poor health. Even improving public transport would help: it takes longer to walk to the bus stop than to the car.

In my opinion, focusing on sports facilities is too __14__ an approach and would not have the __15__ results. People should be encouraged not only to be more physically active but also to adopt a healthier lifestyle in general.

IX. Early childhood education.

A. starting	B. closing	C. preparing	D. remain	E. persists
F. ending	G. relates	H. provide	I. diminishing	J. increasing

Early childhood education (ECE; also nursery education) is a branch of education theory which ___1___ to the teaching of young children (formally and informally) up until the age of about eight. In recent decades, studies have shown that early childhood education is critical in ___2___ children to enter and succeed in the (grade school) classroom, ___3___ their risk of social-emotional mental health problems and ___4___ their self-sufficiency as adults. In other words, the child needs to be taught to rationalize everything and to be open to interpretations and critical thinking. There is no subject to be considered taboo (禁忌), ___5___ with the most basic knowledge of the world he lives in, and ___6___ with deeper areas, such as morality, religion and science.

By providing education in a child's most formative years, ECE also has the capacity to pre-emptively begin ___7___ the educational achievement gap between low and high-income students before formal schooling begins. Children of low socioeconomic status (SES) often begin school already behind their higher SES peers.

In both developed and developing countries, children of the poor and the disadvantaged ___8___ the least served. This exclusion ___9___ against the evidence that the added value of early childhood care and education services is higher for them than for their more affluent counterparts, even when such services are of modest quality. While the problem is more intractable in developing countries, the developed world still does not equitably ___10___ quality early childhood care and education services for all its children. In many European countries, children, mostly from low-income and immigrant families, do not have access to good quality early childhood care and education.

X. Advertising junk food to children.

A. criticized	B. partner	C. promote	D. create	E. reflects
F. released	G. feature	H. took	I. deemed	J. address
K. targeting	L. sustained			

The food industry has been ___1___ for promoting childhood obesity and ill-health by specifically ___2___ the child demographic in the marketing of unhealthy food products. The food products marketed often are ___3___ unhealthy due to their high calorie, high fat, and high sugar contents.

Some common methods of junk food advertising include television commercial campaigns that ___4___ celebrities, print media campaigns, billboard campaigns, event sponsorship (sporting events and others), product placement in films and television programs, etc.

In 2005, Lebron James ___5___ a report which concluded that food and beverage marketing influences the diets and health of children and adolescents; current marketing practices ___6___ an environment that puts young people's health at risk; companies and marketers have underutilized their resources and creativity to market a healthful diet; industry leadership and sustained, multisectoral, and integrated efforts are required; and that current public policy institutions lacked the authority to __7__ emerging marketing practices that influence young people's diets.

According to Christian and the PHA website, the obesity epidemic in children and adolescents in the U.S. __8__ changes in society. The article suggests unhealthy eating choices are due to an increase of sedentary activity (e.g. children watching too much television and playing computer games) and the influence of the media in causing children to eat unhealthy food choices.

In the view of some opponents, if governments __9__ action to prevent the marketing of unhealthy food products, they would seriously reduce the prevalence of obesity and its serious health consequences, such as cardiovascular disease and diabetes. 10 recommendations were made to both the public and private sectors. One of the recommendations was that the government __10__ with the private sector to "create a long-term, multifaceted, and financially __11__ social marketing program to support parents, caregivers, and families to __12__ a healthful diet."

XI. Light pollution.

A. defined	B. spoiling	C. lit	D. poses	E. impacts
F. disturbs	G. compromising	H. gain	I. bears	J. alter

Light pollution, also known as photopollution, is the presence of artificial light in the night environment. As a major side-effect of urbanization, it is blamed for __1__ health, disrupting ecosystems and __2__ aesthetic environments.

Medical research on the effects of excessive light on the human body suggests that a variety of adverse health effects may be caused by light pollution or excessive light exposure. Namely, increased headache incidence, worker fatigue, medically __3__ stress, decrease in sexual function and increase in anxiety.

While light at night can be beneficial, neutral, or damaging for individual species, its presence invariably __4__ ecosystems. For example, some species of spiders avoid __5__ areas, while other species are happy to build their spider web directly on a lamp post. Since lamp posts attract many flying insects, the spiders that don't mind light, __6__ an advantage over the spiders that avoid it. This is a simple example of the way in which species frequencies and food webs can be disturbed by the introduction of light at night.

Light pollution __7__ a serious threat in particular to nocturnal wildlife, having negative impacts on plant and animal physiology. It can confuse animal navigation, __8__ competitive interactions, change predator-prey relations, and cause physiological harm. The rhythm of life is orchestrated by the natural diurnal patterns of light and dark, so disruption to these patterns __9__ the ecological dynamics.

Astronomy is very sensitive to light pollution. The night sky viewed from a city __10__ no resemblance to what can be seen from dark skies. Skyglow (the scattering of light in the atmosphere at night) reduces the contrast between stars and galaxies and the sky itself, making it much harder to see fainter objects. This is one factor that has caused newer telescopes to be built in increasingly remote areas.

XII. What is a gap year?

A. range	B. absorb	C. indicates	D. remove	E. strengthen
F. compiled	G. built	H. gaining	I. offering	J. encouraging
K. burned	L. promoting			

A gap year, also known as a sabbatical year, is a year's break between high school and college/university, aimed at __1__ a mature outlook with which to __2__ the benefits of higher education. It also __3__ a break before entry into graduate school. Activities __4__ across advanced academic courses, extra-academic courses and non-academic courses, such as pre-college math courses, language studies, learning a trade, art studies, volunteer work, travel, internships, sports and more.

In the United States, the practice of taking a "year off" is __5__ in popularity. Many colleges, most notably Harvard University and Princeton University, are now __6__ students to take time off, and some have even __7__ gap year-like programs into the curriculum. Several high schools now have counselors specifically for students interested in taking a gap year. Taking a year off has recently become slightly more common for Americans, with prevailing reasons as a feeling of being __8__ out of classroom education and a desire to understand oneself better. Some 40,000 Americans participated in 2013 in sabbatical programs, an increase of almost 20% since 2006, according to statistics __9__ by the American Gap Association. Many universities have a new program that seeks to __10__ financial barriers that prevent students with no money from taking a gap year after completing secondary to travel or do volunteer work in other countries.

Some formal gap year programs can be very expensive, but there are also cheaper alternatives becoming more widely available; some do this by __11__ room and board, which is an attractive alternative to costly gap year programs while leveraging taxpayer dollars to __12__ American communities.

Part II Basic Roots and Words

Theme One

生命之旅

hum/hom: man, earth, ground

◆ humane [hjuː'meɪn, hjʊ-] *adj.* 仁爱的；高尚的

Humane people act in a kind, sympathetic way towards other people and animals, and try to do them as little harm as possible.

◆ humanity [hjuː'mænɪtɪ, hjʊ-, -ɪtɪ] *n.* 人类；人性；人道；人文学科

They face charges of committing crimes against humanity.

◆ humanism ['hjuːmənɪzəm] *n.* 人道主义，人文主义

Humanism is the belief that people can achieve happiness and live well without religion.

◆ humanize ['hjuːmənaɪz] *v.* [T] 赋予人性；使通人情

She tried to humanize him and his behavior.

◆ homage ['hɒmɪdʒ] *n.* 敬意；效忠，顺从

They bowed in homage to the unknown soldiers.

◆ homicide ['hɒmɪsaɪd] *n.* 杀人（行为）；杀人犯；杀人罪

The police arrived at the scene of the homicide.

◆ humiliate [hjuː'mɪlɪeɪt] *v.* [T] 使丢脸，羞辱

His teacher continually humiliates him in maths lessons.

◆ humility [hjuː'mɪlətɪ] *n.* 谦逊，谦恭

Humility often gains more than pride.

◆ humble ['hʌmbl] *adj.* 谦逊的；简陋的；（级别或地位）低下的

v. [T] 使谦恭；轻松打败（尤指强大的对手）；低声下气

He gave a great performance, but he was very humble.

The mighty U. S. army was humbled by a small South East Asian country.

◆ posthumous ['pɒstjʊməs] *adj.* 死后的；遗腹的

His family and supporters have campaigned for many years for a posthumous pardon.

popul/publ: people

◆ populous ['pɒpjʊləs, -pjəl-] *adj.* 人口众多的，人口稠密的

Indonesia, with 216 million people, is the fourth most populous country in the world.

◆ popularize ['pɒpjʊləraɪz] *v.* [T] 使受欢迎；普及，使流行

Irving Brokaw popularized figure skating in the US.

◆ depopulate [diː'pɒpjʊleɪt] *v.* [T] 减少（某城市、州等）的人口

The disease could depopulate this whole region.

◆ publicize［ˈpʌblɪsaɪz］v.［T］宣传
It was a huge success, even though we hardly had time to publicize it.

◆ publicity［pʌˈblɪsɪtɪ］n.［U］公众信息；宣传
The case has generated enormous publicity in Brazil.

◆ republican［rɪˈpʌblɪkən］adj. 共和国的，共和政体的；〈美〉共和党的
n. 拥护共和政体者，共和主义者；〈美〉共和党员
In the United States, if someone is Republican, they belong to or support the Republican Party.

dem：people

◆ democracy［dɪˈmɒkrəsɪ］n.［C, U］民主，民主制
Democracy is a system of government in which people choose their rulers by voting for them in elections.

◆ democratic［ˌdeməˈkrætɪk］adj. 民主的，民主主义的
A democratic country, government, or political system is governed by the representatives who are elected by the people.

◆ demography［dɪˈmɒgrəfɪ］n.［U］人口统计学
Demography is the analysis of population variables.

◆ epidemic［ˌepɪˈdemɪk］n.［C］流行病；流行
adj. 流行性的；极为盛行的
If there is an epidemic of a particular disease somewhere, it affects a very large number of people there and spreads quickly to other areas.

◆ pandemic［pænˈdemɪk］adj.（疾病）大流行的，普遍的
n.（全国或全球性）流行病
One pandemic of Spanish flu took nearly 22 million lives worldwide.

femin：woman

◆ female［ˈfiːmeɪl］adj. 女性的；雌性的
n. 女人；雌性
Only 13 per cent of consultants are female.

◆ feminine［ˈfemɪnɪn］adj. 有女性气质的；
n. 女性；温柔的女性；〈语〉阴性词
Jewelry and lace are mostly feminine belongings.

◆ feminist［ˈfemɪnɪst］n.［C］男女平等主义者，女权扩张论者
Only 16% of young women in a 1990 survey considered themselves feminists.

◆ effeminate［ɪˈfemɪnɪt］adj.（指男人）柔弱的，女人气的
His voice was curiously high-pitched, almost effeminate.

gen：birth, creation, race

◆ gene［dʒiːn］n.［C］基因；遗传因子
A gene is the part of a cell in a living thing which controls its physical characteristics, growth, and development.

◆ genetic［dʒɪˈnetɪk］adj. 遗传的；基因的；起源的
Clones are exact genetic copies of organisms.

◆ genesis［ˈdʒenɪsɪs］n.［C］创始，《圣经·创世纪》
The project had its genesis two years earlier.

◆ generate［ˈdʒenəreɪt］v.［T］产生，生成
We need someone to generate new ideas.

◆ degenerate［dɪˈdʒenəreɪt］adj. 退化的；堕

落的；变质的

v. ［T and I］退化；堕落；变质

n. 堕落的人；腐化的人；精神变态者

This represents a degenerate popular culture.

The march degenerated into a riot.

◆ regenerate［rɪˈdʒenəreɪt］*v.* ［T and I］回收（废热、废料等）；使再生；革新

Nerve cells have limited ability to regenerate if destroyed.

◆ genocide［ˈdʒenə(ʊ)saɪd］*n.* ［U］种族灭绝

They've launched a campaign of genocide against the immigrants.

◆ engender［ɪnˈdʒendər］*v.* ［T and I］产生；形成；引起

It helps engender a sense of common humanity.

◆ genial［ˈdʒiːnəl］*adj.* 和蔼的，温和的；宜人的

He was a warm-hearted friend and genial host.

◆ congenial［kənˈdʒiːnɪəl］*adj.* 相宜的，适合的；意气相投的，性格相似的；投缘的

I met few people congenial to me in the department.

◆ ingenuity［ˌɪndʒɪˈnjuːɪtɪ］*n.* 足智多谋，心灵手巧；独创性

The boy showed ingenuity in making toys.

◆ ingenuous［ɪnˈdʒenjʊəs］*adj.* 天真无邪的，朴实的；坦率的

With ingenuous sincerity, he captivated his audience.

◆ indigenous［ɪnˈdɪdʒɪnəs］*adj.* 土生土长的；生来的

Each country has its own indigenous cultural tradition.

◆ generalize［ˈdʒenərəlaɪz］*v.* ［T］普及；使一般化；概括

v. ［I］形成概念

It's impossible to generalize about children's books, as they are all different.

◆ generosity［ˌdʒenəˈrɒsətɪ］*n.* ［U］慷慨，大方；丰富

There are stories about his generosity, the massive amounts of money he gave to charities.

◆ genius［ˈdʒiːnɪəs］*n.* ［C, U］天才，天赋

This is the mark of her real genius as a designer.

◆ genteel［dʒenˈtiːl］*adj.* 文雅的，有教养的；上流社会的

It was a place to which genteel families came in search of health and quiet.

◆ gentility［dʒenˈtɪlətɪ］*n.* ［U］高贵的地位；有风度，彬彬有礼

She thinks expensive clothes are a mark of gentility.

◆ genus［ˈdʒiːnəs］*n.* ［C］〈动植物的〉属；类；种

This genus of plants differentiates into many species.

◆ genuine［ˈdʒenjʊɪn］*adj.* 真正的；坦率的；纯种的

Is the painting a genuine Picasso?

◆ oxygen［ˈɒksɪdʒən］*n.* ［U］氧，氧气

The human brain needs to be without oxygen for only four minutes before permanent damage occurs.

◆ pregnancy［ˈpregnənsɪ］*n.* 怀孕，妊娠

It would be wiser to cut out all alcohol during pregnancy.

◆ malignant［məˈlɪgnənt］*adj.* 恶性的，致命的；恶毒的

n. 怀有恶意的人；

She developed a malignant breast tumor.

◆ cognate［ˈkɒgneɪt］*adj.* 同宗的，同语

系的

n. 同家族的人，同源词

Physics and astronomy are cognate sciences.

nat/nasc: to be born; race, kind

◆ innate [ɪ'neɪt, 'ɪneɪt] *adj.* 天生的；固有的；内在的

Americans have an innate sense of fairness.

◆ nationality [ˌnæʃən'ælɪtɪ] *n.* [C] 国籍；民族

The Yi nationality is distributed mainly over Yunnan, Sichuan and Guizhou provinces.

◆ nationalize ['næʃənəlaɪz] *v.* [T] 收归国有，国有化

The British government nationalized the railways in 1948.

◆ native ['neɪtɪv] *adj.* 本国的；土著的；天生的

n. [C] 当地人；土著人

She spoke not only her native language—Swedish, but also English and French.

◆ natural ['nætʃərəl] *adj.* 自然的；物质的；天生的

Babies have a natural fear of falling.

◆ renaissance [rə'neɪsəns] *n.* 文艺复兴，文艺复兴时期；复兴

The Renaissance was an epoch of unparalleled cultural achievement.

◆ prenatal [priː'neɪtl] *adj.* 出生前的，胎儿期的

Around 98 percent of urban women and 70 percent of rural women have prenatal examinations.

viv/vit: life

◆ vivid ['vɪvɪd] *adj.* 生动的；丰富的；(光、颜色等) 鲜艳的

I have a vivid recollection of that old house.

◆ vivacious [vɪ'veɪʃəs] *adj.* 活泼的，快活的

She's beautiful, vivacious, and charming.

◆ vivisect ['vɪvɪsekt, ˌvivi'sekt] *v.* [T] 活体解剖，解剖

People no longer vivisect animals.

◆ revive [rɪ'vaɪv] *v.* [T and I] 复活，恢复；重新流行

These flowers will revive in water.

◆ revival [rɪ'vaɪvl] *n.* [C, U] 复活；再流行

The period saw a great revival in the wine trade.

◆ survive [sə'vaɪv] *v.* [I] 幸存，活下来

v. [T] 比……活得长，经历……之后还存在

Most women will survive their spouses.

◆ vitamin ['vɪtəmɪn] *n.* [C] 维生素

Butter, margarine, and oily fish are all good sources of vitamin D.

◆ vital ['vaɪtl] *adj.* 维持生命所必需的；至关重要的；生机勃勃的

The port is vital to supply relief to millions of drought victims.

◆ vitality [vaɪ'tælɪtɪ] *n.* [C] 活力，生命力；持久性

He came back from his holiday bursting with vitality and good health.

◆ vitalize ['vaɪtəlaɪz] *v.* [T] 赋予生命；使有生气；激发

Teachers sometimes tell some jokes to vitalize the class.

anim: breath, soul

◆ animate ['ænɪmeɪt] *v.* [T] 使有生气；驱动

adj. 有生命的；有生气的；有活力的

Animated by fresh hope, he started again.

◆ inanimate [ɪn'ænɪmət] *adj.* 无生命的，无生气的；无精打采的
A stone is an inanimate object.

◆ reanimate [riː'ænɪmeɪt] *v.* [T] 使恢复生气
Now reanimate yourself again and set up the aim for yourself.

◆ animation [ˌænɪ'meɪʃən] *n.* [C, U] 生气，活泼；动画片
This film is the first British animation sold to an American network.

◆ animism ['ænɪmɪzəm] *n.* [C] 万物有灵论；泛灵论
Animism is the belief that everything has a soul or spirit, including animals, plants, rocks, mountains, rivers, and stars.

◆ equanimity [ˌiːkwə'nɪmɪtɪ] *n.* [U] 平和，镇静
His sense of humor allowed him to face adversaries with equanimity.

◆ magnanimous [mæg'nænɪməs] *adj.* 宽宏大量的，有雅量的；落落大方的
He was magnanimous in defeat and praised his opponent's skill.

◆ unanimous [juː'nænɪməs] *adj.* 全体一致的，无异议的
Editors were unanimous in their condemnation of the proposals.

spir: breath

◆ spiracle ['spaɪərəkl] *n.* 通气孔，气门，喷水孔
The spiracle is a small hole behind each eye that opens to the mouth in some fish.

◆ aspire [ə'spaɪə(r)] *v.* [I] 渴望，立志，追求
They aspired to be gentlemen, though they fell far short of the ideal.

◆ aspirant [ə'spaɪərənt, 'æspɪr-] *adj.* 渴望的，有抱负的，追求名誉或地位的
n. 有志向或渴望获得……的人；候补者
Any aspirant to the presidency here must be seriously rich.

◆ conspire [kən'spaɪə(r)] *v.* [I] 搞阴谋；协力促成
v. [T] 阴谋策划
They were accused of conspiring against the king.

◆ conspiracy [kən'spɪrəsɪ] *n.* [C, U] 阴谋；反叛；共谋
They were charged with conspiracy to murder.

◆ inspire [ɪn'spaɪə(r)] *v.* [T] 鼓舞，激励；赋予灵感
v. [I] 吸，吸入
These herbs will inspire you to try out all sorts of exotic-flavored dishes!

◆ expire [ɪk'spaɪə(r)] *v.* [I] 期满；文件、协议等（因到期而）失效；断气
The chairman's term of office has already expired.

◆ respire [rɪ'spaɪər] *v.* [T] 呼吸
Like other fruits, bananas remain alive after being picked and they actually continue to respire.

◆ perspire [pə'spaɪə(r)] *v.* [I] 出汗，流汗
He began to perspire heavily.

nutr: breed

◆ nutrient ['njuːtrɪənt] *n.* [C] 营养物，养分，养料
The potato is a good nutrient medium for many bacteria.

◆ nutrition [njuː'trɪʃən] *n.* [U] 营养，营养品；营养学
The nutrition plays a role in the prevention of

nearsightedness.

◆ nurture [ˈnɜːtʃə(r)] *v.* [T] 养育，培育；滋养
n. 教养，培育
If you nurture something such as a young child or a young plant, you care for it while it is growing and developing.

◆ nursing [ˈnɜːsɪŋ] *n.* [U] 护理，看护；养育
She started a career in nursing twenty years ago.

◆ nursery [ˈnɜːsərɪ] *n.* [C] 幼儿园；苗圃；滋生地

◆ nourish [ˈnʌrɪʃ] *v.* [T] 滋养，抚养
The food she eats nourishes both her and the baby.

mort: die, dead

◆ mortal [ˈmɔːtl] *adj.* 致命的；不共戴天的；终有一死的
n. 凡人，人类
The police were defending themselves and others against mortal danger.

◆ immortal [ɪˈmɔːtl] *adj.* 不死的，永恒的；神的
n. [C] 神仙；流芳百世的人
Someone or something that is immortal is famous and likely to be remembered for a long time.

◆ mortician [mɔːˈtɪʃən] *n.* [C] 殡仪业者
A mortician is a person whose job is to deal with the bodies of the people who have died and to arrange funerals.

◆ mortuary [ˈmɔːtʃuərɪ] *n.* [C] 停尸房，太平间
adj. 丧葬的
A mortuary is a building or a room in a hospital where dead bodies are kept before they are buried or cremated, or before they are identified or examined.

◆ mortgage [ˈmɔːɡɪdʒ] *n.* [C] 抵押；债权
v. [T] 抵押
Their house was repossessed when they couldn't keep up their mortgage payments.

man/mani/manu: hand

◆ manage [ˈmænɪdʒ] *v.* [T] 使用；完成（困难的事）；经营
v. [I] 能解决（问题）；应付（困难局面等）；支撑
Within two years he was managing the store.

◆ manacle [ˈmænəkl] *n.* [C] 手铐
v. [T] 给……戴上手铐
He was manacled by the police.

◆ emancipate [ɪˈmænsɪpeɪt] *v.* [T] 解放；解脱
This new machine will emancipate us from the hard work.

◆ manicure [ˈmænɪkjʊə(r)] *n.* [C] 修指甲
v. [T] 修剪……的指甲；修剪
I have a manicure occasionally.

◆ manipulate [məˈnɪpjʊleɪt] *v.* [T] 操作；巧妙地控制，操纵
As a politician, he knows how to manipulate public opinion.

◆ manual [ˈmænjʊəl] *adj.* 手的；手工的
n. [C] 手册；指南
They do manual labor in the fields all the year round.
A manual is a book which tells you how to do something or how a piece of machinery works.

◆ manufacture [ˌmænjʊˈfæktʃə(r)] *v.* [T] 制造，生产；捏造
n. [C] 制造；产品
If the media can manufacture stories like

this, who are we supposed to believe?

◆ manuscript [ˈmænjʊskrɪpt] *n.* [C] 手稿，原稿；手写本

adj. 手写的，手抄的

I am grateful to him for letting me read his early chapters in manuscript.

ped: foot; children

◆ pedal [ˈpedl] *n.* [C] 踏板；脚蹬子；垂足线

v. [T and I] 踩自行车的踏板；骑自行车

adj. 脚的；踏板的

He pressed down the accelerator pedal of his car.

◆ peddle [ˈpedl] *v.* [T and I] 传播；叫卖；忙于做琐事

When a drug pusher offered the Los Angeles youngster $100 to peddle drugs, Jack refused.

◆ pedestrian [pɪˈdestrɪən] *n.* [C] 步行者；行人

adj. 徒步的；平淡无奇的

In Los Angeles a pedestrian is a rare spectacle.

◆ expedite [ˈekspɪdaɪt] *v.* [T] 加快进行，迅速完成

The builders promised to expedite the repairs.

◆ expedient [ɪkˈspiːdjənt] *adj.* 应急有效的，权宜之计的

n. 应急办法，权宜之计

Governments frequently ignore human rights abuses in other countries if it is politically expedient to do so.

◆ expedition [ˌekspɪˈdɪʃən] *n.* [C] 考察，远航；远征军

Caroline joined them on the shopping expeditions.

◆ impede [ɪmˈpiːd] *v.* [T] 阻碍；阻止

Fallen rock is impeding the progress of rescue workers.

◆ impediment [ɪmˈpedɪmənt] *n.* [C] 妨碍；口吃；障碍物

He was satisfied there was no legal impediment to the marriage.

◆ pedicure [ˈpedɪkjʊə(r)] *n.* [C] 足部护理，修脚

v. [T] 修脚

I have a manicure and a pedicure every week.

◆ centipede [ˈsentɪpiːd] *n.* [C] 蜈蚣

A centipede is a long and thin creature with a lot of legs.

◆ pediatrician [ˌpiːdɪəˈtrɪʃən] *n.* [C] 儿科医生

He's the best pediatrician in Westchester.

◆ pediatric [ˌpiːdɪˈætrɪk] *adj.* 小儿科的

Pediatric emergency medicine is a rapidly growing area of medicine.

◆ pedagogue [ˈpedəgɒg] *n.* [C] 教师，卖弄学问的教师

He was a French historian and pedagogue.

◆ encyclopedia [enˌsaɪkləʊˈpiːdɪə] *n.* [C] 百科全书

We bought a multimedia encyclopedia.

cap: head

◆ capital [ˈkæpɪtl] *n.* [C, U] 首都；资本；大写字母

adj. 最重要的；资本的；首都的

A large amount of capital is invested in all these branches.

◆ captain [ˈkæptɪn] *n.* [C] 船长，机长；首领；上尉

v. [T] 当首领；统帅或指挥

I'm happy to inform you that you have been promoted to captain.

◆ per capita［pəˈkæpɪtə］*adj.* 每人的；人均的

They have the world's largest per capita income.

◆ decapitate［dɪˈkæpɪteɪt］*v.*［T］杀头

He recently decapitated a tramp on the London Underground.

carn: meat, flesh

◆ carnal［ˈkɑːnl］*adj.* 世俗的；肉体的；性欲的

Our life on Earth is, and ought to be, material and carnal.

◆ carnation［kɑːˈneɪʃən］*n.*［C］康乃馨，麝香石竹；淡红色，肉色

adj. 淡红色的，肉色的

She received a bunch of carnations on her birthday.

◆ carnage［ˈkɑːnɪdʒ］*n.*［C］大屠杀

Refugees crossed the border to escape the carnage in their homeland.

◆ carnivore［ˈkɑːnɪvɔː(r)］*n.*［C］食肉动物，食虫植物

On your left, you have Tyrannosaurus Rex, a carnivore from the Jurassic period.

◆ incarnate［ɪnˈkɑːnɪt, -eɪt］*adj.* 人体化的；拟人化的；肉色的

v.［T］使成化身；使具体化；成为……典型

Why should God become incarnate as a male?

cord: heart

◆ core［kɔː(r)］*n.*［C］核心

Peel the pears and remove the cores.

◆ accord［əˈkɔːd］*n.* 一致；（音调的）谐和；（色彩的）协调

v.［T］给予；使和谐一致；使符合

v.［I］符合，一致

These results are in accord with the earlier research.

The punishments accorded with the current code of discipline.

◆ concord［ˈkɔŋkɔːd］*n.*［U］和谐，和睦

They expressed the hope that he would pursue a neutral and balanced policy for the sake of national concord.

◆ concordant［kənˈkɔːdnt］*adj.* 和谐的，一致的

The results were concordant with our hypothesis.

◆ discord［ˈdɪskɔːd］*n.*［C, U］不和；嘈杂声

A note of discord crept into their relationship.

◆ cordial［ˈkɔːdɪəl］*adj.* 热诚的；诚恳的；兴奋的

n.［C］补品；兴奋剂；甘露酒

He had never known her to be so chatty and cordial.

corp: body

◆ corpse［kɔːps］*n.*［C］尸体

He identified the corpse as the criminal hunted after.

◆ corporal［ˈkɔːpərəl］*adj.* 人体的

n.［C］下士

Nowadays, corporal punishment is banned in many schools.

◆ corporate［ˈkɔːpərɪt］*adj.* 公司的，全体的

The BBC is a corporate body.

◆ incorporate［ɪnˈkɔːpəreɪt］*v.*［T］组成公司；包含；使混合

v. [I] 包含；合并，混合

We had to incorporate the company for tax reasons.

fac/front: face

◆ facial [ˈfeɪʃəl] *adj.* 面部的

n. [C] 美容；面部按摩

Kate bears a strong facial resemblance to her sister.

◆ deface [dɪˈfeɪs] *v.* [T] 损伤外观，丑化，使失面子

It's illegal to deface banknotes.

◆ interface [ˈɪntəfeɪs] *n.* [C] 界面；交界面

v. [T] (使通过界面或接口) 接合，连接

v. [I] 相互作用（或影响）；交流

The new system interfaces with existing telephone equipment.

◆ preface [ˈprefɪs] *n.* [C] 序言；前奏；(弥撒的) 序祷

v. [T and I] 作为……的序言，作为……的开端

The president prefaced his remarks by saying he has supported unemployment benefits all along.

◆ surface [ˈsɜːfɪs] *n.* 表面

v. [T and I] 浮现，浮出水面

The rumors about the killings have begun to surface in the press.

◆ frontier [ˈfrʌntɪə(r)] *n.* 边境，前沿

It wasn't difficult then to cross the frontier.

◆ confront [kənˈfrʌnt] *v.* [T] 使勇敢面对，面临

She knew that she had to confront her fears.

◆ affront [əˈfrʌnt] *n.* (当众) 侮辱，冒犯

v. [T] 公开侮辱；面对

She has taken my enquiry as a personal affront.

◆ frontal [ˈfrʌntl] *adj.* 前面的；正面的

n. [C] 遮挡祭坛前的帷幕；建筑物的正面

Military leaders are not expecting a frontal assault by the rebels.

◆ forefront [ˈfɔːfrʌnt] *n.* [C] 最前部；前列；第一线

The pension issue was not at the forefront of his mind in the spring of 1985.

matr: mother

◆ maternal [məˈtɜːnl] *adj.* 母亲的，母亲般的

She had little maternal instinct.

◆ maternity [məˈtɜːnɪtɪ] *n.* 母性，为母之道；妇产科医院

adj. 产妇用的；产科的；孕妇的

Her going on maternity leave will create a temporary vacancy.

◆ matron [ˈmeɪtrən] *n.* [C] (受人尊敬的) 已婚老妇人；夫人；女看守；女警卫

Sure, everybody in the Second Army knows that matron.

◆ matriarchy [ˈmeɪtrɪɑːkɪ] *n.* [C] 母系社会，母权制

That is due to the matriarchy of its society.

◆ matricide [ˈmætrɪsaɪd, ˈmeɪ-] *n.* 弑母

A crime such as matricide is inconceivable.

patr: father

◆ paternal [pəˈtɜːnl] *adj.* 父亲的；父亲般的；父系的

I was brought up by my paternal aunt.

◆ paternity [pəˈtɜːnɪtɪ] *n.* [U] 父亲身份

The paternity of the child is in dispute.

◆ patriot [ˈpætrɪət, ˈpeɪ] *n.* [C] 爱国者

He was represented as a true patriot.

◆ compatriot [kəmˈpætrɪət] *n.* [C] 同胞；同国人

adj. 同国人的；同胞的

He played against one of his compatriots in the semi-final.

◆ patriarchy [ˈpeɪtrɪɑːkɪ] *n.* 父权制，族长

It is time to challenge standardised doctrines of patriarchy and imperialism.

◆ repatriate [riːˈpætrɪeɪt] *v.* [T] 把（某人）遣送回国，遣返

n. [C] 被遣返回国者

About 300 French hostages are to be repatriated.

◆ expatriate [eksˈpætrɪeɪt] *n.* [C] 移居国外者；被逐出其祖国者

adj. 移居国外的；被逐出其祖国的

v. [T and I]（使）移居国外，（使）放弃原国籍；放逐

The French military is preparing to evacuate the women and children of expatriate families.

◆ patron [ˈpeɪtrən] *n.* [C] 赞助人；老主顾；保护神

Catherine the Great was a patron of the arts and sciences.

◆ patricide [ˈpætrɪsaɪd] *n.* 杀父

When a will was discovered near the man's dead body, patricide was suspected.

Exercises

I. Match the roots with their meanings.

A. corp	( ) 1. mother
B. ped	( ) 2. father
C. carn	( ) 3. heart
D. mort	( ) 4. body
E. nutr	( ) 5. meat, flesh
F. gen	( ) 6. head
G. patr	( ) 7. foot, children
H. spir	( ) 8. die, dead
I. cap	( ) 9. breed
J. cord	( ) 10. breath
K. matr	( ) 11. people
L. dem	( ) 12. birth, creation
M. hum	( ) 13. man, earth
N. front	( ) 14. hand
O. man	( ) 15. face

II. Complete the sentences with the right forms of the best words.

conspire	aspire	respire	perspire	expire	inspire

1. Our challenge is to motivate those voters and ________ them to join our cause.
2. I always ________ when running.
3. They'd ________ to overthrow the government.
4. At that time, all serious artists ________ to go to Rome.

5. However, most of these contracts will ________ next month.

6. Like other fruit, bananas remain alive after being picked and they actually continue to ________.

III. Finish the words according to the definitions. The first letters are given.

1. p ________ to sell or offer for sale from place to place
2. e ________ to speed up the progress of; to facilitate
3. p ________ one who loves and defends his or her country
4. i ________ to make into a whole or make part of a whole
5. i ________ a person of enduring fame
6. p ________ a specialist in the care of babies
7. m ________ hand-written book or document
8. e ________ a long and carefully organized journey, especially to a dangerous or unfamiliar place, or the people that make this journey
9. m ________ to influence or control shrewdly or deviously
10. n ________ to supply with what is necessary for life, health, and growth

IV. Complete the sentences with the right forms of the best words.

humble	republican	feminine	populous	epidemic
mortgage	vitalize	congenial	indigenous	malignant

1. Amelia's report describes the experience from a ________ point of view.
2. She's contemptuous of my ________ home and poor surroundings.
3. He said that we were evil, ________ and mean.
4. That kind of ________ disease has long been stamped out.
5. Kangaroos are ________ to Australia.
6. China is the most ________ developing country in the world.
7. She and he were ________ companion in youth.
8. He's having a lot of trouble paying his ________ every month.
9. We are canvassing for the ________ candidate.
10. We hope the reform plan can ________ our economy.

Theme Two

敢作敢为-1

act/ag: do, perform, move, drive, draw out/forth

◆ activate [ˈæktɪveɪt] *v.* [T] 使活动，激活

The burglar alarm is activated by movement.

◆ actualize [ˈæktʃʊəlaɪz] *v.* [T] 实现

Mistakes are a necessary part of actualizing your vision.

◆ counteract [ˌkaʊntəˈrækt] *v.* [T] 对抗，抵制

They gave him drugs to counteract his withdrawal symptoms.

◆ enact [ɪˈnækt] *v.* [T] 颁布，制定；担任……角色

The authorities have failed so far to enact a law allowing unrestricted emigration.

◆ interact [ˌɪntərˈækt] *v.* [I] 相互作用

Lucy interacts well with other children in the class.

◆ transact [trænˈzækt] *v.* [T and I] 办理，交易

Most deals are transacted over the phone.

◆ agenda [əˈdʒendə] *n.* [C] 议事日程

The government set an agenda for constitutional reform.

◆ agile [ˈædʒaɪl] *adj.* 灵活的

Dogs are surprisingly agile.

◆ agitate [ˈædʒɪteɪt] *v.* [T and I] 煽动；使……焦虑

There are many political groups agitating for social change.

◆ agitation [ˌædʒɪˈteɪʃən] *n.* 烦乱，心焦；鼓动，骚动

She was in a state of considerable agitation.

fact/fect/fict: make, do

◆ factor [ˈfæktə(r)] *n.* [C] 要素，因素

The rise in crime is mainly due to social and economic factors.

◆ benefactor [ˈbenɪfæktə(r)] *n.* [C] 行善者，施主

A private benefactor donated £ 20,000.

◆ benefaction [ˌbenɪˈfækʃən] *n.* 善行

She made many charitable benefactions.

◆ malefactor [ˈmælɪfæktə(r)] *n.* [C] 作恶者，犯罪分子

Malefactors will be pursued and punished.

◆ facile [ˈfæs(a)ɪl] *adj.* 容易做到的；肤浅的

I hated him suggesting facile solutions when I knew very well that the problem was extremely complex.

◆ facilitate [fəˈsɪlɪteɪt] *v.* [T] 使容易，使便利

Computers can be used to facilitate language learning.

◆ affection [əˈfekʃən] *n.* 喜爱，爱

I have a great affection for New York.

◆ affect [əˈfekt] *v.* [T] 影响；感动；假装

We were all deeply affected by her death.

◆ effect [ɪˈfekt] *n.* 效果

My parents' divorce had a big effect on me.

◆ infect [ɪnˈfekt] *v.* [T] 传染，感染

Lucy's enthusiasm soon infected the rest of the class.

◆ fiction [ˈfɪkʃən] *n.* 小说；虚构的事，谎言；杜撰

It can sometimes be difficult to tell fact from fiction.

ten/tain: hold, keep

◆ tenable [ˈtenəbl] *adj.* 守得住的

The old idea that this type of work was not suitable for women was no longer tenable.

◆ tenant [ˈtenənt] *n.* [C] 佃户，承租人

The desk was left by the previous tenant.

◆ tenet [ˈtenɪt, ˈtiːnɪt] *n.* [C] 信条，教义

Non-violence and patience are the central tenets of their faith.

◆ continent [ˈkɒntɪnənt] *adj.* 自制的，克制的

n. [C] 大陆

We're going to spend a weekend on the Continent.

◆ continence [ˈkɒntɪnəns] *n.* [U] 自制，节制

During much of that time, the United States enforced social norms that favored sexual continence, early marriage and low divorce rates.

◆ abstain [əbˈsteɪn] *v.* [I] 戒除，放弃

Pilots must abstain from alcohol for 24 hours before flying.

◆ obtain [əbˈteɪn] *v.* [T and I] 获取，得到

Further information can be obtained from head office.

◆ detain [dɪˈteɪn] *v.* [T] 拘留，耽搁

He was detained in Washington on urgent business.

◆ entertain [ˌentəˈteɪn] *v.* [T and I] 款待，娱乐

A museum should aim to entertain as well as educate.

◆ maintain [meɪnˈteɪn] *v.* [T] 保持，维持；认为

It is important to maintain a constant temperature inside the greenhouse.

◆ retain [rɪˈteɪn] *v.* [T] 留住，保留

Limestone is known to retain moisture.

◆ sustain [səˈsteɪn] *v.* [T] 支撑，维持

They gave me barely enough food to sustain me.

ser (servare): keep, save, protect

◆ conserve [kənˈsɜːv] *v.* [T] 保存；使守恒；将……做成蜜饯

n. 果酱，蜜饯

Conserve your energy. You'll need it!

◆ conservative [kənˈsɜːvətɪv] *n.* [C] 保守的人；(英国)保守党党员

adj. 保守的；(英国)保守党的

Politically, they belonged to the Conservative Party and opposed reform.

◆ observe [əbˈzɜːv] *v.* [T and I] 观察；遵守；保持

We must observe the correct protocol.

◆ observance [əbˈzɜːvəns] *n.* 遵守，奉行；仪式；庆祝

Local councils should use their powers to ensure the strict observance of laws.

◆ observant [əbˈzɜːvənt] *adj.* 善于观察的；严守教规的

She was intelligent and highly observant.

◆ reserve [rɪˈzɜːv] *v.* [T and I] 储备；保留；预订

n. [C, U] 保存，储备；准备金

Say all you know and say it without reserve.

◆ reservoir [ˈrezəvwɑː(r)] *n.* [C] 蓄水池；储藏

A large quantity of water is stored in the reservoir.

◆ preservative [prɪˈzɜːvətɪv] *n.* 防腐剂；预防法；防护层

adj. 防腐的，(能) 保存的

The wood is treated with preservative to prevent decay.

◆ preserve [prɪˈzɜːv] *v.* [T and I] 保护；保存；腌制食物；做蜜饯

n. [C] 蜜饯；禁猎地；独占的事物

The country is fighting to preserve its territorial integrity.

hab/hib: live; have, hold

◆ habitual [həˈbɪtjʊəl, -tʃʊ-] *adj.* 习惯的；习以为常的

He is a habitual criminal.

◆ habitable [ˈhæbɪtəbl] *adj.* 适于居住的

This house is no longer habitable.

◆ habitat [ˈhæbɪtæt] *n.* 栖息地，住处；经常发现某种事物的地方

This creature's natural habitat is the jungle.

◆ habitation [ˌhæbɪˈteɪʃən] *n.* [C, U] 居住；住宅，家

The broken-down old house was not fit for human habitation.

◆ cohabit [kəʊˈhæbɪt] *v.* [I] (未婚者) 同居

The house mouse can cohabit with man and adapt very well to urbanization.

◆ inhabitant [ɪnˈhæbɪtənt] *n.* [C] 居民；(栖息在某地区的) 动物

Panda is the inhabitant of this mountainous area.

◆ rehabilitate [ˌriːəˈbɪlɪteɪt, ˌriːhə-] *v.* [T] 使康复；使复原

He used exercise programs to rehabilitate the patients.

◆ exhibit [ɪgˈzɪbɪt] *v.* [T and I] 陈列，展览；呈现

n. [C] 展览，陈列；〈法〉证据

His work was exhibited in the best galleries in America, Europe and Asia.

◆ prohibit [prəˈhɪbɪt] *v.* [T] 禁止，阻止，防止

Prohibit the sale of alcoholic beverages.

◆ inhibit [ɪnˈhɪbɪt] *v.* [T] 抑制；禁止

It could inhibit the poor from getting the medical care they need.

◆ malady [ˈmælədɪ] *n.* [C] 弊病，弊端；疾病

Malaria is a kind of serious malady.

ple/pli: fill, full

◆ deplete [dɪˈpliːt] *v.* [T and I] 耗尽，损耗；枯竭

It will deplete its cash balance by repaying last week's loan.

◆ replete [rɪˈpliːt] *adj.* 饱食的；充满的，供应充足的

He was replete with food and drink.

◆ replenish [rɪˈplenɪʃ] *v.* [T] 补充；重新装满

In so doing, we can replenish our reservoir of faith.

◆ completion [kəmˈpliːʃən] *n.* 完成，结束；实现

The completion of the building is scheduled for May.

◆ implement [ˈɪmplɪmənt] *v.* [T] 实施，执行；使生效

n. [C] 工具，器械；手段

These policies have never been fully implemented.

The best implement for digging a garden is a

spade.

◆ complement [ˈkɒmplɪmənt] *n.* [C] 补充；补足语；补充物
v. [T] 补足，补充；补助
Rice makes an excellent complement to a curry dish.

◆ supplement [ˈsʌplɪmənt] *v.* [T] 增补，补充
n. [C] 补充；补充物；增刊
A supplement to this dictionary may be published next year.

◆ compliment [ˈkɒmplɪmənt] *n.* [C] 恭维；敬意；道贺
v. [T] 向……道贺；称赞；向……致意
The manager paid her a compliment on her work.

◆ complimentary [ˌkɒmplɪˈmentərɪ] *adj.* 免费赠送的，表示敬意的；赞美的
The supermarket operates a complimentary shuttle service.

pos/pon: put, place

◆ pose [pəʊz] *v.* [T and I] 使摆姿势；以……身份出现
v. [T] 提出；引起
n. 姿势；姿态；装腔作势
The events pose a challenge to the church's leadership.

◆ compose [kəmˈpəʊz] *v.* [T and I] 组成，作曲；使镇静
Water is composed of hydrogen and oxygen.

◆ decompose [ˌdiːkəmˈpəʊz] *v.* [T and I] 分解，腐烂
The meat begins to decompose after some time in the sun.

◆ discompose [ˌdɪskəmˈpəʊz] *v.* [T] 使不安；使烦恼
The grin of his friend discomposed Jack when he tried to make his speech.

◆ impose [ɪmˈpəʊz] *v.* [T] 强加于
The government imposed a ban on the sale of ivory.

◆ expose [ɪkˈspəʊz] *v.* [T] 使暴露，揭发
The report exposes the weaknesses of modern medical practice.

◆ depose [dɪˈpəʊz] *v.* [T] 罢免
The president was deposed in a military coup.

◆ deposit [dɪˈpɒzɪt] *n.* [C] 定金，存款
v. [T and I] 储存，沉淀
We ask for one month's rent in advance, plus a deposit of $500.

◆ dispose [dɪˈspəʊz] *v.* 编排，清除，解决
It's difficult to dispose of nuclear waste.

◆ disposition [ˌdɪspəˈzɪʃən] *n.* 排列，部署，意向，性情
The film is not suitable for the people of a nervous disposition.

◆ interpose [ˌɪntəˈpəʊz] *v.* [T] 介入，插嘴
She interposed herself between the general and his wife.

◆ transpose [trænsˈpəʊz] *v.* [T] 调换位置，颠倒
The director transposes the action from 16th Century France to post-Civil War America.

◆ oppose [əˈpəʊz] *v.* [T] 反对
The Congress is continuing to oppose the President's healthcare budget.

◆ propose [prəˈpəʊz] *v.* [T] 提议；打算；求婚
A number of theories have been proposed to explain the phenomenon.

sert: put in a row, line up, join together

◆ assert [əˈsɜːt] *v.* [T] 声称，断言；坚持
French cooking, she asserted, is the best in

the world.

◆ desert［di'zəːt］*v.*［T］抛弃，遗弃
［'dezət］*n.* 沙漠，荒地
The rise of the price caused many people to desert magazines.
The Sahara Desert is the largest desert in the world.

◆ desertion［dɪ'zɜːʃən］*n.* 离弃；抛弃；擅离职守
The officer was convicted of desertion.

◆ exert［ɪɡ'zɜːt］*v.*［T］发挥；运用；使受（影响等）
He likes to exert his authority.

◆ insert［ɪn'sɜːt］*v.*［T］插入；嵌入
n. 添入物；插页
I wish to insert an advertisement in your newspaper.

ject: throw

◆ inject［ɪn'dʒekt］*v.*［T］注射；添加
We hope to inject new life into our work.

◆ project［'prɒdʒekt］*v.*［T］放映；计划；发射
v.［I］伸出，突出
n. 计划，项目
Four towers projected from the main building.
The project was hung up for lack of funds.

◆ subject［'sʌbdʒɪkt］*n.* 主题，话题；学科
adj. 须服从……的；（在君主等）统治下的
v.［T and I］提供，提出；使……隶属
Prices may be subject to alteration.
He did not want to subject himself to the judgments of his superiors.

◆ reject［rɪ'dʒekt］*v.*［T］拒绝；抛弃；吐出
n. 被拒绝或被抛弃的人或事物
I'm shocked that you rejected her like that.

◆ eject［ɪ'dʒekt］*v.*［T］喷出；驱逐
v.［I］弹射出
The manager threatened to have them ejected if there was any more trouble.

◆ deject［dɪ'dʒekt］*v.*［T］使沮丧，使灰心
The news dejected her.

◆ object［'ɒbdʒɪkt］*n.* 物体；目标；宾语；对象
［əb'dʒekt］*v.*［I］不赞成，反对
v.［T］提出……作反对的理由
The object of the exercise is to raise money for the charity.
I don't object to the children going with us.

◆ abject［'æbdʒekt］*adj.* 卑鄙的，下贱的；厚颜无耻的
He is poor but not abject in his manner.

tract: draw

◆ tractor［'træktə(r)］*n.*［C］拖拉机；牵引器
He learnt tractor maintenance.

◆ attract［ə'trækt］*v.*［T and I］吸引；诱惑
This advertisement is calculated to attract the attention of housewives.

◆ abstract［'æbstrækt］*adj.* 抽象的，理论上的；难解的
n. 抽象概念；摘要；萃取物
v.［T］提取；转移（注意等）；摘录
He is an abstract painter.
An abstract of an article, document, or speech is a short piece of writing that gives the main points of it.
The author has abstracted poems from earlier books.

◆ contract［kən'trækt］*v.*［T and I］染上（恶习、疾病等）；缩小，紧缩
v.［I］订契约，承包

[ˈkɔntrækt] *n.* 合同，契约

Glass contracts as it cools.

The terms of the contract are acceptable to us.

◆ detract [dɪˈtrækt] *v.* [I] 贬低；减损

The publicity could detract from our election campaign.

◆ distract [dɪˈstrækt] *v.* [T] 使分心；使混乱

She jabbered away, trying to distract his attention.

◆ extract [ɪkˈstrækt] *v.* [T] 提取；选取；获得

[ˈekstrækt] *n.* 汁；摘录；提炼物；浓缩物

Oils are extracted from the plants.

◆ protract [prəˈtrækt] *v.* [T] 延长，拖延

The cat can protract its paws.

◆ subtract [sʌbˈtrækt] *v.* [T] 减去；扣除

Please subtract a quarter of the money for your own use.

◆ retract [rɪˈtrækt] *v.* [T and I] 撤回或撤消；缩回；缩进

You may retract that statement.

lev/liev: raise

◆ lever [ˈliːvə(r)] *n.* [C] 杠杆；操作杆；工具

v. [T] 用杠杆撬动

He is repairing the brake lever of an automobile.

◆ levitate [ˈlevɪteɪt] *v.* [T and I] （使）轻轻浮起；（使）飘浮空中

I often dream that I can levitate.

◆ alleviate [əˈliːvɪeɪt] *v.* [T] 减轻，缓和

The doctor gave her an injection to alleviate the pain.

◆ elevate [ˈelɪveɪt] *v.* [T] 举起；提升；鼓舞

Reading good books elevates one's mind.

◆ elevator [ˈelɪveɪtə(r)] *n.* [C] 电梯；升降机；（美）谷仓

The elevator doesn't stop at floors 1, 2 and 3.

◆ levity [ˈlevɪtɪ] *n.* 欠考虑；轻率

Your levity is unseemly at this time.

◆ relieve [rɪˈliːv] *v.* [T] 解除；缓解；换班

The doctors did their best to relieve the patient.

◆ relief [rɪˈliːf] *n.* 宽慰；免除，减轻

She sighed with relief when she heard the good news.

mis/mit: send, throw

◆ missile [ˈmɪsaɪl] *n.* [C] 导弹；投射物

adj. 导弹的；可投掷的

The authorities offered to stop firing missiles if the rebels agreed to stop attacking civilian targets.

◆ mission [ˈmɪʃən] *n.* 代表团；使命；布道所

v. 给……交代任务；派遣；向……传教

A Chinese trade mission has been dispatched to Japan.

◆ dismiss [dɪsˈmɪs] *v.* [T and I] 解雇；遣散；驳回

At first she threatened to dismiss me, but later she relented.

◆ emit [ɪˈmɪt] *v.* [T] 发出；发射；发表

She was heard to emit a cry of horror.

◆ omit [ə(ʊ)ˈmɪt] *v.* [T] 省略；遗漏；删掉

Please don't omit to lock the door when you leave.

◆ permit [pəˈmɪt] *v.* [T and I] 准许；默许，放任

[ˈpɜːmɪt] *n.* [C] 许可；许可证，执照

Hikers need a camping permit for overnight stays in the park.

◆ admit [ədˈmɪt] *v.* [T and I] 许可进入；承认，允许

He will never admit to me that he is lazy.

◆ submit [səbˈmɪt] *v.* [I] 顺从，服从；甘受

v. [T] 使服从，使顺从；提交

Never submit to a threat.

◆ submissive [səbˈmɪsɪv] *adj.* 顺从的，唯命是从的

Their early training programs ask them to be obedient and submissive.

◆ transmit [trænzˈmɪt] *v.* [T] 传输；传送；发射

v. [I] 发送信号

Insects can transmit diseases.

pel/pul: push, drive

◆ compel [kəmˈpel] *v.* [T] 强迫

Do you think you can compel obedience from me?

◆ compelling [kəmˈpelɪŋ] *adj.* 引人入胜的；非常强烈的；不可抗拒的

There is a compelling logic to his main theory.

◆ dispel [dɪˈspel] *v.* [T] 消除（疑虑等）；驱散（云雾等）

I tried in vain to dispel her misgivings.

◆ expel [ɪkˈspel] *v.* [T] 驱逐；赶走；排出（气体等）

They were told at first that they should simply expel the refugees.

◆ impel [ɪmˈpel] *v.* [T] 推动、敦促某人做某事

My final goal is to impel China's renaissance!

◆ propel [prəˈpel] *v.* [T] 推进，推动，驱动

They use oars to propel boats.

◆ repel [rɪˈpel] *v.* [T] 击退；使厌恶；抵制

They have fifty thousand troops along the border ready to repel any attack.

◆ repulse [rɪˈpʌls] *v.* [T] 击退；驳斥；拒绝

n. 击败

Her request for a donation met with a repulse.

◆ repulsive [rɪˈpʌlsɪv] *adj.* 令人厌恶的，可憎的；丑恶的

He was utterly repulsive to her.

◆ expulsion [ɪkˈspʌlʃən] *n.* 驱逐；开除；排出；喷出

His bad behavior resulted in his expulsion from school.

◆ impulse [ˈɪmpʌls] *n.* 凭冲动行事；脉冲；冲动

adj. 冲动的

The plan will give an impulse to industrial expansion.

◆ impulsive [ɪmˈpʌlsɪv] *adj.* 冲动的；任性的；受感情驱使的

She is impulsive in her actions.

◆ compulsion [kəmˈpʌlʃən] *n.* 强迫；冲动；打动人的力量

Compulsion will never result in convincing them.

◆ compulsive [kəmˈpʌlsɪv] *adj.* 极有趣的；令人着迷的；强迫性的

Their story makes compulsive reading.

◆ compulsory [kəmˈpʌlsərɪ] *adj.* 必须做的，强制性的；义务的；必修的

Compulsory schooling ends at sixteen.

crit: judge

◆ critic [ˈkrɪtɪk] *n.* [C] 批评家；评论员；

挑剔的人

She is an outspoken critic of the school system in this city.

◆ critical [ˈkrɪtɪkl] *adj.* 批评的，爱挑剔的；危急的；决定性的

Now that the situation becomes critical, one must keep calm.

◆ hypercritical [ˌhaɪpəˈkrɪtɪkl] *adj.*（尤指对小错误）吹毛求疵的，过于苛刻的

He would be courageous, calm and self-assured, but neither pompous nor hypercritical.

◆ hypocritical [ˌhɪpə(ʊ)ˈkrɪtɪkl] *adj.* 虚伪的；言不由衷的

It's hypocritical to say one thing and do another.

◆ criticize [ˈkrɪtɪsaɪz] *v.* [T and I] 分析，评估；批评

Whenever you criticize him, he always has an excuse.

◆ critique [krɪˈtiːk] *n.* [C] 评论文章；批评

v. [T] 发表评论；批判

They all joined in a very spirited critique upon the party.

◆ criterion [kraɪˈtɪərɪən] *n.* 标准，准则；规范

Practice is the sole criterion of truth.

cure/cur: take care

◆ curious [ˈkjʊərɪəs] *adj.* 好奇的；好求知的；奇妙的

He grew curious about how to make a toy.

◆ secure [sɪˈkjʊə(r)] *adj.* 安全的；牢固的；有把握的

v. [T and I] 保护；获得安全；担保

He found a secure foothold and pulled himself up.

Federal leaders continued their efforts to secure a ceasefire.

◆ security [sɪˈkjʊərɪtɪ] *n.* 安全；保证；保护；有价证券

They lulled her into a false sense of security.

◆ cure [kjʊə(r)] *v.* [T] 治愈；解决

v. [I] 受治疗；被加工处理

n. 治愈；药物；疗法

His cancer can only be controlled, not cured.

◆ curable [ˈkjʊərəbl] *adj.* 可治愈的

Tuberculosis is a curable disease.

◆ curio [ˈkjʊərɪəʊ] *n.* [C] 小件珍奇物

The curio shop is behind the post office.

◆ curator [kjʊəˈreɪtə(r)] *n.* [C]（图书馆等的）馆长；监护人；〈英〉（大学）学监

The curator conducted us round the museum.

◆ accurate [ˈækjʊrɪt] *adj.* 精确的，准确的

He has made an accurate measurement of my garden.

◆ procure [prəˈkjʊə(r)] *v.* [T] 取得，获得

He was accused of procuring weapons for terrorists.

◆ manicure [ˈmænɪkjʊə(r)] *n.* [C] 修指甲

v. [T] 修剪……的指甲；修剪，修平

I have a manicure occasionally.

◆ pedicure [ˈpedɪkjʊə(r)] *n.* [C] 修脚；（修趾甲）医师

v. [T] 修脚

I want to have a manicure and a pedicure.

mon: warn; advise; remind

◆ monitor [ˈmɒnɪtə(r)] *n.* [C] 显示器；监测仪；监控人员

v. [T and I] 监控；记录；监督

If we can know their frequency, we will monitor their talking.

◆ monitory [ˈmɒnɪtərɪ] *adj.* 训诫的

n. 告诫书

She shook a monitory finger at him.

◆ admonish [əd'mɒnɪʃ] *v.* [T] 劝告；训诫；（温和地）责备

Admonish your friend in secret, and commend him in public.

◆ admonition [ˌædmə(ʊ)'nɪʃən] *n.* 告诫；劝告；（温和的）责备

The youth rejected admonition and held to his demand.

◆ premonition [ˌpriːmə'nɪʃən] *n.* [C] 预感，预兆；预诫

The day before her accident, she had a premonition of danger.

◆ premonitory [prɪ'mɒnɪtərɪ] *adj.* 有预兆的

There came a day when the first premonitory blast of winter swept over the city.

◆ monument ['mɒnjʊmənt] *n.* [C] 纪念碑；遗迹；丰碑

A monument was set up as a memorial to the dead soldiers.

Exercises

I. Match the roots with their meanings.

A. mon	( ) 1. judge
B. cur	( ) 2. send, throw
C. crit	( ) 3. throw
D. pel	( ) 4. take care
E. ple	( ) 5. draw
F. mis	( ) 6. raise
G. tract	( ) 7. push, drive
H. ject	( ) 8. advise, remind
I. lev	( ) 9. full, fill
J. pos	( ) 10. live, hold
K. hab	( ) 11. put, place
L. serv	( ) 12. hold, keep
M. act	( ) 13. do
N. fact	( ) 14. make, do
O. ten	( ) 15. serve, keep

II. Complete the sentences with the right forms of the best words.

activate	affection	sustain	detain	actualize
repulsive	infect	abstain	capture	agitate

1. Police have sealed off the ________ areas of the country.
2. The gene is ________ by a specific protein.
3. The women who worked in these mills had begun to ________ for better conditions.
4. Two suspects have been ________ by the police for questioning.
5. She is craving for love and ________.
6. She found it difficult to ________ children's interest.

7. Six countries voted for the change, five voted against, and two ________.
8. Many students hold the opinion that if they study hard, they will ________ their ideals in the future.
9. The sight of him is ________ to me.
10. These photographs ________ the essence of working-class life at the turn of the century.

III. Finish the words according to the definitions. The first letters are given.

1. r ________	to keep something or continue to have something
2. e ________	to make into an act; to represent on the stage
3. d ________	to cease to consider, to terminate the employment of
4. r ________	to make something full again
5. h ________	usual, having a habit of
6. p ________	to put forward something as a plan
7. t ________	capable of being held, maintained, or defended, as against attack or dispute
8. c ________	to act in opposition to
9. b ________	a person who gives money or other help to a person or an organization such as a school or charity
10. f ________	to make things easier or less difficult to do

IV. Choose the best answers.

1. These people ________ to make more than the minimum wage.
   A. conserve B. deserve
   C. reserve D. observe
2. The year 1995 has seen a period of ________ economic growth.
   A. entertained B. detained
   C. maintained D. sustained
3. Millions of people want new and simplified ways of ________ with a computer.
   A. transacting B. counteracting
   C. enacting D. interacting
4. The law ________ tobacco advertising in newspapers and magazines.
   A. exhibits B. cohabits
   C. prohibits D. inhibits
5. You can do no harm by paying a woman ________.
   A. compliments B. complements
   C. supplements D. implements
6. Modern industry produces many things, from coal ash to computers, which are difficult to ________ of properly.
   A. impose B. compose
   C. depose D. dispose
7. Environmental groups ________ pressure on the government to tighten pollution laws.

A. insert B. exert
C. assert D. desert

8. His son was ________ with strong drugs.

A. rejected B. injected
C. subjected D. ejected

9. Don't let yourself be ________ by fashionable theories.

A. detracted B. contracted
C. distracted D. protracted

10. They ________ their reports to the Chancellor yesterday.

A. submitted B. omitted
C. emitted D. permitted

Theme Two

敢作敢为-2

car/cur: go, run

◆ career [kəˈrɪə(r)] *v.* [I] 全速前进，猛冲
n. 事业
His car careered into a river.

◆ cargo [ˈkɑːgəʊ] *n.* [C, U] 飞机、船等装载的货物；负荷，荷重
The tanker began to spill its cargo of oil.

◆ cart [kɑːt] *n.* [C] 运货马车，手推车；一车之量
v. [T] 用推车或卡车运送；费力搬运
We carted all the furniture upstairs.

◆ charge [tʃɑːdʒ] *v.* [T] 装载；控诉；使充电
v. [T and I] 指责；进攻
v. [I] 收费；要求支付
n. 费用；掌管；指责；指控
He will be sent back to England to face a charge of armed robbery.

◆ current [ˈkʌrənt] *adj.* 现在的；最近的；流行的
n. [C] 趋势；电流；水流
The factory cannot continue its current level of production.

◆ concur [kənˈkɜː(r)] *v.* [I] 同时发生；共同作用
Historians have concurred with each other in this view.

◆ cursory [ˈkɜːsərɪ] *adj.* 粗略的，草率的，仓促的
I gave the letter a fairly cursory reading.

◆ cursor [ˈkɜːsər] *n.* [C] 光标
You can move the cursor by using the mouse.

◆ excursion [ɪkˈskɜːʃən] *n.* [C] (尤指集体) 远足；短途旅行；离题
In Bermuda, Sam's father took him on an excursion to a coral barrier.

◆ excursive [ɪkˈskɜːsɪv] *adj.* 离题的，散漫的
His speech was filled with excursive statements.

◆ incur [ɪnˈkɜː(r)] *v.* [T] 招致，引起；遭受
The government had also incurred huge debts.

◆ occur [əˈkɜː(r)] *v.* [I] 发生，出现；闪现
If headaches only occur at night, lack of fresh air and oxygen is often the cause.

◆ recur [rɪˈkɜː(r)] *v.* [I] 再发生；重现；回想
Economic crises recur periodically.

ced/ceed/cess: go, give away, yield

◆ cede [siːd] *v.* [T] 割让；放弃
Cuba was ceded by Spain to the US in 1898.

◆ cession [ˈseʃən] *n.* [C, U] (领土的) 割

让，（财产的）转让

Third-party states have no title to object to cession.

◆ accede［æk'siːd］*v.*［I］（正式）加入；答应

Britain would not accede to France's request.

◆ access［'ækses］*n.*［U］入口；进入

v.［T］接近，进入；获取

Scientists have only recently been able to gain access to the area.

◆ ancestor［'ænsestə(r)，-sɪs-］*n.*［C］祖先，祖宗

He could trace his ancestors back seven hundred years.

◆ antecedent［ˌæntɪ'siːdənt］*n.*［C］前情，先行词，祖先

adj. 在前的，先行的

It was permissible to take account of antecedent legislation.

◆ concede［kən'siːd］*v.*［T］不情愿地承认；让步

I conceded that I had made a number of errors.

◆ concession［kən'seʃən］*n.*［C，U］让步，承认或允许

The firm will be forced to make concessions if it wants to avoid a strike.

◆ exceed［ɪk'siːd］*v.*［T］超过；超越

v.［I］突出，领先

Its research budget exceeds ＄700 million a year.

◆ excess［ɪk'ses，'ek-］*n.*［C，U］超过；超额量；放肆

adj. 超重的，过量的，额外的

An excess of house plants in a small flat can be oppressive.

Cut any excess fat from the meat.

◆ proceed［prə'siːd］*v.*［I］继续进行；前进

n.（plural）收入，获利

The government was determined to proceed with the election.

The proceeds of the concert went to the charity.

◆ process［'prəʊses］*n.* 过程；工序；工艺流程

v.［T］加工；处理；审核

v.［I］列队行进

There was total agreement to start the peace process as soon as possible.

◆ precede［prɪ'siːd］*v.*［T and I］在……之前发生或出现，优于

The earthquake was preceded by a loud roar and lasted 20 seconds.

◆ precedent［'presɪdənt］*n.*［C］前例；先例

adj. 在前的，在先的

Is there a precedent for what you want me to do?

◆ precedence［'presɪdəns］*n.*［U］领先；优先权

Have as much fun as possible at college, but don't let it take precedence over work.

◆ recede［rɪ'siːd］*v.*［I］后退；减弱

As she receded, he waved goodbye.

◆ recess［rɪ'ses，'riːses］*n.*［C］休息；隐蔽处；凹处

v.［T］把某物放在凹处；（暂时）休息

v.［I］休息，休会，休庭

The conference broke for a recess.

◆ secede［sɪ'siːd］*v.*［T］从……中脱离

v.［I］脱离；退出

The Republic of Panama seceded from Colombia in 1903.

◆ secession［sɪ'seʃən］*n.*［U］退出，脱离

Croatia was ready for its secession from Yugoslavia.

◆ recession［rɪ'seʃən］*n.* 经济衰退；撤退；凹处

The recession caused sales to drop off.

◆ succeed [səkˈsiːd] *v.* [I] 成功；继承
v. [T] 继承；随……之后
Who will succeed him to the throne?

◆ success [səkˈses] *n.* [C, U] 成功
The jewelry was a great success.

◆ succession [səkˈseʃən] *n.* [C, U] 继承人，继承权
She is now the seventh in line of succession to the throne.

◆ successor [səkˈsesə(r)] *n.* 接替的人或事物；继承人
He set out several principles that he hopes will guide his successors.

◆ successive [səkˈsesɪv] *adj.* 连续的，继承的，逐次的
Jackson was the winner for a second successive year.

fer: go, carry; bear

◆ ferry [ˈferɪ] *n.* [C] 渡船；渡口；摆渡
v. [T and I] 渡运，摆渡
A helicopter ferried in more soldiers to help in the search.

◆ circumference [səˈkʌmfərəns] *n.* [C, U] 周围，圆周；胸围
It's a mile round the circumference of the field.

◆ confer [kənˈfɜː(r)] *v.* [T] 授予，颁与；比较
v. [I] 商议，磋商
An honorary degree was conferred on him by the University.
He wanted to confer with his colleagues before reaching a decision.

◆ conference [ˈkɒnfərəns] *n.* 会议
v. [I] 举行或参加（系列）会议
She is attending a three-day conference on AIDS education.

◆ differ [ˈdɪfə(r)] *v.* [I] 不同；意见相左
French differs from English in this respect.

◆ indifferent [ɪnˈdɪfərənt] *adj.* 不感兴趣的，漠不关心的
People have become indifferent to the suffering of others.

◆ defer [dɪˈfɜː(r)] *v.* [T and I] 推迟；延期；服从
The department deferred the decision for six months.

◆ deference [ˈdefərəns] *n.* [U] 顺从；尊重
The flags were lowered out of deference to the bereaved family.

◆ infer [ɪnˈfɜː(r)] *v.* [T] 推断；猜想，暗示
I inferred from what she said that you have not been well.

◆ prefer [prɪˈfɜː(r)] *v.* [T] 更喜欢
Does he prefer a particular sort of music?

◆ preference [ˈprefərəns] *n.* [C, U] 偏爱；优先权
The choice was to him a matter of personal preference.

◆ suffer [ˈsʌfə(r)] *v.* [I] 受痛苦；受损害
v. [T] 忍受；遭受
I realized he was suffering from shock.

◆ fertile [ˈfɜːtaɪl] *adj.* 肥沃的；可繁殖的；丰富的
The land is not fertile enough to repay cultivation.

◆ fertility [fɜːˈtɪlɪtɪ] *n.* 肥沃；繁殖力
He was able to bring large sterile acreages back to fertility.

◆ fertilize [ˈfɜːtɪlaɪz] *v.* [T] 使肥沃；使受孕；施肥
Reading will fertilize his vocabulary.

ger/gest: carry; bear

◆ congest [kən'dʒest] v. [T and I] 充满，拥挤

He knew how the traffic congested at the junction of Seventh Avenue and Forty-second Street.

◆ digest [dɪ'dʒest,daɪ-] v. [T and I] 消化；吸收；整理

n. 文摘；法律汇编

Humans cannot digest plants such as grass.

◆ ingest [ɪn'dʒest] v. [T] 咽下；获取；吸收

You will ingest only the lightest of substances.

◆ exaggerate [ɪg'zædʒəreɪt] v. [T and I] 夸张，夸大

It's difficult to exaggerate the importance of sleep.

◆ belligerent [bɪ'lɪdʒərənt] adj. 交战的；好战的

He was almost back to his belligerent mood of twelve months ago.

◆ gesture ['dʒestʃə(r)] n. 手势，姿势；姿态，表示

v. [I] 打手势，用动作示意

Sarah made a menacing gesture with her fist.

He gestured for her to take a seat.

◆ gesticulate [dʒe'stɪkjʊleɪt] v. [I] 做手势示意或强调

We sometimes gesticulate even when talking on the telephone.

◆ registered ['redʒɪstəd] adj. 注册的；登记过的；已挂号的

He asked his mother to send it by registered mail.

◆ registry ['redʒɪstrɪ] n. 记录，登记

He agreed to set up a central registry of arms sales.

port: carry; gate

◆ porter ['pɔːtə(r)] n. 门童；搬运工人

The hotel porter will help you.

◆ portable ['pɔːtəbl] adj. 手提的；轻便的

I always carry a portable computer with me.

◆ portage ['pɔːtɪdʒ] n. （两条水路间货物、小船等的）陆上运输，陆上运输路线

Finally, after a month of hard labor, the portage was complete.

◆ portfolio [ˌpɔːt'fəʊlɪəʊ] n. 公文包；文件夹

After dinner that evening, Edith showed them a portfolio of her own political cartoons.

◆ disport [dɪ'spɔːt] v. [T and I] 嬉戏，玩乐，自娱

Every Sunday, they disport themselves either in the parks or in the mountains.

◆ rapport [ræ'pɔː] n. 友好关系；融洽，和谐

He said he wanted to establish a rapport with the Indian people.

◆ import ['ɪmpɔːt] n. 进口，进口商品

v. [ɪm'pɔːt] [T] 输入，进口；对……有重大关系

Germany, however, insists on restrictions on the import of Polish coal.

◆ export ['ekspɔːt] n. 输出，出口

v. [ɪk'spɔːt] [T and I] 出口，输出

The nation also exports beef.

◆ transport [træn'spɔːt] v. [T] 运送，运输；

n. 运输

Transport networks need to be expanded to remote rural areas.

◆ deport [dɪ'pɔːt] v. [T] 把……驱逐出境

More than 240 England football fans are being deported from Italy following riots last night.

◆ opportune [ˈɒpətjuːn] *adj.* 恰好的；及时的；适时的

Her arrival was very opportune.

◆ opportunity [ˌɒpəˈtjuːnɪtɪ] *n.* 机会

I want to see more opportunities for young people.

grad/gress: step, go

◆ grade [greɪd] *n.* 等级，班级

v. [T] 依序排列；评分

v. [I] 属于……等级；缓缓地变化或发展

All the materials used were of the highest grade.

◆ gradient [ˈgreɪdjənt] *n.* 梯度，陡度

adj. 倾斜的；步行的

The car slid down the steep gradient into the river.

◆ graduate [ˈgrædʒʊət, -djʊ-] *v.* [I] 渐变

v. [T] 授予学位或毕业证书

n. 毕业生；研究生

adj. 〈美〉毕业了的，研究生的；有（学士）学位的

She recently graduated from being a dancer to having a small role in a movie.

◆ degrade [dɪˈgreɪd] *v.* [T] 使降级；降低……身份；使丢脸

v. [T and I] 退化；降低价值

This poster is offensive and degrades women.

◆ upgrade [ˈʌpgreɪd] *n.* 向上的斜坡

v. [T] 提升；升级

Medical facilities are being reorganized and upgraded.

◆ aggress [əˈgres] *v.* [T] 挑衅，发动攻击

The three were aggressed by angry mobs.

◆ aggressive [əˈgresɪv] *adj.* 好攻击的，有闯劲的

Some children are much more aggressive than others.

◆ congress [ˈkɒŋgres] *n.* 国会；代表大会

v. [I] 开会，集合

Congress is the legislative branch of the U. S. government.

◆ digress [daɪˈgres] *v.* [I] 离题

adj. 离题的，枝节的

I've digressed a little to explain the situation.

◆ egress [ˈiːgres] *n.* 外出；出口

Safe access and egress can be achieved by various methods.

◆ ingress [ˈɪngres] *n.* 进入；进食

There are several gates providing ingress to the meadow in this picture.

◆ progress [ˈprəʊgres] *n.* 进步；进化

[prəˈgres] *v.* [T and I] 进步，进行；发展

The two sides made little progress if any towards agreement.

◆ regress [rɪˈgres] *v.* [T and I] 逆行，倒退；退化

n. 退回；退化

Such countries are not developing at all, but regressing.

◆ regressive [rɪˈgresɪv] *adj.* 倒退的，退步的

This regressive behavior is more common in boys.

◆ transgress [trænzˈgres] *v.* [T] 超越；违反

v. [I] 做坏事；违反道德

His plays transgress accepted social norms.

vad/vas: go

◆ evade [ɪˈveɪd] *v.* [T and I] 逃避；规避

He evaded taxes as a Florida real-estate speculator.

◆ invade [ɪnˈveɪd] *v.* [T and I] 侵略；干扰

The Romans invaded Britain 2,000 years

ago.

◆ invasion［ɪnˈveɪʒən］n. 侵略；侵犯

Is reading a child's diary always a gross invasion of privacy?

◆ pervade［pɜːˈveɪd, pəˈv-］v.［T］弥漫；渗透，充满

The smell of sawdust and glue pervaded the factory.

◆ pervasion［pɜːˈveɪʒən］n. 弥漫，遍布

At present, the spread of Christianity in this area is in an unordered pervasion and rapid development.

◆ wade［weɪd］v.［T and I］（从水、泥等）蹚，走过；跋涉

n. 跋涉

Rescuers had to wade across a river to reach them.

◆ waddle［ˈwɒdl］v.［I］（像鸭子一样）摇摇摆摆地走

n. 摇摆的步子，蹒跚

In the evenings, ducks waddle up to the front door to be fed.

mob/mov/mot: move

◆ mobile［ˈməʊbaɪl］adj. 移动的；变化的

n. 风铃，（可随风摆动的）悬挂饰物

We're a very mobile society, and people move after they get divorced.

◆ immobile［ɪˈməʊbaɪl］adj. 不能活动的，静止的

Joe remained as immobile as if he had been carved out of rock.

◆ mobility［məʊˈbɪlɪtɪ］n. 流动性

Prior to the nineteenth century, there were almost no channels of social mobility.

◆ immobility［ˌɪməʊˈbɪlɪtɪ］n. 不动

He maintained the rigid immobility of his shoulders.

◆ mobilize［ˈməʊbɪlaɪz］v.［T］调动；动员；组织

v.［I］动员起来

Faced with crisis, people mobilized.

◆ demobilize［diːˈməʊbɪlaɪz］v.［T and I］使复原；遣散；使退伍

Both sides have agreed to demobilize 70% of their armies.

◆ automobile［ˌɔːtəˈməʊbɪl, -mə-］n.〈美〉汽车

v. 开汽车，坐汽车

He is repairing the brake lever of an automobile.

◆ mob［mɒb］n. 暴徒，犯罪团伙；乌合之众

v.［T］聚众包围；蜂拥进入

The inspectors watched a growing mob of demonstrators gathering.

◆ move［muːv］v.［T and I］移动，搬动

v.［I］搬家；行动；进展

v.［T］使感动；摇动

n. 改变；迁移

Things moved quickly once the contract was signed.

◆ remove［rɪˈmuːv］v.［T and I］开除；脱掉，迁移

n. 差距；移动

The student senate voted to remove Fuller from office.

◆ motion［ˈməʊʃən］n. 运动；手势；动机

v.［T］打手势；向某人点头或摇头示意

v.［I］运动；打手势

He made a neat chopping motion with his hand.

◆ motionless［ˈməʊʃənlɪs］adj. 静止的

He stood there motionless.

◆ motivate［ˈməʊtɪveɪt］v.［T］使有动机；刺激；激发……的积极性

They are motivated by a need to achieve.

◆ motive［ˈməʊtɪv］n. 动机；（艺术作品的）

主题

adj. 运动的；动机的

Police have ruled out robbery as a motive for the killing.

◆ motif [məʊ'tiːf] *n.* 主题；动机；基本图案

The jacket has a rose motif on the collar.

◆ motor ['məʊtə(r)] *n.* 马达，发动机

v. [I] 开汽车

v. [T] 用汽车运送

adj. 有发动机的；机动车的

He worked as a motor mechanic.

◆ demote [dɪ'məʊt] *v.* [T] 使降级，使降职

If they prove ineffective, they should be demoted or asked to retire.

◆ promote [prə'məʊt] *v.* [T] 促进；提升

I was promoted to editor and then editorial director.

◆ emotion [ɪ'məʊʃən] *n.* 情感，感情

Her voice trembled with emotion.

◆ locomotion [ˌləʊkə'məʊʃən] *n.* 运动；移动

He specializes in the mechanics of locomotion.

◆ locomotive [ˌləʊkə'məʊtɪv] *n.* 火车头，机车；动力

adj. 移动的；起推动作用的

Steam locomotives pumped out clouds of white smoke.

◆ remote [rɪ'məʊt] *adj.* 遥远的；偏远的；微小的

n. 遥控器

I'm afraid your chances of success are rather remote.

vag: wander

◆ vagabond ['vægəbɒnd] *n.* 流浪者，游手好闲者

adj. 流浪的；漂泊的；声名狼藉的

For the next three decades she lived the life of a vagabond moving restlessly from one city to another.

◆ vagary ['veɪgərɪ, və'geərɪ] *n.* [C] 奇想，奇特行为

He was unable to deal with the perplexing vagaries of politics.

◆ vagarious [və'geərɪəs] *adj.* 异想天开的，越出常规的，奇特的

I took different kinds of clothes with me in case of vagarious weather.

◆ vagrant ['veɪgrənt] *n.* 流浪者；无业游民；乞丐

adj. 流浪的；游移不定的

He lived on the street as a vagrant.

◆ vague [veɪg] *adj.* 不清楚的，含糊的；暧昧的

n. 模糊不定状态

A lot of the talk was apparently vague and general.

◆ extravagant [ɪk'strævəgənt] *adj.* 过度的；浪费的；放肆的

Her Aunt Sallie gave her an extravagant gift.

migr: move from one place to another; wander

◆ migrate [maɪ'greɪt] *v.* [I] 迁移；随季节而移居

v. [T] 使移居；使移植

People migrate to cities like Jakarta in search of work.

◆ migration [maɪ'greɪʃən] *n.* [U] 迁移，移居

Swallows begin their migration south in autumn.

◆ migrant ['maɪgrənt] *n.* [C] 候鸟；移民；

随季节迁移的工作者

adj. 移居的；流浪的

Migrant birds fly to the warm places every winter.

◆ emigrate [ˈemɪgreɪt] *v.* [T] 移居国外

He emigrated to Belgium.

◆ emigrant [ˈemɪgrənt] *n.* [C] (从本国移往他国的) 移民

adj. 移居的，移民的，侨居的

The emigrant found his livelihood almost immediately on arrival.

◆ immigrate [ˈɪmɪgreɪt] *v.* [I] 移入

v. [T] 移居外国，迁移

He immigrated from Ulster in 1848.

◆ immigrant [ˈɪmɪgrənt] *n.* (自外国移入的) 移民，侨民

adj. 移民的，移来的；侨民的

Immigrant tales have always been popular themes in fiction.

◆ transmigrate [ˌtrænzmaɪˈgreɪt] *v.* [I] 移居，轮回，转生

Hindus believe that we transmigrate.

ven: come, move forward

◆ venture [ˈventʃə(r)] *n.* 冒险；商业冒险

v. [T] 冒……的危险；用……进行投机

v. [I] 冒险行事；猜测

People are afraid to venture out for fear of sniper attacks.

◆ venturous [ˈventʃərəs] *adj.* 好冒险的，大胆的

Hunters need a venturous spirit.

◆ advent [ˈædvənt, -vent] *n.* 出现；将临期；基督降临(圣诞节前的4个星期)

The advent of war led to a greater austerity.

◆ adventurous [ədˈventʃ(ə)rəs] *adj.* 爱冒险的；大胆的

Warren was an adventurous businessman.

◆ adventure [ədˈventʃə(r)] *n.* 冒险活动；奇遇

I set off for a new adventure in the United States on the first day of the New Year.

◆ avenue [ˈævənuː, -njuː] *n.* 林荫路；大街；途径

The Fifth Avenue has become a symbol of New York.

◆ revenue [ˈrevɪnjuː] *n.* 税收，收入

One study said the government would gain about $12 billion in tax revenues over five years.

◆ venue [ˈvenjuː] *n.* 犯罪地点；会场

Birmingham's International Convention Centre is the venue for a three-day arts festival.

◆ souvenir [ˌsuːvəˈnɪə(r)] *n.* 纪念品；礼物

v. [T] 把……留作纪念

Please accept this little gift as a souvenir.

◆ circumvent [ˌsɜːkəmˈvent] *v.* [T] 绕行，规避

They found a way of circumventing the law.

◆ convene [kənˈviːn] *v.* [T] 召集；聚集；传唤

v. [I] 集合

A Board of Inquiry was convened immediately after the accident.

◆ convention [kənˈvenʃən] *n.* 大会；习俗

By convention the deputy leader was always a woman.

◆ covenant [ˈkʌvənənt] *n.* 协议；盖印合同；契约条款

v. [T and I] 立誓；订立盟约；订立契约

They covenanted with Judas for 30 pieces of silver.

◆ convent [ˈkɒnvənt] *n.* 女修道院

She entered a convent at the age of 16.

◆ convenient [kənˈviːnjənt] *adj.* 方便的；实用的

The house is very convenient for several schools.

◆ invent [ɪn'vent] *v.* [T] 发明，创造；虚构

He invented the first electric clock.

◆ inventory ['ɪnvəntərɪ] *n.* 存货清单；财产目录

v. [T] 编制……的目录；开列……的清单；盘存

Before starting, he made an inventory of everything that was to stay.

◆ prevent [prɪ'vent] *v.* [T and I] 预防；阻止

Further treatment will prevent cancer from developing.

◆ event [ɪ'vent] *n.* 事件，项目比赛

A new book by Grass is always an event.

◆ intervene [ˌɪntə'viːn] *v.* [I] 干涉；插嘴；介于……之间

The situation calmed down when police intervened.

Exercises

I. List at least 5 words for each of the roots below.

1. car/cur ________ ________ ________ ________ ________
2. ger/gest ________ ________ ________ ________ ________
3. fer ________ ________ ________ ________ ________
4. port ________ ________ ________ ________ ________
5. mot/mov/mob ________ ________ ________ ________ ________
6. vad/vas ________ ________ ________ ________ ________
7. vag ________ ________ ________ ________ ________
8. grad/gress ________ ________ ________ ________ ________
9. migr ________ ________ ________ ________ ________
10. ced/ceed/cess ________ ________ ________ ________ ________
11. ven ________ ________ ________ ________ ________

II. Complete the sentences with the right forms of the best words.

mobilize	intervene	belligerent	fertility	occur
invade	immigrant	motivate	indifferent	recede

1. The time when a solar eclipse will ________ can be calculated.
2. Every so often the kitchen would be ________ by ants.
3. Our country is in great danger, so we must ________ the army.
4. This country has large numbers of expatriates or ________ populations.
5. A green manure is a crop grown mainly to improve soil ________.
6. We can't remain ________ when any comrade is in difficulty.
7. The mountain peaks ________ into the distance as one leaves the shore.
8. Our government has forbidden the export of petroleum to the ________ countries.
9. You have first got to ________ the children and then to teach them.
10. When riot broke out, the police were obliged to ________.

III. Finish the words according to the definitions. The first letters are given.

1. w ________	walk (through relatively shallow water)
2. a ________	4-wheeled motor vehicle; usually propelled by an internal combustion engine
3. e ________	spending or costing a lot of money, especially more than is necessary; wasteful
4. p ________	continue with one's activities
5. a ________	anything that precedes something similar in time
6. p ________	something of the same type that has happened or existed before
7. i ________	reason by deduction; establish by deduction
8. f ________	capable of reproducing
9. e ________	to enlarge beyond bounds or the truth
10. l ________	a wheeled vehicle consisting of a self-propelled engine that is used to draw trains along railway tracks

IV. Complete the sentences with the right forms of the best words.

transmigrate	migrate	emigrate	immigrate

1. The family left Greece in 1974 and ________ to America.
2. His family ________ here from England three years ago.
3. These birds ________ to North Africa in winter.
4. Do you believe that people ________ after death?

transgress	digress	regress	progress	congress
ingress	egress	aggress		

5. Some rooms may require large windows, called "________" windows, for fire safety.
6. When people or things ________, they return to an earlier and less advanced stage of development.
7. This sealing mechanism is used to prevent the ________ of dirt.
8. No one is permitted to have privileges to ________ the law.
9. She ________ from her prepared speech to pay tribute to the President.
10. The enemies are ahead. You can either ________ or run.
11. Jack worked so hard and his ________ is obvious.
12. The national people's ________ meets once a year.

Theme Two

敢作敢为-3

sec/sequ：follow

◆ second［ˈsekənd］*n.* 助手；第二名；秒

v.［T］支持；临时调派；赞成

We never use second quality ingredients in building Construction.

The motion has been seconded.

◆ persecute［ˈpɜːsɪkjuːt］*v.*［T］迫害；烦扰

They persecute those who do not conform to their ideas.

◆ consecutive［kənˈsekjʊtɪv］*adj.* 连续的，连贯的

She was absent for nine consecutive days.

◆ sequence［ˈsiːkwəns］*n.*［C］数列；顺序；连续

v.［T］使按顺序排列

The project is nothing less than mapping every gene sequence in the human body.

◆ sequent［ˈsiːkwənt］*adj.* 随后的；连续的

In the sequent ten years, he travelled almost the whole country.

◆ consequent［ˈkɒnsɪkwənt］*adj.* 随之发生的；作为结果或后果发生的

This fall of prices is consequent on the rise in production.

◆ subsequent［ˈsʌbsɪkwənt］*adj.* 后来的；随后的

They won only one more game subsequent to their Cup semi-final win last year.

◆ sequel［ˈsiːkwəl］*n.*［C］继续；续集；结局

The police said the clash was a sequel to yesterday's nationwide strike.

fug：flee

◆ fugitive［ˈfjuːdʒɪtɪv］*n.* 逃命者；难捕捉之物

adj. 逃亡的；难以捉摸的；短暂的

The rebel leader was a fugitive from justice.

◆ lucifugous［luːˈsɪfjʊgəs］*adj.* 畏光的，怕光的

Such lucifugous creature can only live in the dark.

◆ refuge［ˈrefjuːdʒ］*n.*［C, U］避难；避难所；救急疗法

v.［T and I］给予……庇护；避难

Father Rowan took refuge in silence.

◆ febrifuge［ˈfebrɪfjuːdʒ］*n.* 解热药，退热药

adj. 退热的，解热的

Take some febrifuge if you still have fever.

frag/fract：break

◆ fracture［ˈfræktʃə(r)］*v.*［T and I］（使）折断，破碎

n.［C］破裂；骨折

You've fractured a rib, maybe more than

one.

◆ fraction［ˈfrækʃən］*n.*［C］分数；一小部分

The car missed me by a fraction of an inch.

◆ fragment［ˈfrægmənt］*n.*［C］碎片；片段

v.［T and I］碎裂，分裂

This was only a fragment of a long conversation with John.

◆ fragile［ˈfrædʒaɪl］*adj.* 易碎的，脆的；虚弱的

The Prime Minister's fragile government was on the brink of collapse.

◆ diffract［dɪˈfrækt］*v.*［T］衍射；绕射

Laser light diffracts electrons.

◆ refract［rɪˈfrækt］*v.*［T and I］折射

As we age, the lenses of the eyes thicken, and thus refract light differently.

◆ infract［ɪnˈfrækt］*v.*［T］违反，侵害

I am proving that the fact of the authorization letter is true, and it doesn't infract the law of the People's Republic of China.

rupt: break

◆ interrupt［ˌɪntəˈrʌpt］*v.*［T and I］打断；阻止

v.［T and I］暂停；中断；打扰

n. 中断；暂停

He tried to speak, but she interrupted him.

◆ disrupt［dɪsˈrʌpt］*v.*［T］使混乱；使分裂；使中断

Demonstrators succeeded in disrupting the meeting.

◆ bankrupt［ˈbæŋkrʌpt］*adj.* 破产的；（智力等）完全丧失的

v.［T］使破产，使枯竭

If the firm cannot sell its products, it will go bankrupt.

◆ bankruptcy［ˈbæŋkrʌptsɪ, -rəpsɪ］*n.* 破产；彻底失败

Many established firms were facing bankruptcy.

◆ corrupt［kəˈrʌpt］*adj.* 道德败坏的；贪污的；腐烂的

v.［T and I］腐败；腐烂；堕落

The whole system is inefficient and corrupt.

◆ corruption［kəˈrʌpʃən］*n.*［C, U］腐败；贪污；贿赂

The President faces 54 charges of corruption and tax evasion.

◆ rupture［ˈrʌptʃər］*n.*［C］断裂，破裂；疝气

v.［T and I］使破裂；断绝（关系等）

The eleventh century saw the formal rupture between the East and West.

◆ irrupt［ɪˈrʌpt］*v.*［I］突然冲入，突然闯入

She irrupted into our sitting room.

◆ erupt［ɪˈrʌpt］*v.*［I］爆发；喷发；突然发生

v.［T］爆发

Heavy fighting erupted there today after a two-day ceasefire.

vers/vert: change; turn

◆ controvert［ˌkɒntrəˈvɜːt］*v.*［T］争论，反驳，否定

The statement of the last witness controverted the evidence of the first two.

◆ controversy［ˈkɒntrəvɜːsɪ, kənˈtrɒvəsɪ］*n.* 争论，公开辩论

The President resigned amid considerable controversy.

◆ controversial［ˌkɒntrəˈvɜːʃəl］*adj.* 有争议的

Winston Churchill and Richard Nixon were both controversial figures.

◆ converse［kənˈvɜːs］*v.*［I］谈话；对话

adj. 相反的，逆的
She enjoyed the chance to converse with another French speaker.

◆ convert [kənˈvɜːt] v. [T] (使) 转变；使皈依；兑换
v. [I] 经过转变；被改变
n. 皈依者；改变宗教信仰者
The hotel is going to be converted into a nursing home.

◆ convertible [kənˈvɜːtəbl] adj. 可改变的；(货币) 可以自由兑换的；(汽车等) 有顶篷的
n. 敞篷车
They don't have access to a convertible currency.

◆ divert [daɪˈvɜːt] v. [T] 使转移，转向
Northbound traffic will have to be diverted onto minor roads.

◆ diversion [daɪˈvɜːʃən] n. [C, U] 转向，绕行；消遣
We made a short diversion to go and look at the castle.

◆ diversify [daɪˈvɜːsɪfaɪ] v. [T and I] 使不同，使多样化
Farmers are being encouraged to diversify into new crops.

◆ invert [ɪnˈvɜːt] v. [T] 使……前后倒置；使反转
[ˈɪnvɜ˞t/ˈɪnvɜːt] n. 颠倒的事物；变性者
Invert the cake onto a cooling rack.

◆ inverse [ɪnˈvɜːs] adj. 相反的；倒转的
n. 相反；倒转；相反的事物
There is no sign that you bothered to consider the inverse of your logic.

◆ retrovert [ˌretrəʊˈvɜːt] v. [T] 向后弯曲，使后倾
We retroverted our bodies.

◆ revert [rɪˈvɜːt] v. [I] 恢复；重提；回到
v. [T] 使恢复原状
Jackson said her boss became increasingly depressed and reverted to smoking heavily.

◆ reversion [rɪˈvɜːʃən] n. 返回，恢复
I'm trying to prevent the reversion of my garden to nature.

◆ subvert [səbˈvɜːt] v. [T] 颠覆，破坏
The rebel army is attempting to subvert the government.

◆ subversion [səbˈvɜːʃən] n. [U] 颠覆，破坏
He was charged with subversion and stealing state secrets.

◆ subversive [səbˈvɜːsɪv] adj. 颠覆性的，破坏性的
n. [C] 危险分子，颠覆分子
Agents regularly rounded up suspected subversives.

◆ transverse [ˈtrænzvɜːs,-ˈ-] adj. 横向的；横切的
The transverse abdominis is made up of muscle fibers that run horizontally around the abdomen.

◆ extrovert [ˈekstrə(ʊ)vɜːt] n. 性格外向者
She's a good person to invite to a party because she's such an extrovert.

◆ introvert [ˈɪntrə(ʊ)vɜːt] n. 内向的人
That young man is an introvert.

◆ versatile [ˈvəːsətail] adj. 多才多艺的；多功能的
This versatile summer jacket is a great buy.

◆ obverse [ˈɒbvɜːs] n. 对立面；前面或上面；钱币或奖章的正面
The head of the Queen appears on the obverse of British coins.

◆ advertise [ˈædvətaɪz] v. [T] 做广告；通知；宣扬
v. [I] 做广告；做宣传
Are lawyers allowed to advertise?

◆ anniversary [ˌænɪˈvɜːsərɪ] n. 周年纪念日

adj. 周年的
Today is my parents' 30th wedding anniversary.

◆ avert［ə'vɜːt］*v.*［T］防止，避免；转移
When someone tells a lie, he will usually avert his eyes.

◆ averse［ə'vɜːs］*adj.* 不乐意的；反对的
I don't smoke cigarettes, but I'm not averse to the occasional cigar.

◆ adverse［'ædvɜːs］*adj.* 不利的；有害的
Dirt and disease are adverse to the best growth of children.

◆ inadvertent［ˌɪnəd'vɜːtənt］*adj.* 不经意的，出于无心的；粗心大意的
The suffering is inadvertent and unwanted.

◆ universe［'juːnɪvɜːs］*n.* 宇宙，全世界，全人类
We still don't know how many galaxies there are in the universe.

◆ universal［ˌjuːnɪ'vɜːsl］*adj.* 普遍的；通用的；全世界的
First of all we should make primary education universal.

◆ version［'vɜːʃən］*n.* 版本；译本
His version of the events is pure supposition.

◆ vertical［'vɜːtɪkl］*adj.* 垂直的；顶点的
The climber inched up a vertical wall of rock.

◆ vertigo［'vɜːtɪgəʊ］*n.*［U］眩晕，头晕
He had a dreadful attack of vertigo.

volv/volu: turn; roll

◆ evolve［ɪ'vɒlv］*v.*［T and I］发展；进化；发出
We can evolve the truth from a mass of confused evidence.

◆ convolution［ˌkɒnvə'luːʃən］*n.* 回旋，盘旋，卷绕
Let's now examine the convolution a bit more as a mathematical entity.

◆ voluble［'vɒljʊbl］*adj.* 喋喋不休的；（指说话）快的；口若悬河的
Bert is a voluble and gregarious man.

◆ devolve［dɪ'vɒlv］*v.*［T and I］移交；交给下属；衰落
The central government devolved most tax-raising powers to the regional authorities.

◆ devolution［ˌdiːvə'luːʃən］*n.* 移交，授权；授权代理
The majority of people in the province are in favor of devolution.

◆ involve［ɪn'vɒlv］*v.*［T］包含；使参与，牵涉
Don't involve me in your quarrel.

◆ revolve［rɪ'vɒlv］*v.*［T and I］使旋转；反复考虑；使循环
v.［I］旋转；循环出现；反复考虑
The planets revolve around the sun.

◆ revolving［rɪ'vɒlvɪŋ］*adj.* 旋转的，轮转式的；循环的
He spun the revolving door round and round.

◆ revolution［ˌrevə'luːʃən］*n.*［C］革命；旋转；公转
This volume records the history of the country's revolution.

◆ revolutionary［ˌrevə'luːʃənərɪ］*adj.* 革命的；创新的；旋转的
Do you know anything about the revolutionary movement?

◆ revolt［rɪ'vəult］*v.*［T］（使）厌恶
v.［I］背叛；厌恶，反感
n.［C］造反，起义
The revolt was suppressed in a matter of hours.

press: press

◆ press［pres］*v.*［T］压，按；逼迫
v.［I］压；逼迫
n. 新闻报道，出版物

He hastened to assure us that the press would not be informed.

◆ compress [kəm'pres] *v.* [T] 压缩；精简

n. [C] 止血敷布；打包机

Some courses such as engineering had to be compressed.

◆ depress [dɪ'pres] *v.* [T] 压低；使沮丧；使萧条

Wet weather always depresses me.

◆ depression [dɪ'preʃən] *n.* 萎靡不振，沮丧；衰弱

She suffered from severe depression after losing her job.

◆ express [ɪk'spres] *v.* [T] 表达；快递

adj. 明确的；迅速的；专门的

n. 快车；专使；捷运公司

You have to pay a premium for express delivery.

◆ impress [ɪm'pres] *v.* [T] 印；给……以深刻印象

I was very impressed by one young man at my lectures.

◆ oppress [ə'pres] *v.* [T] 压迫；使烦恼

A good ruler will not oppress the poor.

◆ repress [rɪ'pres] *v.* 抑制；镇压；压抑

He could hardly repress a smile at her simplicity.

◆ suppress [sə'pres] *v.* [T] 镇压，压制；防止被人知道

The police were accused of suppressing evidence.

tect: cover

◆ detect [dɪ'tekt] *v.* [T] 发现；侦察

The tests are designed to detect the disease early.

◆ detective [dɪ'tektɪv] *adj.* 侦探的；用于探测的

n. [C] 侦探

Despite careful detective work, many items have never been recovered.

◆ detectaphone [dɪ'tektəfəʊn] *n.* 窃听器，侦探用电话机

◆ protect [prə'tekt] *v.* [T] 保卫；贸易保护

Many manufacturers have policies to protect themselves against blackmailers.

◆ protective [prə'tektɪv] *adj.* 保护的，防护的

Protective measures are necessary if the city's monuments are to be preserved.

◆ protectionism [prə'tekʃənɪzəm] *n.* [U] 保护主义

Racial quotas and protectionism are scaring away some foreign investors.

plic/pli/ply/plex/plo: fold

◆ complicate ['kɒmplɪkeɪt] *v.* [T] 使复杂化；使混乱

I do not wish to complicate the task more than is necessary.

◆ duplicate ['djuːplɪkɪt] *adj.* 复制的；成对的，二倍的

n. 复制品；复印件

Is this a duplicate or the original?

◆ duplication [ˌdjuːplɪ'keɪʃən] *n.* 复制；重复；成倍

Duties have been reassigned to avoid wasteful duplication of work.

◆ duplicity [djuː'plɪsɪtɪ] *n.* [U] 表里不一；欺骗；双重性

His duplicity caused us to distrust him.

◆ replicate ['replɪkeɪt] *v.* [T] 复制；重复；折转

Cells can reproduce but only molecules can replicate.

◆ implicate ['ɪmplɪkeɪt] *v.* [T] 牵涉；表

明……是起因；暗示

His investigation would eventually implicate his brother in the crime.

◆ complicity［kəmˈplɪsɪtɪ］*n.*［U］合谋，串通；共犯

He denied complicity in the murder.

◆ accomplice［əˈkʌmplɪs，-ˈkɒm-］*n.*［C］共犯，帮凶；同谋

He is suspected as an accomplice of the murder.

◆ apply［əˈplaɪ］*v.*［T］应用，运用；申请

v.［I］申请，请求；适用

You may apply for tickets in person or by letter.

◆ applicable［ˈæplɪkəbl］*adj.* 适当的；可应用的

This section of the law is applicable only to corporations.

◆ appliance［əˈplaɪəns］*n.*［C］器具，装置；家用电器

Do not use appliance for other than intended use.

◆ imply［ɪmˈplaɪ］*v.*［T and I］暗示；意味；隐含

Cheerfulness doesn't always imply happiness.

◆ implicit［ɪmˈplɪsɪt］*adj.* 含蓄的；无疑问的，绝对的

A soldier must give implicit obedience to his officers.

◆ explicit［ɪkˈsplɪsɪt］*adj.* 明确的，清楚的

It's an explicit statement.

◆ inexplicable［ˌɪnɪkˈsplɪkəbl，ɪnˈe-］*adj.* 无法解释的；费解的；莫名其妙的

Her inexplicable absence worried me.

◆ multiply［ˈmʌltɪplaɪ］*v.*［T and I］乘；（使）增加；（使）繁殖

These creatures can multiply quickly.

◆ complex［ˈkɒmpleks］*adj.* 复杂的；合成的

n. 复杂；合成体

He put over a complex and difficult business deal.

◆ complexion［kəmˈplekʃən］*n.*［C］肤色，气色；局面

She had short brown hair and a pale complexion.

◆ perplex［pəˈpleks］*v.*［T］使迷惑，使混乱；使复杂化

This problem is hard enough to perplex even the teacher.

◆ diploma［dɪˈpləʊmə］*n.* 毕业文凭；学位证书；奖状

She worked hard to earn her music diploma.

◆ diplomacy［dɪˈpləʊməsɪ］*n.*［U］外交；外交使团；处世之道

This was done through the skill in diplomacy.

◆ diplomat［ˈdɪpləmæt］*n.*［C］外交官；有外交手腕的人

He's a U.S. diplomat assigned to the embassy in London.

◆ exploit［ˈeksplɔɪt］*v.*［T］开采；开拓；剥削

n.［C］功绩；功劳

His wartime exploits were later made into a film.

lav: wash

◆ lave［leɪv］*v.*［T］洗涤；给……沐浴

The waves laved the shore.

◆ lavatory［ˈlævətərɪ］*n.*［C］厕所，洗手间

Is the lavatory vacant?

◆ lavish［ˈlævɪʃ］*adj.* 过分慷慨的；非常浪费的；过分丰富的

v.［T］浪费，挥霍；慷慨地给予

American reviewers are lavish in their praise of this book.

◆ laundry［ˈlɔːndrɪ］*n.* 洗衣店；洗好的衣

服；待洗的衣服；洗熨

He'd put his dirty laundry in the clothes basket.

◆ ablution [ə'bluːʃən] *n.* 净身礼；（常用复数）沐浴；洗礼水

He is performing his ablutions.

◆ dilute [daɪ'luːt] *v.* [T] 稀释，冲淡

adj. 稀释的，冲淡的

The paint can be diluted with water to make a lighter shade.

sist/sta/stit: stand

◆ assist [ə'sɪst] *n.* 帮助；辅助装置

v. [T and I] 帮助；援助；参加

You will be employed to assist in the development of new equipment.

◆ insistence [ɪn'sɪstəns] *n.* [U] 坚持；强调；极力主张

Her parents were united in their insistence that she go to college.

◆ persist [pə'sɪst] *v.* 坚持；存留；继续存在

Contact your doctor if the cough persists.

◆ persistent [pə'sɪstənt] *adj.* 持续的；坚持不懈的；持久的

Steady progress can only be the result of persistent study.

◆ resist [rɪ'zɪst] *v.* [T] 抵抗；忍耐；反对

n. 防染剂；防腐剂

One cannot help being old but one can resist being aged.

◆ resistance [rɪ'zɪstəns] *n.* [U] 抵抗；阻力；电阻

After two hours' heavy fighting, we bore down the enemy's resistance.

◆ desist [dɪ'zɪst] *v.* [I] 停止

The judge told the man to desist from threatening his wife.

◆ estate [ɪ'steɪt] *n.* [C] 财产，遗产，房地产

He used to live on the estate.

◆ ecstasy ['ekstəsɪ] *n.* 狂喜；出神，忘形；迷幻药

He listened to the music with ecstasy.

◆ obstacle ['ɒbstəkl] *n.* [C] 障碍（物）

The fallen tree lying across the road is an obstacle.

◆ obstinate ['ɒbstɪnɪt] *adj.* 顽固的；固执的

She's too obstinate to let anyone help her.

◆ instant ['ɪnstənt] *n.* [C] 瞬间；此刻；速食食品

adj. 立即的；目前的；即食的

The current account offers savers instant access to funds.

◆ instantaneous [ˌɪnstən'teɪnjəs] *adj.* 瞬间的；即刻的；猝发的

He had an instantaneous response.

◆ stability [stə'bɪlɪtɪ] *n.* [U] 稳定（性）；坚定，恒心

It could threaten the peace and stability of the region.

◆ destitute ['destɪtjuːt] *adj.* 极度缺乏的；贫乏的

When he died, his family was left completely destitute.

◆ institute ['ɪnstɪtjuːt] *v.* [T] 建立；开始

n. [C] 协会；学会；学院

We had no choice but to institute court proceedings against the airline.

◆ constitution [ˌkɒnstɪ'tjuːʃən] *n.* [C, U] 组成；体格；宪法

The nation's constitution provided a model that other countries follow.

◆ constituent [kən'stɪtjʊənt] *n.* 选民；成分；委托人

Caffeine is the active constituent of drinks such as tea and coffee.

◆ prostitute ['prɒstɪtjuːt] *n.* [C] 卖淫者，

妓女

He admitted last week he paid for sex with a prostitute.

◆ substitute [ˈsʌbstɪtjuːt] *v.* [T and I] 代替，替换

n. [C] 代替者；替代物；代用词

Vitamin pills are no substitute for a healthy diet.

◆ superstition [ˌsuːpəˈstɪʃən, ˌsjuː-] *n.* 迷信；〈古〉邪教

Superstition results from ignorance.

sid：sit

◆ preside [prɪˈzaɪd] *v.* [I] 主持，指挥；担任会议主席

Mr. Smith will preside at the next meeting.

◆ president [ˈprezɪdənt] *n.* [C] 校长；总统；董事长

Angry shareholders called for the resignation of the company president.

◆ dissident [ˈdɪsɪdənt] *n.* [C] 持异议者，持不同政见者

adj. 持不同意见的（人）

He was exiled as a dissident.

◆ reside [rɪˈzaɪd] *v.* [I] 居住，（官吏）留驻；（权力、权利等）属于

They reside abroad.

◆ resident [ˈrezɪdənt] *adj.* 定居的，常驻的

n. [C] 居民；（旅馆的）住宿者

The resident population of mental hospitals has fallen by 20%.

◆ subside [səbˈsaɪd] *v.* [I] 减弱，平息；退去

The excitement began subside at midnight.

◆ subsidence [səbˈsaɪdəns, ˈsʌbsɪdəns] *n.* 沉淀，下沉；沉淀物

There has been an intermittent uplift of the land and subsidence of the sea going on.

◆ assiduous [əˈsɪdjʊəs] *adj.* 刻苦的；殷勤的；百折不挠的

The book was the result of ten years' assiduous research.

tend/tens/tent：stretch

◆ contend [kənˈtend] *v.* [I] 争夺；竞争；争斗

v. [T] 主张；争辩；斗争

Three armed groups were contending for power.

◆ attend [əˈtend] *v.* [I] 出席；致力于；照顾

v. [T] 出席，参加；陪伴

Thousands of people attended the funeral.

◆ attentive [əˈtentɪv] *adj.* 周到的，殷勤的；细心的

The vast majority of the attentive audience applauded these sentiments.

◆ distend [dɪˈstend] *v.* [T and I] 膨胀，肿胀

Air is introduced into the stomach to distend it for easier visualisation.

◆ intend [ɪnˈtend] *v.* [T] 意欲，计划；为特定用途而打算

v. [I] 怀有某种意图或目的

I didn't intend coming to Germany to work.

◆ intension [ɪnˈtenʃən] *n.* 紧张；加剧；内涵

All versions of externalism have in common that intensions don't determine extensions.

◆ tendency [ˈtendənsɪ] *n.* 倾向，趋势

He is spoiled, arrogant and has a tendency towards snobbery.

◆ tender [ˈtendə(r)] *adj.* 纤弱的；嫩的；温柔的

v. （正式）提出；投标

As company secretary, you must tender the

proposal.

◆ tension [ˈtenʃən] *n.* 紧张；紧张气氛；张力，拉力

The tension between the two countries is likely to remain.

◆ ostensible [ɒsˈtensəbl] *adj.* 表面上的；假装的；貌似真实的

The ostensible purpose of these meetings was to gather information on financial strategies.

◆ ostentatious [ˌɒstenˈteɪʃəs] *adj.* 好夸耀的；自负的；讲排场的；浮华的

Obviously he had plenty of money and was generous in its use without being ostentatious.

◆ pretend [prɪˈtend] *v.* [T] 假装，伪装；假称

v. [I] 扮演；自称；假装

adj. 假装的

I had no option but to pretend ignorance.

◆ pretense [prɪˈtens] *n.* 借口；(无事实根据的) 要求；假装

You can't keep up the pretense any longer.

◆ pretentious [prɪˈtenʃəs] *adj.* 狂妄的，自负的；虚伪的

His response was full of pretentious nonsense.

◆ extensive [ɪkˈstensɪv] *adj.* 广阔的，广大的；范围广泛的

The facilities available are very extensive.

◆ intensive [ɪnˈtensɪv] *adj.* 强烈的；精耕细作的；集约的

Each counselor undergoes an intensive training program before beginning work.

Exercises

I. Match the roots with their meanings.

A. tend ( ) 1. wash
B. sid ( ) 2. press
C. lav ( ) 3. break
D. tect ( ) 4. follow
E. pli ( ) 5. fold
F. press ( ) 6. flee
G. vers ( ) 7. sit
H. rupt/frag ( ) 8. turn
I. fug ( ) 9. stretch
J. sec ( ) 10. cover

II. Complete the sentences with the right forms of the best words.

duplication	constitution	subside	tendency	intensive
reversion	laundry	diplomat	explicit	revolt

1. The suppression of the ________ took a mere two days.
2. Prices continue to show an upward ________.
3. This is a ________ to the system under which the Royals were paid for nearly 300 years.

4. We had to have the washing done at the ________.

5. The President has suspended the ________ and assumed total power.

6. ________ care in hospital is given to the seriously ill.

7. He served as a ________ in Russia before the war.

8. About 2 a. m. , however, the excitement began to ________.

9. If you say that there has been ________ of something, you mean that someone has done a task unnecessarily because it has already been done before.

10. The lease is ________ in saying the rent must be paid by the 10th of every month.

III. Finish the words according to the definitions. The first letters are given.

1. a ________ the date on which an event occurred in some previous year (or the celebration of it)

2. d ________ to change something or to make it change so that there is more variety

3. c ________ lack of integrity or honesty (especially susceptibility to bribery); use of a position of trust for dishonest gain

4. b ________ the state of being unable to pay debts

5. c ________ marked by or capable of arousing disagreement

6. f ________ easily broken or damaged or destroyed

7. s ________ following in time or order

8. r ________ a shelter from danger or hardship

9. p ________ to treat someone cruelly or unfairly

10. f ________ a piece broken off or cut off of something larger

IV. Choose the best word for each sentence.

1. The atoms in the crystal ________ the X-ray light, and the diffraction pattern allows scientists to reconstruct the arrangement of the atoms in the crystal.

A. diffract B. refract C. infract D. fracture

2. Heavy fighting ________ there today after a two-day ceasefire.

A. irrupted B. erupted C. disrupted D. interrupted

3. They have made a ________ of her to Christianity.

A. subvert B. invert C. revert D. convert

4. Before too long he started ________ me in the more confidential aspects of the job.

A. involving B. revolving C. evolving D. devolving

5. I know he is too optimistic but I don't want to ________ him.

A. oppress B. suppress C. depress D. repress

6. He was obliged to resign when one of his own aides was ________ in a financial scandal.

A. duplicated B. implicated C. supplicated D. replicated

7. Local officials say the flood waters have ________.

A. presided B. resided C. subsided D. decided

8. Julia was ________ him with his speech.

A. resisting B. insisting C. assisting D. desisting

9. Coming on as a ________, he scored four crucial goals for Cameroon.

A. substitute B. constitute C. institute D. prostitute

10. The meeting will be ________ by finance ministers from many countries.

A. contended B. attended C. distended D. intended

Theme Two

敢作敢为-4

scend/scal: climb

◆ ascend [ə'send] *v.* [T] 攀登；继承；占领

v. [I] 上升；爬坡；追溯

We watched the airplane ascend higher and higher.

◆ ascent [ə'sent] *n.* [C] 上升；登高；追溯

Burke pushed the button and the elevator began its slow ascent.

◆ descend [dɪ'send] *v.* [T] 下来；遗传下来；来源于

v. [I] (from) 起源 (于)；是……的后裔；(to) 把身份降至

The title descends to me from my father.

◆ descent [dɪ'sent] *n.* [C, U] 下降；血统；倾斜

She is of German descent.

◆ condescend [ˌkɒndɪ'send] *v.* [I] 屈尊，俯就；故意表示和蔼可亲

She did not condescend to have dinner with him.

◆ transcend [træn'send] *v.* [T] 超越；优于；高于或独立于 (宇宙) 而生存

Such matters transcend human understanding.

◆ escalate ['eskəleɪt] *v.* [T] 使逐步升级；乘自动梯上升

v. [I] 逐步上升；(战争) 逐步升级；像乘自动梯上升

Her fear was escalating into panic.

◆ escalator ['eskəleɪtə(r)] *n.* 自动扶梯

I don't take the escalator and I'll climb the stairs.

mount: hill, rise

◆ mount [maʊnt] *v.* [T and I] 登上；骑；上升；安装

n. 山峰；攀，登；底座

Tension here is mounting, as we await the final result.

◆ dismount [dɪs'maʊnt] *v.* [I] 下车，下马

He who rides a tiger is afraid to dismount.

◆ surmount [sə'maʊnt] *v.* [T] 战胜；攀登；顶上覆盖着

He tried to surmount his embarrassment.

◆ paramount ['pærəmaʊnt] *adj.* 最高的，至上的；最重要的

n. 最高，至上；有最高权力的人

During a war the interests of the state are paramount, and those of the individual come last.

◆ promontory ['prɒməntərɪ] *n.* 岬，隆起的部分，海角

The mansion was on a promontory, high over the Pacific.

cad/cas/cid: fall

◆ decadence ['dekədəns, dɪ'keɪ-] *n.* (道德、

文学、艺术等）衰落，颓废

The decadence of morals is bad for a nation.

◆ casual [ˈkæʒuəl] *adj.* 偶然的；临时的；随便的；非正式的

n. 临时工人；待命士兵

Among her friends, casual dress and a relaxed manner are the rule.

◆ casualty [ˈkæʒuəltɪ] *n.* [C, U] 伤亡（人数）；事故；死伤者

Casualty lists were published the day after the train accident.

◆ accident [ˈæksɪdənt] *n.* [C] 意外；事故；偶然

5, 000 people die every year because of accidents at home.

◆ accidental [ˌæksɪˈdentl] *adj.* 意外的，偶然的；附属的

Our meeting in New York was quite accidental.

◆ incident [ˈɪnsɪdənt] *n.* 事件，事变小插曲；敌对行动

The incident left him angry and upset.

◆ incidence [ˈɪnsɪdəns] *n.* 发生率；影响范围；接合

The incidence of this disease has dropped considerably in the past few years.

◆ coincide [ˌkəʊɪnˈsaɪd] *v.* [I] 同时发生；与……一致；想法、意见等相同

The exhibition coincides with the 50th anniversary of his death.

◆ coincident [kəʊˈɪnsɪdənt] *adj.* 同时发生的；巧合的；一致的

These parallels cannot be merely coincident.

◆ occasion [əˈkeɪʒən] *n.* [C] 机会，时机；场合

On this occasion the plane diverted from its usual flight path.

◆ occident [ˈɒksɪdənt] *n.* 西方；欧美；西欧诸国

Chapter three narrates the economy of the Occident.

rad/ras: scrape

◆ abrade [əˈbreɪd] *v.* [T] 刮擦；使筋疲力尽

v. [I] 经受磨损，受擦伤

My skin was seriously abraded.

◆ abrader [əˈbreɪdə] *n.* 磨石，研磨器

◆ abrasion [əˈbreɪʒən] *n.* 磨损；擦伤处

Diamonds have extreme resistance to abrasion.

◆ erase [ɪˈreɪz] *v.* [T] 擦掉；抹去；清除

He tried to erase the idea from his mind.

◆ eraser [ɪˈreɪzə(r)] *n.* [C] 橡皮擦，板擦

Rub out chalk marks with an eraser.

◆ raze [reɪz] *v.* [T] 彻底摧毁，将……夷为平地

The owners intend to raze the hotel and erect an office building on the site.

◆ razor [ˈreɪzə(r)] *n.* [C] 剃刀，刮面刀

v. [T] 剃；用剃刀刮

A sharp razor gives a close shave.

tang/tact/tag: touch

◆ tangency [ˈtændʒənsɪ] *n.* 接触，相切

◆ tangent [ˈtændʒənt] *n.* 〈数〉正切；突然转移话题；突兀的转向

adj. 〈数〉正切的；切线的；离题的

It's not easy to follow her thought because she's always going off at a tangent.

◆ tangible [ˈtændʒəbl] *adj.* 可触知的；真实的；有形的

n. 有形资产；可触知的或具体的某事物

The policy has not yet brought any tangible benefits.

◆ intangible [ɪnˈtændʒəbl] *adj.* 触不到的；难以理解的

n.〈商〉（指企业资产）无形的

Sound and light are intangible.

◆ tact［tækt］*n.*［U］机智；老练，圆滑

He has no tact in dealing with people.

◆ tactful［ˈtæktf(ʊ)l］*adj.* 机智的；老练的，圆滑的

I made a tactful retreat before they started arguing.

◆ tactless［ˈtæktlɪs］*adj.* 不圆通的；不得体的；粗鲁的

His tactless words had incurred his father's deep displeasure.

◆ tactics［ˈtæktɪks］*n.*［C］战术；策略

They planned the tactics for the next day's battle.

◆ tactician［tækˈtɪʃən］*n.*［C］战术家，策士

He is more of a strategist than of a tactician.

◆ contact［ˈkɒntækt］*n.*［C, U］接触；触点；门路

v.［T］使接触；与……联系；与……通信

I don't have much contact with my uncle.

◆ intact［ɪnˈtækt］*adj.* 完整无缺的，未受损伤的；原封不动的

He can scarcely survive this scandal with his reputation intact.

◆ contagion［kənˈteɪdʒən］*n.*［C, U］传染；道德败坏

They have been reluctant to admit AIDS patients, in part because of unfounded fears of contagion.

◆ contagious［kənˈteɪdʒəs］*adj.* 有传染性的；有感染力的；会蔓延的

Scarlet fever is highly contagious.

prehend/pris: seize, catch

◆ apprehend［ˌæprɪˈhend］*v.*［T］理解；逮捕；忧虑

The police have failed to apprehend the culprits.

◆ apprehensible［ˌæprɪˈhensɪbl］*adj.* 可理解的，可了解的

His worry about his wife is apprehensible.

◆ apprehension［ˌæprɪˈhenʃən］*n.* 不安，忧虑；理解（力）；拘捕

They were filled with apprehension as they approached the building.

◆ misapprehend［ˌmɪsæprɪˈhend］*v.*［T］误解，误会

She misapprehended my words.

◆ comprehend［ˌkɒmprɪˈhend］*v.*［T］理解，领会；包含

She could not comprehend how someone would risk people's lives in that way.

◆ comprehensive［ˌkɒmprɪˈhensɪv］*adj.* 广泛的；综合的；有理解力的

n.（常用复数）专业综合考试；综合学校

An objective test can be quite comprehensive.

◆ comprehension［ˌkɒmprɪˈhenʃən］*n.*［C, U］理解，理解力；内涵

She had no comprehension of what was involved.

◆ reprehend［ˌreprɪˈhend］*v.*［T］斥责，责备

His conduct deserves to be reprehended.

◆ prison［ˈprɪzn］*n.*［C］监狱；监禁

v.［T］监禁，关押；紧紧抱住

He was sentenced to life in prison.

◆ imprison［ɪmˈprɪzn］*v.*［T］关押，监禁；使……不自由

You can lock up a person physically, but you cannot imprison his heart.

◆ imprisonment［ɪmˈprɪznmənt］*n.* 关押，监禁

He was sentenced to one year's imprisonment for stealing.

◆ apprise [ə'praɪz] *v.* [T] 告知，通知；评价
We must apprise them of the dangers that may be involved.

◆ comprise [kəm'praɪz] *v.* [T] 包含，包括；由……组成
The collection comprises 327 paintings.

◆ enterprise ['entəpraɪz] *n.* [C，U] 企(事)业单位；事业；事业心，进取心
He has no enterprise at all in his studies.

◆ enterprising ['entəpraɪzɪŋ] *adj.* 有事业心的；有进取心的；有魄力的
You are no longer the enterprising cook that once you were.

◆ reprisal [rɪ'praɪzl] *n.* 报复；(特指国家间的)暴力性报复，报复行为
They shot ten hostages in reprisal for the assassination of their leader.

◆ surprise [sə'praɪz] *v.* [T] 使惊奇；意外发现；突袭
n. [C，U] 令人吃惊的事物；惊奇
Sue was overcome by surprise when Peter walked in.

◆ prize [praɪz] *n.* [C] 奖赏；战利品
v. [T] 珍视，珍惜；估价
adj. 获奖的；理应获奖的
He won the first prize at the Leeds Piano Competition.

rap/rav: seize, snatch

◆ rape [reɪp] *v.* [T] 掠夺；强奸
n. 掠夺，强夺
The invading troops were guilty of rape and pillage.

◆ rapacious [rə'peɪʃəs] *adj.* 贪婪的；(尤指)贪财的；掠夺的
He had a rapacious appetite for a bird's nest soup.

◆ rapacity [rə'pæsɪtɪ] *n.* [C] 贪婪，贪心，劫掠的欲望
Some people think most criminals are attributed to the rapacity of money.

◆ rapid ['ræpɪd] *adj.* 快速的；感光快的；险峻的
n. 急流；高速交通工具
A rapid rise in price makes the life even harder for poor people.

◆ rapids ['ræpɪdz] *n.* [C] 急流；险滩
The canoe shot the rapids.

◆ rapine ['ræpaɪn] *n.* 〈文〉劫掠，强夺
The soldiers got their food by rapine.

◆ rapt [ræpt] *adj.* 全神贯注的，入迷的
She sat with rapt expression reading her book.

◆ rapture ['ræptʃə(r)] *n.* [U] 极度欢喜
v. [T] 使……狂喜
I have read this book a hundred times with new rapture.

◆ enrapture [ɪn'ræptʃə(r)] *v.* [T] 使狂喜
The beautiful place at once enraptured me.

◆ raptor ['ræptə(r)] *n.* 猛禽，肉食鸟
Some raptors never attack birds, and others only occasionally.

◆ raptorial [ræp'tɔːrɪəl] *adj.* 捕食生物的，猛禽类的
Eagles are raptorial birds.

cap/cept/ceiv: take

◆ capable ['keɪpəbl] *adj.* 能干的；有才能的；能胜任的
You are capable of better work than this.

◆ captivate ['kæptɪveɪt] *v.* [T] 迷住，迷惑；〈古〉逮捕
The allure and charm of Paris captivate all who visit there.

◆ capture ['kæptʃə(r)] *v.* [T] 俘获；引起

（注意、想象、兴趣）

n. 捕获；占领

The city was captured in 1941.

◆ captive［ˈkæptɪv］*adj.* 被俘的；被监禁的；无法逃离的

n. 俘虏；自保公司

The rock star had a captive audience.

◆ conceive［kənˈsiːv］*v.*［T and I］怀孕；构思；设想

v.［I］怀孕；设想；考虑

He conceived the idea of transforming the old power station into an arts centre.

◆ perceive［pəˈsiːv］*v.*［T］意识到；察觉；理解

I can't perceive any difference between these coins.

◆ except［ɪkˈsept］*v.*［T］把……除外；不计

prep. 除……外

High technology equipment would be excepted from any trade agreement.

sume：take

◆ assume［əˈsjuːm］*v.*［T］取得（权力）；承担；假设

We can't just assume her guilt.

◆ consume［kənˈsjuːm］*v.*［T］消耗；耗尽，毁灭

The electricity industry consumes large amounts of fossil fuels.

◆ resume［rɪˈz(j)uːm］*v.*［T］重新取得；取回

v.［I］再开始；重返

We'll stop now and resume at two o'clock.

◆ résumé［ˈrezjuːmei］*n.* 摘要；履历

A well-designed résumé helps a lot when hunting for a job.

◆ sumptuous［ˈsʌmptjʊəs］*adj.* 豪华的；奢侈的；美轮美奂的

The guests turned up dressed in sumptuous evening gowns.

empt/em：take

◆ peremptory［pəˈremptərɪ］*adj.* 断然的；不容置辩的；傲慢的；专横的

The officer issued peremptory commands.

◆ preempt［ˌpriːˈempt, prɪ-］*v.*［T］先占；取代；先发制人

They do not preempt the land surface that is useful for other purposes.

◆ exempt［ɪgˈzempt］*v.*［T］使免除，豁免

adj. 被免除的，被豁免的

n. 被免除（义务、责任）的人；免税人

These goods are exempt from customs duties.

◆ exemplary［ɪgˈzemplərɪ］*adj.* 典型的；示范的；惩戒性的

An exemplary person may well have the great charisma to affect others.

◆ impromptu［ɪmˈprɒmptjuː］*adj.* 即席的；临时的；无准备的

adv. 即席地；临时地；无准备地

n. 即席演出；即席之作；即席演说

The announcement was made in an impromptu press conference at the airport.

◆ prompt［prɒmpt］*adj.* 敏捷的；立刻的；即期付款的

v. 提示；促进；激起

n. 刺激物；提示；

adv. 准时地；正好

The company was prompt in its response to these accusations.

◆ promptitude［ˈprɒmptɪtjuːd］*n.* 敏捷，迅速

Their own promptitude in retreating at the critical moment saved them.

◆ premium［ˈpriːmjəm］*n.* 费用，额外费用；

保险费；奖励
You have to pay a premium for express delivery.

◆ redeem [rɪ'diːm] *v.* [T] 赎回；偿还；兑现
You can redeem the coupon at any store.

◆ redemption [rɪ'dempʃən] *n.* 赎回；偿还；补救
Have you seen the movie *Shawshank Redemption*?

tort: twist

◆ contort [kən'tɔːt] *v.* [T and I] 扭曲，扭弯
His face contorted with anger.

◆ contortionist [kən'tɔːʃənɪst] *n.* [C] 柔软体操演员
A contortionist is someone who twists his/her body into strange and unnatural shapes and positions in order to entertain other people.

◆ distort [dɪ'stɔːt] *v.* [T] 扭曲；曲解；使变形
v. [I] 扭曲；变形
The loudspeaker seemed to distort his voice.

◆ extort [ɪk'stɔːt] *v.* [T] 敲诈
The evil police used torture to extort a confession from him.

◆ retort [rɪ'tɔːt] *v.* [T] 反驳；报复
v. [I] 回嘴；反驳
n. 反驳，回嘴；反驳的回答
He opened his mouth to make a caustic retort.

◆ torsion ['tɔːʃən] *n.* [U] 扭转；扭曲
A portable torsion balance is used for weighing.

◆ torture ['tɔːtʃə(r)] *n.* [U] 拷问；折磨
v. [T] 使痛苦；使苦恼；曲解
He would not torture her further by trying to argue with her.

◆ tortuous ['tɔːtjuəs] *adj.* 弯曲的；曲折的；不正派的
We have travelled a tortuous road.

◆ torment ['tɔːment] *n.* [C, U] 折磨，痛苦；刑罚
v. [tɔː'ment] [T and I] 使折磨，使烦乱；纠缠
It was wicked of you to torment the poor girl.

stinct/sting/stig/sti: prick

◆ extinct [ɪk'stɪŋkt] *adj.* 灭绝的；绝种的；消逝的
All her hopes were extinct.

◆ extinguish [ɪk'stɪŋgwɪʃ] *v.* [T] 熄灭；使（希望、爱情等）不复存在；偿清
You may extinguish a nation, but not the love of liberty.

◆ distinct [dɪ'stɪŋkt] *adj.* 明显的；卓越的；有区别的
There was a distinct smell of gas.

◆ distinctive [dɪ'stɪŋktɪv] *adj.* 有特色的，与众不同的；独特的
The male bird has distinctive white markings on its head.

◆ distinction [dɪ'stɪŋkʃən] *n.* 区别；荣誉；特质；卓越
She had the distinction of being the first woman to fly the Atlantic.

◆ distinguish [dɪ'stɪŋgwɪʃ] *v.* [I] 区分，分清；辨别是非
v. [T] 区分；引人注目；使著名
She has already distinguished herself as an athlete.

◆ distinguished [dɪ'stɪŋgwɪʃt] *adj.* 卓越的；著名的；受人尊敬的

I think grey hair makes you look very distinguished.

◆ instinct［ˈɪnstɪŋkt］*n.* 本能，天性；冲动；天才

He always knew what time it was, as if by instinct.

◆ sting［stɪŋ］*v.*［T and I］叮，螫；精神上刺痛

n.［C］螫伤处；（某些昆虫的）毒刺；（身体或心灵的）剧痛

Sprays can sting sensitive skin.

◆ stingy［ˈstɪndʒɪ］*adj.* 小气的，吝啬的

Don't be so stingy with the money!

◆ instigate［ˈɪnstɪgeɪt］*v.*［T］教唆；煽动；激起

It would not prove worthwhile to instigate a nuclear attack.

◆ stigma［ˈstɪgmə］*n.*［C］耻辱，污名；烙印

It's a stigma to ask for money.

◆ stigmatize［ˈstɪgmətaɪz］*v.*［T］使受耻辱，指责，污辱

IQ testing can stigmatize a child permanently, causing more harm than good.

◆ stimulate［ˈstɪmjʊleɪt］*v.*［T］刺激；激励，鼓舞

v.［I］起兴奋作用；起刺激作用

Your encouragement will stimulate me to further efforts.

◆ stimulus［ˈstɪmjʊləs］*n.*［C］刺激物；刺激因素

Poverty is a stimulus to industry.

◆ stimulant［ˈstɪmjʊlənt］*n.* 兴奋剂；刺激物；酒精饮料

adj. 刺激的，激励的；使人兴奋的

It is used in medicine for its stimulant quality.

min: hang, project

◆ eminent［ˈemɪnənt］*adj.* 知名的，杰出的；（指品质、特性）明显的

We are expecting the arrival of an eminent scientist.

◆ preeminent［prɪˈemɪnənt］*adj.* 卓越的，杰出的

He is the preeminent tenor of the modern era.

◆ imminent［ˈɪmɪnənt］*adj.*（通常指不愉快的事）即将发生的；迫切的；迫在眉睫的

The black clouds show that a storm is imminent.

◆ prominent［ˈprɒmɪnənt］*adj.* 突出的，杰出的；突起的

He is prominent in science.

◆ menace［ˈmenɪs］*n.*［C, U］威胁；恐吓

v.［T and I］威胁；恐吓

In my view you are a menace to the public.

pend: hang; weigh; pay

◆ append［əˈpend］*v.*［T］附加；添加；贴上

Organizers may amend or append the terms and conditions without prior notification.

◆ appendix［əˈpendɪks］*n.*［C］附录；阑尾；附加物

I have recently had my appendix removed.

◆ impending［ɪmˈpendɪŋ］*adj.* 即将发生的，迫在眉睫的；悬挂的

Against a background of impending famine, heavy fighting took place.

◆ stipend［ˈstaɪpend］*n.*［C］（尤指牧师的）薪俸；奖学金

This sum was nearly a third of his total stipend.

◆ pendant［ˈpendənt］*n.*［C］（装在项链等上的）垂饰，吊坠

The pendant was hanging by a thin gold chain.

◆ pending [ˈpendɪŋ] *prep.* 直到；在等待……期间
adj. 未决的；待定的；即将发生的
The matter is still pending in court.

◆ suspend [səˈspend] *v.* [T] 暂停；延缓；悬浮
v. [I] 暂缓；悬浮；无力支付
Balloons suspend easily in the air.

◆ suspension [səˈspenʃən] *n.* 悬浮，暂停
The athlete received a two-year suspension following a positive drug test.

◆ propensity [prəˈpensɪtɪ] *n.* [C] 倾向；习性，癖好
He has a propensity for drinking too much alcohol.

◆ dispense [dɪˈspens] *v.* [T] 分配；实施；免除
The machine dispenses a range of drinks and snacks.

◆ indispensable [ˌɪndɪˈspensəbl] *adj.* 不可缺少的；责无旁贷的；不可避开的
For a successful class, humour is indispensable.

◆ expend [ɪkˈspend] *v.* [T] 花费；耗尽
Don't expend all your time on such a useless job.

◆ expenditure [ɪkˈspendɪtʃə(r)] *n.* [C, U] 花费，支出
I'm getting short of money. I have to draw in my expenditure.

◆ compensate [ˈkɒmpenseɪt] *v.* [T] 补偿；报酬；抵消
v. [I] 补偿，弥补
Nothing can compensate for the loss of a loved one.

◆ recompense [ˈrekəmpens] *v.* [T] 赔偿；补偿；酬谢
n. [U] 报酬；报应；惩罚
He was given £ 1,000 in recompense for his loss.

◆ dependant [dɪˈpendənt] *n.* [C] 家眷；侍从；受赡养者
adj. 相关的；附属的
A sick dog is as much a dependant as a sick child.

◆ pension [ˈpenʃən] *n.* [C] 退休金，养老金
v. [T] 发给……养老金，退休金
I would have been much wiser to start my own pension plan when I was younger.

spond: promise, answer

◆ respond [rɪˈspɒnd] *v.* [T and I] 回答，响应
v. [I] 做出反应，回复
n. 对称，回复
He was noticeably slow to respond.

◆ correspond [ˌkɒrɪˈspɒnd] *v.* [I] 符合；相应；通信
Your account of events does not correspond with hers.

◆ corresponding [ˌkɒrɪˈspɒndɪŋ] *adj.* 对应的；通信的；符合的
A change in the money supply brings a corresponding change in expenditure.

◆ sponsor [ˈspɒnsə(r)] *n.* 发起者，主办者；担保者
v. [T] 赞助
A wealthy sponsor came to our rescue with a generous donation.

◆ spouse [spaʊz, spaʊs] *n.* 配偶，夫或妻
Her spouse will come to see her on Sunday.

prob/prov: test, try

◆ approbation [ˌæprəˈbeɪʃən] *n.* 许可，批准；赞许
The manager surveyed her report with

approbation.

◆ probation［prə'beɪʃən］*n.* 试用（期）；缓刑（期）

That company puts all new employees on a three-month probation.

◆ reprobate［'reprə(ʊ)beɪt］*n.* 道德败坏的人，恶棍

v.［T］斥责，遗弃

He ventured to reprobate that common system.

◆ approval［ə'pruːvəl］*n.* 同意；批准

The bill will be submitted for approval by Congress.

◆ disprove［dɪs'pruːv］*v.*［T］反驳；证明……是虚假的

The theory has now been disproved.

◆ reprove［rɪ'pruːv］*v.*［T］〈正〉责骂，指摘，非难

She again found herself unable to reprove him.

Exercises

I. Match the roots with their meanings.

A. probe	(　　) 1. hang, weigh
B. min	(　　) 2. hang, project
C. pend	(　　) 3. test, try
D. stinct	(　　) 4. climb
E. tort	(　　) 5. twist
F. empt	(　　) 6. take
G. spond	(　　) 7. prick
H. prehend	(　　) 8. promise, answer
I. scend	(　　) 9. scrape
J. tang	(　　) 10. seize, catch
K. rad	(　　) 11. touch
L. mount	(　　) 12. fall
M. cid	(　　) 13. hill, rise

II. Complete the sentences with the right forms of the best words.

paramount	indispensable	escalate	compensate	contagious
probation	distinguished	torture	casualty	prompt

1. No ________ would make him speak.
2. The child's welfare must be seen as ________.
3. There's a three-month period of ________ for new recruits.
4. It is universally acknowledged that trees are ________ to us.
5. Defeat could cause one side or other to ________ the conflict.
6. The people with ________ diseases should be isolated.
7. Troops fired on demonstrators near the Royal Palace causing many ________.
8. Elephants are ________ from other animals by their long noses.

9. She used her good looks to ________ for her lack of intelligence.

10. His ________ action prevented the fire from spreading.

III. Finish the words according to the definitions. The first letters are given.

1. s ________	someone who financially supports something
2. e ________	money spent
3. c ________	to be compatible, similar or consistent
4. s ________	to stop a process or a habit by imposing a freeze on it
5. s ________	to make sth. develop or become more active; to encourage something
6. i ________	inborn pattern of behavior often responsive to specific stimuli
7. e ________	being or serving as an illustration of a type
8. c ________	to succeed in catching or seizing, especially after a chase
9. a ________	capable of being understood
10. c ________	occurring or happening at the same time

IV. Choose among the words with similar roots and fill in the blanks in the right forms.

contort	distort	retort	extort	torture

1. French police are convinced that she was ________ and killed.
2. The minister has said his remarks at the weekend have been ________.
3. Brenner was breathing hard, his face ________ with pain.
4. He opened his mouth to make a sharp ________.
5. Corrupt government officials were ________ money from him.

V. Give the antonyms of the following words.

1. tangible
2. mount
3. apprehend
4. orient
5. ascend

Theme Two

敢作敢为-5

duc/duct: lead

◆ reduce [rɪ'djuːs] *v.* [T] 使变为；使变弱
v. [I] 减少；（液体）浓缩变稠
It reduces the risks of heart disease.

◆ introduce [ˌɪntrə'djuːs] *v.* [T] 提出；介绍；引进
The Government has introduced a number of other money-saving moves.

◆ produce [prə'djuːs] *v.* [T and I] 生产；产生；制作
A mental vision of success would help produce real success.

◆ induce [ɪn'djuːs] *v.* [T] 引诱；引起；归纳
The medicine will induce sleep.

◆ educe [ɪ'djuːs] *v.* [T] 引出；推断；演绎（出）
The teacher was unable to educe an answer from her pupils.

◆ deduce [dɪ'djuːs] *v.* [T] 推断；演绎；追溯根源
The police were able to deduce where the fugitive was hiding.

◆ seduce [sɪ'djuːs] *v.* [T] 勾引；诱奸，使入迷
She has set out to seduce Stephen.

◆ traduce [trə'djuːs] *v.* [T] 诋毁；诽谤；背叛
n. 诽谤，中伤；诽谤者
It is not easy to traduce his character.

◆ conduce [kən'djuːs] *v.* [I] 有益，有贡献于；导致
Wealth does not always conduce to happiness.

◆ conduct [kən'dʌkt] *v.* [T] 组织；实施；引导
v. [I] 当指挥；当售票员；导电
['kɔndʌkt] *n.* 举止；行为；实施
I decided to conduct an experiment.
For Europeans, the law is a statement of the basic principles of civilised conduct.

◆ abduct [æb'dʌkt] *v.* [T] 劫持；诱拐；使外展
The police caught the man who tried to abduct the boy for ransom.

◆ aqueduct ['ækwɪdʌkt] *n.* 沟渠；引水渠；高架渠
The ancient aqueduct stood out against the clear sky.

◆ ventiduct ['ventɪdʌkt] *n.* 通风管
Midea has made a world-wide breakthrough of its wind turbine and ventiduct technology in air-conditioner.

◆ viaduct ['vaɪədʌkt] *n.* 高架桥（通常有多孔）
An overhead road for cars or trains is called a viaduct.

don/dot/dow: give

◆ donate [dəʊ'neɪt] *v.* [T and I] (尤指向慈善机构) 捐赠; 献 (血); 捐献 (器官)
n. 捐赠; 捐献
He frequently donates large sums to charity.

◆ donation [dəʊ'neɪʃən] *n.* [C] 捐赠; 捐款; 捐赠物
I'll be sending them a donation in appreciation of their help.

◆ donor ['dəʊnə(r)] *n.* [C] 捐赠者; 输血者; 施主
As the donor of this elementary school, he is greatly respected by the people in this small town.

◆ condone [kən'dəʊn] *v.* [T] 容忍, 宽恕, 原谅
I cannot condone the use of violence.

◆ antidote ['æntɪdəʊt] *n.* 解药; 矫正方法, 对抗手段
There is no known antidote to the poison.

◆ anecdote ['ænɪkdəʊt] *n.* [C] 趣闻, 轶事; (复数) 秘史
He departed from the text to tell an anecdote.

◆ dose [dəʊs] *n.* 剂量; (酒中的) 配料, 增味剂
v. [I] 服药
v. [T] 把 (药等) 配分剂量; 在 (酒) 中加料
In the accident, the workers received a heavy dose of radiation.

◆ pardon ['pɑːdn] *v.* [T] 宽恕; 赦免; 劳驾
n. 原谅; 赦免; 请再说一遍
I hope you will pardon me for that slip.

◆ dowry ['daʊərɪ] *n.* [C] 嫁妆
His family hoped that his bride would bring a large dowry.

◆ endow [ɪn'daʊ] *v.* [T] 捐赠, 资助; 赋予
Mathematics seems to endow one with something like a new sense.

◆ endowment [ɪn'daʊmənt] *n.* 捐赠; 基金; 天赋
Is it true that Chinese students lack the endowment of learning foreign languages?

tribute: give

◆ tribute ['trɪbjuːt] *n.* 称赞; 证据; 贡品
The couple paid tribute to the helicopter crew who rescued them.

◆ attribute [ə'trɪbjuːt] *v.* [T] 认为……是; 把……归于
['ætrɪbjuːt] *n.* 属性; 特征; 定语
I attribute our success to him.

◆ retribution [ˌretrɪ'bjuːʃən] *n.* [U] 应得的惩罚, 报应; 报答
Evil actions will bring retribution.

◆ contribute [kən'trɪbjuːt] *v.* [T and I] 贡献; 捐赠; 出力
The three sons also contribute to the family business.

◆ distribute [dɪ'strɪbjuːt] *v.* [T] 分配, 散布; 分发
Distribute these pamphlets among them before you leave, will you?

quire/quest/quisit: ask, seek

◆ questionable ['kwestʃənəbl] *adj.* 可疑的, 有疑问的
There are still a few questionable points in the case.

◆ questionnaire [ˌkwestʃə'neə(r)] *n.* [C] 调查表; 调查问卷
Use a questionnaire to survey attitudes to smoking.

◆ acquire [əˈkwaɪə(r)] *v.* [T] 获得，取得；学到

We must work hard to acquire a good knowledge of English.

◆ acquisition [ˌækwɪˈzɪʃən] *n.* [C, U] 获得；取得；获得物

He devotes his time to the acquisition of knowledge.

◆ inquire [ɪnˈkwaɪə(r)] *v.* [T and I] 打听，询问；查究

We must inquire into the matter.

◆ inquisition [ˌɪnkwɪˈzɪʃən] *n.* [C] 调查，审讯

The police subjected him to an inquisition that lasted two hours.

◆ inquisitive [ɪnˈkwɪzətɪv] *adj.* 好问的，好奇的；爱打听的

n. 好询问的人；爱打听别人事情的人

Children are usually inquisitive.

◆ inquiring [ɪnˈkwaɪərɪŋ] *adj.* 咨询的，打听的；爱追根究底的

As a child he had a lively inquiring mind.

◆ inquiry [ɪnˈkwaɪərɪ] *n.* [C, U] 调查；询问；打听

Many parents have been pressing for an inquiry into the problem.

◆ require [rɪˈkwaɪə(r)] *v.* [T] 要求；需要；命令

These pets require a lot of care and attention.

◆ request [rɪˈkwest] *n.* 要求；需要

v. [T] 请求；索取

He turned a deaf ear to my request for help.

◆ requisite [ˈrekwɪzɪt] *n.* [C] 必需品；要素

adj. 需要的，必要的

He hasn't got the requisite qualifications for the job.

◆ conquer [ˈkɒŋkə(r)] *v.* [T] 征服；攻克；克服

v. [I] 得胜，胜利

Will can conquer habit.

◆ conquest [ˈkɒŋkwest] *n.* [C, U] 征服，击败；战利品

They succeeded in the conquest of that city.

◆ exquisite [ˈekskwɪzɪt, ɪkˈs-] *adj.* 精致的；细腻的；优美的

n. 过分讲究穿戴的人

I was admiring the exquisite workmanship in the mosaic.

pet: seek, rush

◆ repetition [ˌrepɪˈtɪʃən] *n.* 重复；背诵；复制品

That is a mere repetition of what you said before.

◆ petition [pɪˈtɪʃən] *n.* [C] 请愿书，请愿；上诉状

v. [I] 祈求；请愿

v. [T]（向法庭）申诉

Thousands of citizens subscribed the petition.

◆ competition [ˌkɒmpɪˈtɪʃən] *n.* 竞争；比赛

There is keen competition between the two motorcar firms.

◆ competence [ˈkɒmpɪtəns] *n.* [C, U] 能力；技能；相当的资产

The ability to write is a supreme test of linguistic competence.

◆ appetite [ˈæpɪtaɪt] *n.* [C] 欲望；胃口；嗜好

He has a gigantic appetite and eats gigantic meals.

◆ perpetual [pəˈpetʃʊəl] *adj.* 永久的；不断的；无期限的

He is on a perpetual search for truth.

◆ impetus [ˈɪmpɪtəs] *n.* [U] 动力；促进；势头

This is the primary impetus behind the

economic recovery.

◆ impetuous [ɪmˈpetjʊəs] *adj.* 冲动的；鲁莽的；猛烈的

The headstrong impetuous man rushed into things without forethought.

◆ petulant [ˈpetjʊlənt] *adj.* 易怒的，使性子的，脾气坏的

She could be wayward, petulant, and disagreeable.

◆ propitiate [prəˈpɪʃɪeɪt] *v.* [T] 劝解，抚慰，使息怒

They offer a sacrifice to propitiate the god.

◆ propitious [prəˈpɪʃəs] *adj.* 有利的；吉祥的；合适的

Conditions were propitious for development.

fuse: pour, melt

◆ fuse [fjuːz] *v.* [T and I] 熔化；融合；给……装信管

n. [C] 保险丝；导火线；引信

The metal will fuse at a relatively low temperature.

◆ defuse [diːˈfjuːz] *v.* [T] 拆除（爆炸物）的引信；减少……的危险性；平息

The bomb blew up as experts tried to defuse it.

◆ confuse [kənˈfjuːz] *v.* [T and I] 使困窘；使混乱；使困惑

His comments only served to confuse the issue further.

◆ diffuse [dɪˈfjuːz] *v.* [T and I] 传播；使分散；漫射

adj. 散开的；冗长的；累赘的

Critics believe that such action will diffuse the power of Congress.

◆ infuse [ɪnˈfjuːz] *v.* [T] 灌输；使充满；激发

v. [I] 沏（茶），泡（草药）

Add the tea leaves and leave to infuse for five minutes.

◆ effuse [ɪˈfjuːz] *v.* [T] 涌出，流出

The room effuses happiness.

◆ refuse [ˈrefjuːs] *n.* 废物，垃圾

[rɪˈfjuz] *v.* [T and I] 拒绝，回绝

He refused to comment after the trial.

◆ suffuse [səˈfjuːz] *v.* [T]（指颜色、水汽等）弥漫于，布满

They want to move everyone with their behaviors and suffuse the world with love.

◆ transfuse [trænsˈfjuːz] *v.* [T] 输（血或别的液体）；渗透；使……被灌输或传达

He cannot transfuse the knowledge into your brain.

◆ profuse [prəˈfjuːs] *adj.* 毫不吝惜的；慷慨的；挥霍的

He was so profuse with his money that he is now poor.

◆ circumfuse [ˌsɜːkəmˈfjuːz] *v.* [T] 从四面浇灌，围绕，充溢

form: form

◆ formal [ˈfɔːml] *adj.* 正规的；方式上的；礼仪上的

Her dress was too showy for such a formal occasion.

◆ formalize [ˈfɔːməlaɪz] *v.* [T and I] 使正式，形式化；拘泥于形式

Formalize and obtain final acceptance for the project.

◆ formalism [ˈfɔːməlɪzəm] *n.* 形式主义

The development of formalism is contrary to the spirit of the legislation.

◆ informal [ɪnˈfɔːməl] *adj.* 非正式的；口语体的；友好随便的

Discussions are held on an informal basis within the department.

◆ formation [fɔːˈmeɪʃən] *n.* 形成；构成；队形

The aircraft are flying in formation.

◆ malformation [ˌmælfɔːˈmeɪʃən] *n.* [C] 难看，畸形

This treatment could result in malformation of the arms.

◆ formula [ˈfɔːmjʊlə] *n.* [C, U] 公式，准则；配方

No one has a magic formula for keeping youngsters away from crime.

◆ formulate [ˈfɔːmjʊleɪt] *v.* [T] 构想出；确切地阐述；用公式表示

He took care to formulate his reply very clearly.

◆ conform [kənˈfɔːm] *v.* [I] 符合；遵照；适应环境

He did not feel obliged to conform to the rules that applied to ordinary men.

◆ inform [ɪnˈfɔːm] *v.* [T] 通知；使活跃，使充满

v. [I] 告发；检举

Please inform us of your decision and we will act accordingly.

◆ deform [dɪˈfɔːm] *v.* [T] 使变形；使残废；毁伤……的形体

v. [I] 变形；变畸形

The shoes that are too tight deform the feet.

◆ perform [pəˈfɔːm] *v.* [T and I] 表现；执行；表演

This play was first performed in 411 BC.

◆ reform [rɪˈfɔːm] *n.* 改革，改良

v. [T and I] 改善，改革；重组

All their efforts at reform have been set back.

◆ transform [trænsˈfɔːm] *v.* [T] 改变；变换

In order to transform their environment, he drew up the project with painstaking accuracy.

◆ uniform [ˈjuːnɪfɔːm] *n.* [C] 制服；军服

adj. 一样的；始终如一的

v. [T] 使规格一律；使均一；使穿制服

The town police wear dark blue uniforms and flat caps.

ori: rise, begin

◆ orient [ˈɔːrɪənt] *v.* [T and I] 标定方向；使……向东方；以……为参照

adj. 东方的；(太阳等) 上升的，新生的

n. 东亚各国；日出之处，东方

The people in the Orient are mainly yellow or brown.

◆ oriental [ˌɔːrɪˈentl] *adj.* 东方的；东方人的；东方文化的；优质的

n. [C] 东方人；东亚人

He has oriental blood in his veins.

◆ origin [ˈɒrɪdʒɪn] *n.* 起源，根源；起点

There are many theories about the origin of life.

◆ original [əˈrɪdʒənəl] *adj.* 原始的；最初的；新颖的

n. 原文；原型；怪人

I don't think George is capable of having original ideas!

◆ originate [əˈrɪdʒɪneɪt] *v.* [T] 引起；创作；开始

v. [I] 起源于，来自；产生

All theories originate from practice and in turn serve practice.

◆ abortion [əˈbɔːʃən] *n.* 流产；夭折

Is abortion morally defensible?

◆ disorient [dɪsˈɔːrɪent] *v.* [T] 使迷失方向；使迷惑；使不知所措

They were disoriented by the smoke and were firing blindly into it.

termi: end; limit, boundary

◆ terminate [ˈtɜːmɪneɪt] *v.* [T and I] 结束；使终结；到达终点站

You have no right to terminate the contract.

◆ exterminate [ɪkˈstɜːmɪneɪt] *v.* [T] 消灭；根除

This spray will exterminate the ants.

◆ interminable [ɪnˈtɜːmɪnəbl] *adj.* 冗长的；无止境的；没完没了的

For several seemingly interminable seconds no one spoke.

◆ determine [dɪˈtɜːmɪn] *v.* [T and I] 下决心，做出决定；限定；结束

We both looked up to determine the source of the water.

◆ determinant [dɪˈtɜːmɪnənt] *n.* [C] 决定物；决定因素；行列式

adj. 决定因素的；限定性的

The windows and the views beyond them are major determinants of a room's character.

◆ predetermine [ˌpriːdɪˈtɜːmɪn] *v.* [T and I] 预先裁定；注定

These factors predetermine to a large extent the outcome.

◆ terminal [ˈtɜːmɪnl] *adj.* 末期的；晚期的；末端的

n. [C] 终端；终点站；航空站

Plans are underway for a fifth terminal at Heathrow Airport.

◆ terminus [ˈtɜːmɪnəs] *n.* [C] 终点；终点站；界限

What time does the train reach the terminus?

◆ terminology [ˌtɜːmɪˈnɒlədʒɪ] *n.* 专门名词；术语，术语学

It is important that lawyers use the correct terminology when they prepare contracts.

fin: end, limit

◆ affinity [əˈfɪnɪtɪ] *n.* [C] 密切关系，姻亲关系；(男女之间的) 吸引力

I felt a great affinity with the people of the Highlands.

◆ definitive [dɪˈfɪnɪtɪv] *adj.* 确定的，决定性的；限定的

n. 限定词

We got a definitive victory.

◆ infinitive [ɪnˈfɪnɪtɪv] *n.* (动词) 不定式

adj. 不定式的

In English an infinitive is often used with the word "to".

◆ infinity [ɪnˈfɪnɪtɪ] *n.* 〈数〉无穷大；无限的时间或空间

It is impossible to count up to infinity.

◆ infinite [ˈɪnfɪnɪt] *adj.* 无限的，无穷的；无数的

n. 无限；无穷大；〈宗〉造物主

The universe seems infinite.

◆ definite [ˈdefɪnɪt] *adj.* 明确的；一定的；肯定的

Our ideas began to crystallize into a definite plan.

◆ define [dɪˈfaɪn] *v.* [T] 规定；精确地解释；画出……的线条

v. [I] 下定义，构成释义

Please define the words.

◆ confine [kənˈfaɪn] *v.* [T] 限制；局限于；禁闭

n. 界限，范围；国界

Doctors are trying to confine the disease within the city.

◆ finalize [ˈfaɪnəlaɪz] *v.* [T] 完成；使结束；使落实

Franck and his crew had arrived to finalize all the details of the wedding.

◆ finance [ˈfaɪnæns, fɪˈnæns] *n.* 财政；金融；资金

v. [T] 为……供给资金，从事金融活动；掌握财政

A finance house made a bid to buy up the entire company.

cide/cise: kill; cut

◆ concise [kənˈsaɪs] *adj.* 简明的，简洁的；精练的

Teaching content should be concise.

◆ precise [prɪˈsaɪs] *adj.* 清晰的；精确的；精密的

She gave me clear and precise directions.

◆ decide [dɪˈsaɪd] *v.* [T] 决定；决心；解决

v. [I] 决定；下决心

I can't decide who is the winner.

◆ excise [ekˈsaɪz] *v.* [T] 切除；向……征税；向……索取高价

n. 国内货物税，消费税；执照税；（英国的）国产税务局

Customs and excise receipts rose 2.5 percent.

◆ excision [ɪkˈsɪʒən] *n.* 切除，删除；切割

Most surgeons agree that radical excision should be performed.

◆ incise [ɪnˈsaɪz] *v.* [T]（在表面）雕，刻

After the surface is polished, a design is incised or painted.

◆ insecticide [ɪnˈsektɪsaɪd] *n.* 杀虫剂

Many pests are resistant to the insecticide.

◆ rodenticide [rəʊˈdentɪsaɪd] *n.* 灭鼠剂

The researchers studied the clinical feature of acute rodenticide.

◆ pesticide [ˈpestɪsaɪd] *n.* 杀虫剂，农药

It is claimed that current levels of pesticide do not pose a threat to health.

◆ suicide [ˈs(j)uːɪsaɪd] *n.* 自杀；自杀者；自杀行为

Police are treating the man's death as suicide.

clud/clus/clos: shut, close

◆ conclude [kənˈkluːd] *v.* [T and I] 得出结论；结束；推断

What do you conclude from that?

◆ exclude [ɪkˈskluːd] *v.* [T] 排除，不包括；驱除

This was intended to exclude the direct rays of the sun.

◆ exclusive [ɪkˈskluːsɪv] *adj.* 专用的；高级的；排外的

n. 独家新闻；专有物；排外者

This bathroom is for the President's exclusive use.

◆ preclude [prɪˈkluːd] *v.* [T] 阻止；排除；妨碍

We try to preclude any possibility of misunderstanding.

◆ seclude [sɪˈkluːd] *v.* [T] 使隔开；使隔绝，使隐退

She would seclude herself from the world forever.

◆ recluse [rɪˈkluːs] *n.* [C] 隐居者，隐士

All these years, Eric had lived as a recluse.

◆ disclose [dɪsˈkləʊz] *v.* [T] 公开；揭露；使显露

Science can disclose the mysteries of nature.

◆ enclose [ɪnˈkləʊz] *v.* [T] 围起来；把……装入信封；附入

I enclose here with a draft for the sum of 100 dollars.

lect/leg: choose, gather; speak

◆ collect [kəˈlekt] *v.* [T and I] 收集；收款；聚积

adj. 由受话人付费的（美国英语）

adv.（电话、电报等）由受话人付费

He gave me not even a moment to collect my thoughts.

◆ recollect [ˌrekəˈlekt] v. [T] 记起，想起，回忆

He tried to recollect things and drown himself in them.

◆ select [sɪˈlekt] v. [T] 选择；挑选；选拔

adj. 精选的；苛择的

The book is a select collection of poetry from various authors.

◆ selective [sɪˈlektɪv] adj. 精心选择的；不普遍的

She is selective about the clothes she buys.

◆ elegant [ˈelɪgənt] adj.（人或其举止）优美的；漂亮的；简练的

She was an elegant and accomplished woman.

◆ eligible [ˈelɪdʒəbl] adj. 合适的；合格的；有资格当选的

n. 合格者；合适者；称心如意的人

He was not eligible for the examination because he was over age.

◆ intellect [ˈɪntɪlekt] n. [C] 智力；有才智的人；知识分子

Newton is a man of great intellect.

◆ intellectual [ˌɪntɪˈlektjʊəl,-tʃʊ-] adj. 智力的；有才智的；智力发达的

n. [C] 知识分子；脑力劳动者；有极高智力的人

◆ intelligent [ɪnˈtelɪdʒənt] adj. 聪明的；理解力强的；有智力的

I have not arrived at a very intelligent opinion on that matter.

◆ intelligible [ɪnˈtelɪdʒəbl] adj. 可理解的，明白易懂的，清楚的

His lecture was readily intelligible to all the students.

◆ neglect [nɪˈglekt] v. [T] 疏忽；忽略；疏于照顾

n. 玩忽；被忽略的状态；怠慢

Today's housing problems are the product of years of neglect.

◆ negligent [ˈneglɪdʒənt] adj. 疏忽的；粗心大意的；不留心的

The committee heard that he had been negligent in his duty.

◆ negligible [ˈneglɪdʒəbl] adj. 可以忽略的；微不足道的；无足轻重的

There was a negligible amount of rain in that region last year.

◆ colleague [ˈkɒliːg] n. [C] 同事；同僚；同行

We were friends and colleagues for more than 20 years.

◆ legion [ˈliːdʒən] n. [C] 大批部队；大量；古罗马军团

adj. 众多的；大量的

Each legion contained between 3,000 and 6,000 soldiers.

flu: flow

◆ fluent [ˈfluːənt] adj. 流畅的；流利的；液态的

Long practice enabled that American to speak fluent Chinese.

◆ influent [ˈɪnflʊənt] adj. 流入的

n. 支流

◆ influence [ˈɪnflʊəns] n. [C, U] 影响；势力；〈占星学〉星力

v. [T] 影响；支配

They were accused of exerting too much influence on voters.

◆ effluent [ˈeflʊənt] adj. 发出的，流出的

n.（注入河里等的）污水，工业废水；（从湖等）流出的水流

Industrial effluent often causes problems to

people's health.

◆ refluent [ˈreflʊənt] *adj.* 回流的，退潮的，倒流的

◆ confluence [ˈkɒnflʊəns] *n.* 汇流处；汇合；汇流

They built the city at the confluence of two rivers.

◆ superfluous [suːˈpɜːflʊəs, sjuː-] *adj.* 过多的；多余的；奢侈的

He had already been told, so our comments were superfluous.

◆ superfluity [ˌsuːpəˈfluːɪtɪ, ˌsjuː-] *n.* [C] 过多；过剩；过剩品

The city has a superfluity of five-star hotels.

◆ affluent [ˈæflʊənt] *adj.* 富足的；流畅的，滔滔不绝的

n. 富裕的人；支流

We live in an affluent society.

◆ flush [flʌʃ] *v.* [T and I] 脸红；奔流；冲刷

adj. 满面红光的；富足的；在同一平面的，同高的

n. 奔流；脸红或发亮；强烈情感的冲动

Father asked me to flush off the garage floor.

◆ fluid [ˈfluːɪd] *n.* 液体，流体

adj. 流动的，液体的；流畅优美的

Air, whether in the gaseous or liquid state, is a fluid.

◆ fluctuate [ˈflʌktʃʊeɪt] *v.* [I] 波动；涨落

v. [T] 使波动；使动摇

Body temperature fluctuates if you are ill.

Exercises

I. Match the roots with their meanings.

A. flu	( ) 1. pour, melt
B. lect	( ) 2. lead
C. termi	( ) 3. form
D. cide	( ) 4. give
E. form	( ) 5. end, limit
F. fuse	( ) 6. rise
G. pet	( ) 7. kill, cut
H. quest	( ) 8. ask, seek
I. tribute	( ) 9. choose, gather
J. ori	( ) 10. seek, rush
K. duct	( ) 11. flow

II. Complete the sentences with the right forms of the best words.

concise	affluent	fluctuate	neglect	intellectual
distribute	deduce	acquisition	diffuse	conform

1. We can ________ a conclusion from the premise.
2. The explanation in this dictionary is ________ and to the point.
3. Do you know the ________ property rights?
4. The building does not ________ to safety regulations.

5. Prices ________ from year to year.
6. Cigarette smoking used to be commoner among ________ people.
7. Employees complained of the company's ________ of safety standards.
8. Please ________ the examination papers round the class.
9. He devotes his time to the ________ of knowledge.
10. Many presidential candidates have used humor to ________ criticism.

III. Finish the words according to the definitions. The first letters are given.

1. e ________ not divided or shared with others
2. o ________ the place where something begins, where it springs into being
3. c ________ to accept something wrong and let it happen
4. p ________ a chemical used to kill pests
5. d ________ give to a charity or good cause
6. q ________ a form containing a set of questions; submitted to people to gain statistical information
7. c ________ the quality of being adequately or well qualified physically and intellectually
8. e ________ natural qualities or talents
9. o ________ coming from or associated with Eastern Asia, especially China and Japan
10. t ________ change or alter in form, appearance, or nature

IV. Choose the best answers.

1. Doctors said surgery could ________ a heart attack.
   A. induce B. deduce C. traduce D. conduce
2. Women tend to ________ their success to external causes such as luck.
   A. tribute B. contribute C. attribute D. distribute
3. He has ________ a reputation as this country's premier solo violinist.
   A. acquired B. inquired C. required D. conquered
4. Charlie, do you want to sign this ________?
   A. repetition B. competition C. petition D. competence
5. Many of the girls seemed to be ________ with excitement on seeing the snow.
   A. confused B. infused C. defused D. transfused
6. They were ________ in their compliments.
   A. suffuse B. circumfuse C. profuse D. effuse
7. He did not feel obliged to ________ to the rules that applied to ordinary men.
   A. transform B. conform C. deform D. perform
8. But I felt it my duty to ________ evil.
   A. terminate B. exterminate C. terminal D. interminable
9. It helps you improve yourself and ________ your skills.
   A. refine B. definitive C. infinitive D. confine
10. The village is almost ________ from the world for the bad communications.
   A. excluded B. precluded C. secluded D. concluded

Theme Three

听说睹写-1

audi: hear

◆ audible [ˈɔːdəbl,-dɪ-] *adj.* 听得见的

The noise was audible even above the roar of the engines.

◆ audience [ˈɔːdjəns,ˈɔːdɪəns] *n.* [C] 听众

Some of the magic tricks called for audience participation.

◆ audio [ˈɔːdɪəʊ] *adj.* 声音的

Often, the meeting is recorded on audio or video media for later reference.

◆ auditor [ˈɔːdɪtə(r)] *n.* [C] 听者，审计员

The auditor examines the accounts of all county officers and departments.

◆ auditorial [ˌɔːdɪˈtɔːrɪəl] *adj.* 审计员的，查账的；听觉的

Many problems in auditorial principle, legal basis and mode are exposed.

◆ auditorium [ˌɔːdɪˈtɔːrɪəm] *n.* 观众席，礼堂

No smoking in the auditorium.

◆ auditory [ˈɔːdɪtərɪ] *adj.* 有关听觉的

Finally he overcame the auditory difficulties by three years' efforts.

son: sound

◆ sonata [səˈnɑːtə] *n.* 奏鸣曲

He played a Beethoven sonata yesterday.

◆ sonic [ˈsɒnɪk] *adj.* 声音的，声波的

The signals will travel at sonic speeds.

◆ supersonic [ˌsuːpəˈsɒnɪk,ˌsjuː-] *adj.* 超声的，超声速的

These planes travel at supersonic speeds.

◆ sonorous [səˈnɔːrəs] *adj.* 洪亮的

The sonorous voice of the speaker echoed round the room.

◆ consonant [ˈkɒnsənənt] *n.* [C] 辅音 *adj.* 符合的；一致的

"N" is a syllabic consonant in "ton."

I found their work very much consonant with this way of thinking.

◆ dissonant [ˈdɪsənənt] *adj.* 不和谐的，不一致的

His voice is drowned by the dissonant scream of a siren outside.

◆ resonate [ˈrezəneɪt] *v.* [I] 共鸣，共振

The bass guitar was so loud that it resonated in my head.

◆ resonant [ˈrezənənt] *adj.* 回响的，回荡的

His voice sounded oddly resonant in the empty room.

phon: sound

◆ phoneme [ˈfəʊniːm] *n.* [U] 音素，音位

simple phoneme

◆ phonetic [fə(ʊ)ˈnetɪk] *adj.* 语音的

A list of phonetic symbols is given in the

front of the dictionary.

◆ phonetics [fə(ʊ)ˈnetɪks] *n.* [U] 语音学

◆ phonic [ˈfɒnɪk] *adj.* 声音的
His story is not phonic, but told by body language.

◆ phonics [ˈfɒnɪks] *n.* [U] 发音学

◆ phonograph [ˈfəʊnəgrɑːf] *n.* [C] 留声机
Put a record on the phonograph and let's have some music.

◆ phonology [fə(ʊ)ˈnɒlədʒɪ] *n.* [U] 音位学

◆ euphony [ˈjuːfənɪ] *n.* [C] 悦耳的声音
Such euphony is hard to resist.

◆ euphonious [juːˈfəʊnɪəs] *adj.* 悦耳的
He was enchanted with the euphonious music.

◆ interphone [ˈɪntəfəʊn] *n.* [C] 对讲机
Interphone is a telephone system for linking different rooms within a building, ship, etc.

◆ homophone [ˈhɒmə(ʊ)fəʊn] *n.* [C] 同音异义词，同音异形词
Drinking cup (beiju) is a homophone for "tragedy" in Chinese.

◆ microphone [ˈmaɪkrəfəʊn] *n.* [C] 麦克风
He gave a tap at the microphone before speaking.

◆ symphony [ˈsɪmfənɪ] *n.* [C] 交响乐
The Ninth Symphony of Beethoven is a famous one.

◆ telephone [ˈtelɪfəʊn] *n.* [C] 电话

ton：tone

◆ tonal [ˈtəʊnl] *adj.* 音调的
There is little tonal variety in his voice.

◆ tone [təʊn] *n.* [C] 音调；语气；格调；色调
Her tone implied that her patience was limited.

◆ monotone [ˈmɒnətəʊn] *n.* [C] 单调
The evidence was read out to the court in a dull monotone.

◆ monotonic [ˌmɒnəˈtɒnɪk] *adj.* 单调的，无变化的
The crickets sang their everlasting monotonic note.

◆ monotonous [məˈnɒtənəs] *adj.* 单调无聊的
She thought life in the small town was monotonous.

◆ monotony [məˈnɒtənɪ] *n.* [U] 单调乏味
A night on the town may help to break the monotony of the week.

◆ intonation [ˌɪntə(ʊ)ˈneɪʃən] *n.* [C] 语调，声调
Questions are spoken with a rising intonation.

dic：say

◆ diction [ˈdɪkʃən] *n.* [U] 说话的风格；措辞
His diction is noted for its freshness and vividness.

◆ dictionary [ˈdɪkʃənərɪ] *n.* [C] 词典
She bought an English dictionary for me.

◆ dictate [dɪkˈteɪt] *v.* [T] 口授；读出(文字)，做听写或录音
He dictated a letter to his secretary.

◆ dictation [dɪkˈteɪʃən] *n.* [C] 口授；听写
We have a dictation every English class.

◆ dictator [dɪkˈteɪtə(r)] *n.* [C] 口授者；专制者
The dictator's first step was to strangle the free press.

◆ abdicate [ˈæbdɪkeɪt] *v.* [I] 退位；逊位
The last French King was Louis Philippe, who abdicated in 1848.

◆ addict [ˈædɪkt] *n.* [C] 上瘾的人

v. ［T］使上瘾

He's only 24 years old and a drug addict.

He was addicted to heroin at the age of 17.

◆ contradict［ˌkɒntrəˈdɪkt］v. ［I and T］反驳，与……矛盾

The two stories contradict each other.

◆ contradictory［ˌkɒntrəˈdɪktərɪ］adj. 相矛盾的

We are faced with two apparently contradictory statements.

◆ dedicate［ˈdedɪkeɪt］v. ［T］奉献

He dedicated his life to helping the poor.

◆ dedication［ˌdedɪˈkeɪʃən］n. 对某事业的忠诚，奉献

I admire her dedication to the job.

◆ edict［ˈiːdɪkt］n. ［C］法令，公告

The emperor issued an edict forbidding doing trade with foreigners.

◆ indicate［ˈɪndɪkeɪt］v. ［T］表示；表明或暗示什么的可能性

Dreams can help indicate your true feelings.

◆ indication［ˌɪndɪˈkeɪʃən］n. ［C］指示，表示，迹象

He gave no indication that he was ready to compromise.

◆ indict［ɪnˈdaɪt］v. ［T］控告、起诉或告发某人

He was later indicted on corruption charges.

◆ indictment［ɪnˈdaɪtmənt］n.［C］控诉，起诉书

He handed up the indictment to the supreme court.

◆ jurisdiction［ˌdʒʊərɪsˈdɪkʃən］n. ［U］司法权，裁判权

The British police have no jurisdiction over foreign bank accounts.

◆ malediction［ˌmælɪˈdɪkʃən］n.［C］诅咒，咒骂

He was answered with a torrent of malediction.

◆ predicate［ˈpredɪkeɪt］v. 宣称，断言［ˈpredɪkət］n. 谓语

Most religions predicate life after death.

◆ predict［prɪˈdɪkt］v. ［T］预言

No one had enough foresight to predict the winner.

◆ verdict［ˈvɜːdɪkt］n. ［C］裁决

Three judges will deliver their verdict in October.

◆ vindicate［ˈvɪndɪkeɪt］v. ［T］证明……无辜；为……辩护

He tried hard to vindicate his honesty.

log/loqu/locut：speak

◆ logic［ˈlɒdʒɪk］n. ［U］逻辑性，逻辑

I didn't follow the logic of your argument.

◆ logician［lə(ʊ)ˈdʒɪʃən, lɒ-］n. 逻辑学家

◆ analogy［əˈnælədʒɪ］n. ［C］类比，比拟

It is sometimes easier to illustrate an abstract concept by analogy with something concrete.

◆ anthropology［ˌænθrəˈpɒlədʒɪ］n. ［U］人类学

◆ astrology［əˈstrɒlədʒɪ,-trɑ-］n. ［U］占星术

◆ biology［baɪˈɒlədʒɪ］n.［U］生物学

◆ etymology［ˌetɪˈmɒlədʒɪ］n. ［U］词源学

◆ eulogy［ˈjuːlədʒɪ］n. ［C］颂词，颂歌，悼词

He needs no eulogy from me or from any other man.

When Levy died at the age of 93, Rudoph, his friend, delivered a eulogy at the funeral.

◆ eulogize［ˈjuːlədʒaɪz］v. ［T］称赞，颂扬

The media world seemed to prematurely eulogize Steve Jobs.

◆ genealogy［ˌdʒiːnɪˈælədʒɪ］n. ［U］家谱学 n. ［C］家系，宗谱

He had sat and repeated his family's genealogy to her, twenty minutes of nonstop names.

◆ geology [dʒɪ'ɒlədʒɪ] *n.* [U] 地质学

◆ neology [niː'ɒlədʒɪ, nɪ-] *n.* 新词

◆ psychology [saɪ'kɒlədʒɪ] *n.* [U] 心理学

◆ meteorology [ˌmiːtɪə'rɒlədʒɪ] *n.* [U] 气象学

◆ trilogy ['trɪlədʒɪ] *n.* [C] 三部曲
He is best known for his trilogy on working life.

◆ apology [ə'pɒlədʒɪ] *n.* [C] 道歉
He made a public apology for the team's performance.

◆ apologize [ə'pɒlədʒaɪz] *v.* [I] 道歉
I apologize for being late.

◆ catalogue ['kætəlɒg] *n.* [C] 目录，目录册
The librarian entered a new book in the catalogue.

◆ Decalogue ['dekəlɒg] *n.* 摩西十诫

◆ prologue ['prəʊlɒg] *n.* [C] 开场白，序幕
The prologue to the novel is written in the form of a newspaper account.

◆ epilogue ['epɪlɒg] *n.* [C]（书、剧本、电影、节目等的）结尾部分，后记；跋
Besides the epilogue, there are four chapters in this paper.

◆ dialogue ['daɪəlɒg] *n.* [C] 对话，对白
They have begun dialogues to promote better understanding between both communities.

◆ monologue ['mɒnəlɒg] *n.* [C] 独白
The comedian gave a long monologue of jokes.

◆ loquacious [lə(ʊ)'kweɪʃəs, lɒ'-] *adj.* 多话的
The normally loquacious Mr O'Reilly has said little.

◆ colloquial [kə'ləʊkwɪəl] *adj.* 口语的
"Movie" is a colloquial word for "motion picture."

◆ soliloquy [sə'lɪləkwɪ] *n.* [C] 独白，自言自语
Hamlet's soliloquy is probably the most famous in English drama.

◆ eloquence ['eləkwəns] *n.* 口才；雄辩
He expressed his sentiments about the war with great eloquence.

◆ obloquy ['ɒbləkwɪ] *n.* 辱骂；诽谤
I have had enough obloquy for one lifetime.

◆ elocution [ˌelə'kjuːʃən] *n.* [U] 演说艺术
When I was 11, my mother sent me to elocution lessons.

◆ interlocution [ˌɪntələʊ'kjuːʃən, -lɒ-] *n.* 会谈，问答
The mutual interlocution after the speeches was a highlight of the lecture.

◆ circumlocution [ˌsɜːkəmlə'kjuːʃən] *n.* [C] 迂回累赘的陈述
It was always when you most wanted a direct answer that Greenfield came up with a circumlocution.

ora: speak, pray

◆ oral ['ɔːrəl] *adj.* 口头的
No oral test will be required for admission to that university.

◆ orate [ɔː'reɪt] *v.* [I] 当众演说，祈祷
It certainly is a fine thing to be able to orate.

◆ oratorical [ˌɒrə'tɒrɪkl] *adj.* 演说的，演说术的；雄辩的
We'll organize an oratorical contest.

◆ oratory ['ɒrətərɪ] *n.* [U] 演讲术
n. [C] 私人小礼拜堂
He displayed determination as well as powerful oratory.

◆ oracle ['ɒrəkl] *n.* [C] 神谕；神示所
In times of difficulty, she prays for an oracle

to guide her.

◆ adore［əˈdɔː(r)］*v.*［I and T］崇拜，爱慕
I adore good books and the theatre.

◆ exorable［ˈeksərəbl］*adj.* 可说服的
Scientists are establishing a new math model, trying to make the numbers exorable.

◆ inexorable［ɪnˈeksərəbl］*adj.* 不可阻挡的；坚持不懈的；无情的
The downward trend is inexorable.

◆ perorate［ˈperəreɪt］*v.*［I］做结语，以夸张的口气做长篇演讲
She perorates with an innocent conclusion.

fam/fat/fab/fess: speak

◆ fame［feɪm］*n.*［U］名声，名望
v.［T］获取名利，使闻名
He owed his fame to good fortune.

◆ defame［dɪˈfeɪm］*v.*［T］破坏（某人）的声誉；诽谤，中伤
We expect politicians to defame each other in an election year.

◆ infamous［ˈɪnfəməs］*adj.* 恶名昭著的
He was infamous for his anti-feminist attitudes.

◆ infamy［ˈɪnfəmɪ］*n.*［U］臭名，丑行
His name will live in infamy.

◆ infant［ˈɪnfənt］*n.*［C］婴儿
The operation on the new born infant was a failure.

◆ infantile［ˈɪnfəntaɪl］*adj.* 婴儿期的；幼稚的
This kind of humour is infantile and boring.

◆ infantry［ˈɪnfəntrɪ］*n.*［U］步兵
The infantry were advancing to attack the ridge.

◆ fate［feɪt］*n.* 命运
Her fate rests with her father.

◆ fatal［ˈfeɪtl］*adj.* 致命的
One moment of inattention when driving could be fatal.

◆ fable［ˈfeɪbl］*n.* 寓言
This fable was written after the manner of Aesop.

◆ fabulous［ˈfæbjʊləs］*adj.* 极好的，寓言中的
The scenery and weather were fabulous.

◆ affable［ˈæfəbl］*adj.* 易于交谈的，和蔼的
He is an affable man, always willing to stop and talk.

◆ ineffable［ɪnˈefəbl］*adj.* 不可言喻的，难以用语言表达的
The gift brought her ineffable joy.

◆ confess［kənˈfes］*v.*［I and T］供认，坦白
Her husband confessed to having had an affair.

◆ confession［kənˈfeʃən］*n.* 招供；向神父忏悔
The police stenographer recorded the man's confession word by word.

◆ profess［prəˈfes］*v.*［T］自称，妄称
She professed to hate her nickname.

◆ professor［prəˈfesə(r)］*n.*［C］教授
We were laughing about that absent-minded professor.

◆ profession［prəˈfeʃən］*n.*［C］需高等教育级专业培训的职业
First of all, you should know what profession suits you.

nounc/nunci: say, report

◆ renounce［rɪˈnaʊns］*v.*［I and T］放弃，抛弃；断绝关系
It was painful for him to renounce his son.

◆ announce［əˈnaʊns］*v.*［I and T］宣布；述说
It was announced that the groups have agreed

to a ceasefire.

◆ denounce [dɪˈnaʊns] *v.* [T] 公开指责；正式指控；告发

Some 25,000 demonstrators denounced him as a traitor.

◆ pronouncement [prəˈnaʊnsmənt] *n.* [C] 声明；公告；宣告；判决

Occasionally, Paulson would make a bold policy pronouncement.

◆ enunciate [ɪˈnʌnsɪeɪt] *v.* [I and T]（清晰地）发音；确切地说明

He was ever ready to enunciate his views to all who would listen.

lingu: tongue

◆ language [ˈlæŋgwɪdʒ] *n.* [C] 语言

We learn a language in order to communicate.

◆ linguist [ˈlɪŋgwɪst] *n.* [C] 语言学家

He used to be a linguist till he turns writer.

◆ linguistics [lɪŋˈgwɪstɪks] *n.* [U] 语言学

◆ bilingual [baɪˈlɪŋgwəl] *adj.* 会说两种语言的；双语的

Many parents oppose bilingual education in schools.

◆ monolingual [ˌmɒnə(ʊ)ˈlɪŋgwəl] *adj.* 仅用一种语言的

In fact, America is one of the most stubbornly monolingual nations on Earth.

◆ multilingual [ˌmʌltɪˈlɪŋgwəl] *adj.* 多语言的

As a multilingual society, Singapore has an extremely complicated language environment.

voc/vok: call, speak, voice

◆ voice [vɔɪs] *n.* [C] 嗓音；发言权；影响

Your partners will have no voice in how you operate your company.

◆ vocal [ˈvəʊkl] *adj.* 嗓音的，直言的

He has been very vocal in his displeasure over the results.

◆ vocalist [ˈvəʊkəlɪst] *n.* [C] 歌手

The pianist had to tailor his style to suit the vocalist's distinctive voice.

◆ vocabulary [və(ʊ)ˈkæbjʊlərɪ] *n.* 词汇

The basic vocabulary of a language is those words that must be learnt.

◆ vocation [və(ʊ)ˈkeɪʃən] *n.* 使命感（尤指社会上的或宗教上的）；行业

She felt it was her vocation to take care of the sick.

◆ advocate [ˈædvəkeɪt] *v.* [T] 拥护，提倡 *n.* [C] 倡导者

He was a strong advocate of free market policies and a multi-party system.

◆ advocacy [ˈædvəkəsɪ] *n.* 鼓吹，主张

I support your advocacy of free trade.

◆ equivocal [ɪˈkwɪvəkl] *adj.* (= ambiguous) 模棱两可的；意义不明的

You must state your position on the matters of principles. Don't be equivocal.

◆ equivocate [ɪˈkwɪvəkeɪt] *v.* [I] 说模棱两可的话；支吾

Don't equivocate with me. I want a straight answer to a straight question!

◆ evoke [ɪˈvəʊk] *v.* [T] 唤起，引起

These images are likely to evoke a strong response in the viewer.

◆ evocation [ˌevə(ʊ)ˈkeɪʃən, ˌiː-] *n.* 引起；唤起

Her novel is a brilliant evocation of life in 18th century India.

◆ invoke [ɪnˈvəʊk] *v.* [T] 祈求；援用法律等为行动依据

Let us invoke the blessings of peace.

◆ invocation [ˌɪnvə(ʊ)ˈkeɪʃən] *n.* 援用，求

助，用法术召唤

◆ provoke［prəˈvəʊk］*v.*［T］激怒，引起

I provoked him into doing something really stupid.

◆ provocative［prəˈvɒkətɪv］*adj.* 挑衅的；挑逗的

He has made a string of outspoken and sometimes provocative speeches in recent years.

◆ revoke［rɪˈvəʊk］*v.*［T］撤回，吊销

The university may revoke my diploma.

◆ revocable［ˈrevəkəbl］*adj.* 可撤销的

We confirm that it is opened as revocable documentary.

◆ irrevocable［ɪˈrevəkəbl］*adj.* 不能取消的

His life was set on an irrevocable course.

cite: call

◆ cite［saɪt］*v.*［T］引用，表彰，传讯

She cites a favourite poem by George Herbert.

◆ citation［saɪˈteɪʃən］*n.*［C］引用；引文；表彰

One thing that's very important to note: we must provide a citation for every question we write.

◆ recite［rɪˈsaɪt］*v.*［I and T］列举；背诵

I repeated them until I could recite seventy stories without dropping a word.

◆ solicit［səˈlɪsɪt］*v.*［I and T］恳求

He's already solicited their support on health care reform.

claim/clar: cry, shout

◆ claim［kleɪm］*v.*［T］声称；索要，索赔

You should be able to claim against the car insurance.

◆ acclaim［əˈkleɪm］*v.*［I and T］称赞；为……喝彩

He was acclaimed as England's greatest modern painter.

◆ disclaim［dɪsˈkleɪm］*v.*［T］声称没有，否认，放弃

He disclaimed any interest in the plan.

◆ exclaim［ɪkˈskleɪm］*v.*［I and T］惊叫，呼喊

She exclaimed in delight when she saw the presents.

◆ proclaim［prəˈkleɪm］*v.*［T］宣告，公布（某事物）；声明，表明

His manners proclaim him a scholar.

◆ reclaim［rɪˈkleɪm］*v.*［T］要回；回收；开拓，开垦

The Netherlands has been reclaiming farmland from water.

◆ clamorous［ˈklæmərəs］*adj.* 吵闹的

He hated the crowded and clamorous streets.

◆ acclamation［ˌækləˈmeɪʃən］*n.* 欢呼

The news was greeted with considerable popular acclamation.

◆ declaim［dɪˈkleɪm］*v.*［I and T］（像演讲般）说（话），慷慨陈词

He raised his right fist and declaimed: "Liar and cheat!"

◆ declamation［ˌdekləˈmeɪʃən］*n.* 朗诵，演说（尤指慷慨陈词）

Declamation is a traditional Chinese teaching method.

◆ declamatory［dɪˈklæmətərɪ］*adj.* 正式讲究遣词的，慷慨激昂的

Katharine has made a name for bold and declamatory statements.

◆ declare［dɪˈkleə(r)］*v.*［I and T］宣布；向海关申报需纳税物品

She had nothing to declare, and was starting to go through the "Green" channel.

Exercises

I. Read the clues and complete the crossword.

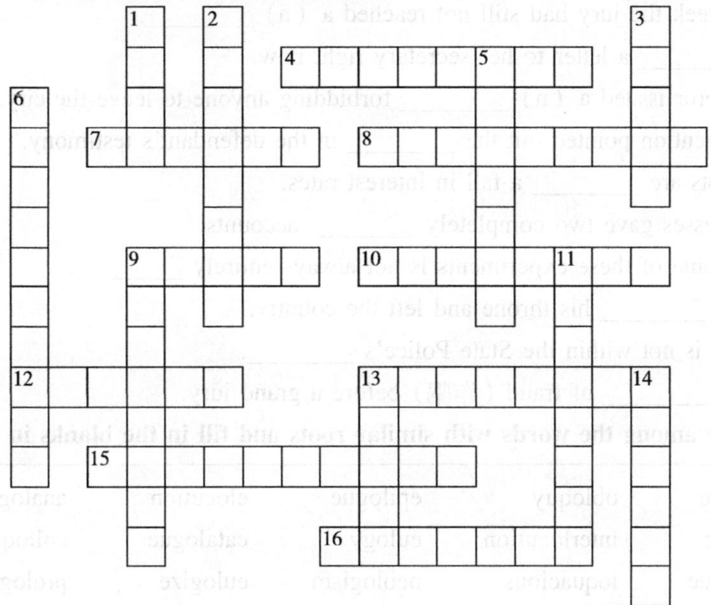

Across:

4. vibrate and produce a deep and strong sound
7. repeat aloud from memory
8. sounded or spoken in a tone unvarying in pitch
9. involving the use of the human voice
10. someone who studies or teaches linguistics
12. a baby or very young child
13. speak in favor of something or somebody and defend them
15. a device that is used to make sounds louder
16. a new word or expression

Down:

1. quote something or mention it, especially as an example or proof
2. the group of people watching or listening to a performance
3. relating to sound that is recorded or broadcast
5. an expression of regret at having caused trouble for someone
6. disagree with something, especially by saying that opposite is true
9. a period of the year when schools are officially closed
11. soldiers who fight on foot rather than in tanks or on horses
13. love intensely

14. a speech or piece of writing in which you praise someone or something very much

II. Complete the sentences with the right forms of the best words.

contradiction	jurisdiction	dictate	verdict	indict
predictable	contradictory	edict	predict	abdicate

1. After a week the jury had still not reached a（n）________.
2. She's ________ a letter to her secretary right now.
3. The emperor issued a（n）________ forbidding anyone to leave the city.
4. The prosecution pointed out the ________ in the defendant's testimony.
5. Economists are ________ a fall in interest rates.
6. The witnesses gave two completely ________ accounts.
7. The outcome of these experiments is not always entirely ________.
8. The king ________ his throne and left the country.
9. That area is not within the State Police's ________.
10. He was ________ of fraud（诈骗）before a grand jury.

III. Choose among the words with similar roots and fill in the blanks in the right forms.

eloquence	obloquy	epilogue	elocution	analogy
eulogistic	interlocution	eulogy	catalogue	colloquial
monologue	loquacious	neologism	eulogize	prologue

1. The Vice President gave the ________ at the general's funeral.
2. The author made up a lot of ________ in his novels, and few people can figure out the meanings of the new words she invented.
3. To everyone's surprise, the satire（讽刺）was ________ rather than critical.
4. He wrote a poem ________ the bravery of the nation's warriors.
5. The mutual ________ after the speeches was a highlight of the conference.
6. I resent the ________ that you are casting upon my reputation.
7. Dr. Wood explained the movement of light by ________ with the movement of water.
8. The book is about a terrible disease, and the author added a（n）________ about recent research into a cure.
9. Businesses mail out a ________ of their products of customers.
10. While the comedian was giving a long ________ of jokes, the other actors were silent.
11. She is very ________ and can talk on the telephone for hours.
12. The young man took lessons in ________ to improve his ability to speak in front of a large crowd.
13. The book has a short ________ written by the author.
14. After many speeches the senator（参议员）is now able to speak with ________ before the Senate.
15. The guests talked in a（n）________ language at the party instead of a formal language.

IV. Choose the best answers.

1. He had ________ trouble and could not hear clearly.

   A. phonic B. auditory C. tonal D. sonic

2. ________ is the study of the origins and historical development of words.

   A. Etymology B. Astrology C. Genealogy D. Meteorology

3. The group's debut album was immediately ________ a hip hop classic.

   A. exclaimed B. proclaimed C. acclaimed D. declaimed

4. He ________ his claim to the French throne.

   A. pronounced B. announced C. denounced D. renounced

5. You'd better not ________ that fellow.

   A. provoke B. invoke C. revoke D. evoke

6. The quality of the dress isn't quite ________ with its price.

   A. resonant B. consonant C. dissonant D. supersonic

7. We'll have the meeting in the classroom rather than in the ________.

   A. auditor B. auditorial C. auditorium D. audible

8. The ________ traitor was sentenced to death.

   A. affable B. fabulous C. infantile D. infamous

Theme Three

听说睹写-2

spect/spic: look

◆ spectacle [ˈspektəkl] *n.* 景象；壮观，大场面；(*pl.*) 眼镜

It was a spectacle not to be missed.

He looked at me over the tops of his spectacles.

◆ spectacular [spekˈtækjʊlə(r)] *adj.* 壮观的；令人惊叹的

The ceremonial opening of the exhibition was very spectacular.

◆ spectator [spekˈteɪtə(r)] *n.* [C] 观众

Thirty thousand spectators watched the final game.

◆ speculate [ˈspekjʊleɪt] *v.* [I and T] 推测；投机

Big farmers are moving in, not in order to farm, but in order to speculate with rising land prices.

◆ aspect [ˈæspekt] *n.* 方面；外观

Climate and weather affect every aspect of our lives.

◆ circumspect [ˈsɜːkəmspekt] *adj.* 慎重的

The banks should have been more circumspect in their dealings.

◆ expect [ɪkˈspekt] *v.* [T] 预料；要求；怀孕

She was expecting another baby.

◆ inspect [ɪnˈspekt] *v.* [I and T] 检查，视察

Cut the fruit in half and inspect the pips.

◆ introspect [ˌɪntrə(ʊ)ˈspekt] *v.* [I and T] 反省，内省

It's time for everyone to introspect.

◆ prospect [ˈprɒspekt] *n.* 前景，景象；希望，前程

The prospect of war loomed large in everyone's mind.

◆ prospective [prəˈspektɪv] *adj.* 预期的，未来的

When his prospective employers learned that he smoked, they said they wouldn't hire him.

◆ perspective [pəˈspektɪv] *n.* 远景；看法；透视法

You can get a perspective of the whole city from here.

◆ respect [rɪˈspekt] *v.* &*n.* 尊重

All students should respect their teachers.

◆ respectful [rɪˈspektfəl] *adj.* 恭敬的，尊重人的

The children in our family are always respectful to their elders.

◆ respective [rɪˈspektɪv] *adj.* 各自的

Steve and I were at very different stages in our respective careers.

◆ retrospect [ˈretrəʊspekt] *v.* &*n.* 回顾

It was, in retrospect, the happiest day of her life.

◆ suspect [sə'spekt] *v.* [I and T] 怀疑 *n.* [C] 嫌疑犯

The police suspect him of having taken the money.

The suspect was identified by the scar on his face.

◆ auspice ['ɔːspɪs] *n.* [C] 吉兆，预兆

He took that as an auspicc of happincss.

◆ auspicious [ɔː'spɪʃəs] *adj.* 吉利的，吉祥的

His career as a playwright had an auspicious start.

◆ conspicuous [kən'spɪkjʊəs] *adj.* 显眼的，明显的

It is conspicuous that smoking is harmful to health.

◆ despise [dɪ'spaɪz] *v.* [T] 鄙视，轻视

How I despised myself for my cowardice!

◆ despicable ['despɪkəbl] *adj.* 可鄙的，卑劣的

From beginning to end his conduct had been despicable and wicked.

◆ suspicion [sə'spɪʃən] *n.* 怀疑

The suspicion that she was lying continued to nag at me.

◆ suspicious [sə'spɪʃəs] *adj.* 表示怀疑的；可疑的

He's so suspicious that he would distrust his own mother.

vis/vid/view: see

◆ visa ['viːzə] *n.* [C] 签证

You'll have to get a passport, and you'll also need a visa.

◆ visible ['vɪzɪbl] *adj.* 看得见的，明显的

They found a bacterium visible to the human eye.

◆ vision ['vɪʒn] *n.* 视力；洞察力；幻影

Education and experience breed a breadth of vision and understanding to him.

◆ visionary ['vɪʒənərɪ] *adj.* 有远见卓识的；幻想的

All we lack is the next generation of visionary leaders to make this strategic alliance happen.

◆ vista ['vɪstə] *n.* [C] 远景；展望

From my bedroom window I looked out on a crowded vista of hills and rooftops.

◆ visit ['vɪzɪt] *v.* [T] 参观，访问；看望

This afternoon we're going to visit a friend in hospital.

◆ visual ['vɪzjʊəl] *adj.* 看得见的，视觉的

The opera was an aural as well as a visual delight.

◆ visualize ['vɪʒʊəlaɪz,-zjʊ-] *v.* [I and T] 想象或设想某人（某事物）；使可见

He could not visualize her as old.

◆ advise [əd'vaɪz] *v.* [I and T] 建议，劝告

She advised him to leave immediately.

◆ advisory [əd'vaɪzərɪ] *adj.* 顾问的，劝告的

He was appointed to the advisory committee last month.

◆ improvise ['ɪmprəvaɪz] *v.* [I and T] 即兴创作；临时就现有条件做

He was giving an improvised speech.

◆ provision [prə'vɪʒən] *n.* 供应，提供；食品；（法律文件中的）规定，条款

On board were enough provisions for two weeks.

It is a clear provision.

◆ provisional [prə'vɪʒənl] *adj.* 临时的，暂时的

All these conclusions are provisional.

◆ revise [rɪ'vaɪz] *v.* [I and T] 修订，校正

The United Nations has been forced to revise its estimates of population growth upwards.

◆ devise［dɪˈvaɪz］*v.*［T］设计，想出；遗赠给

Scientists are working to devise a means of storing this type of power.

◆ supervise［ˈsuːpəvaɪz,ˈsjuː-］*v.*［I and T］监督，指导

He had left her at the car to supervise the baggage.

◆ supervisor［ˈsuːpəvaɪzə(r)，ˈsjuː-］*n.*［C］监察员，导师

He was too flighty to be a good supervisor.

◆ television［ˈtelɪvɪʒən,--ˈ--］*n.*［C］电视机

There are too many ads on television.

◆ evident［ˈevɪdənt］*adj.* 显而易见的

His progress is evident.

◆ provide［prəˈvaɪd］*v.*［I and T］提供；赡养；规定

The agreement provided that the two sides should meet once a month.

◆ provident［ˈprɒvɪdənt］*adj.* 未雨绸缪的，节俭的

He is provident of his money.

◆ improvident［ɪmˈprɒvɪdənt］*adj.* 不顾及将来的，浪费的

You will pay for your improvident behavior.

◆ providence［ˈprɒvɪdəns］*n.* 天意；先见之明；远见

These women regard his death as an act of providence.

◆ providential［ˌprɒvɪˈdenʃəl］*adj.* 天赐的，及时的

The pistols were loaded so our escape is indeed providential.

◆ view［vjuː］*n.* 观点；景色；视野

Each of the rooms has a superb view of Boston Bay.

◆ interview［ˈɪntəvjuː］*n.* & *v.* 面试；采访

Not everyone who writes in can be invited for interview.

◆ review［rɪˈvjuː］*n.* & *v.* 复习，复查；汇报；评论

Let's set aside an hour a day for review purpose.

◆ viewpoint［ˈvjuːpɔɪnt］*n.* 观点，意见；角度，视角

His social viewpoint, since going to London, had changed.

◆ envious［ˈenvɪəs］*adj.* 嫉妒的；羡慕的

I don't think I'm envious of your success.

◆ surveillance［sɜːˈveɪləns］*n.* 盯梢，监督

The army carried out covert surveillance of the building for several months.

test：witness

◆ detest［dɪˈtest］*v.*［T］憎恶，嫌恶，痛恨

Jean detested being photographed.

◆ attest［əˈtest］*v.*［I and T］宣称……为真实的；证明，证实

Police records attest to his long history of violence.

◆ contest［kənˈtest］*v.*［I and T］竞争，为……而奋争；辩驳

［ˈkɔntest］*n.* 比赛；竞赛

She had to contest against a very strong opponent for the championship.

Are you going to enter yourself for the writing contest?

◆ pretest［ˈpriːtest］*n.* 预备考试

Each group was given three tests—a pretest, a test and a posttest.

◆ protest［prəˈtest］*v.*［I and T］抗议；断言

［ˈprəʊtest］*n.* 抗议；反对

I can't pass the matter by without a protest.

◆ protestation［ˌprəʊteˈsteɪʃən，ˌprɒ-］*n.*（严正的）声明

Despite his constant protestations of

devotion and love, her doubts persisted.

◆ protestant [ˈprɒtɪstənt] *n.* 抗议人

A lot of protestants were arrested.

◆ testament [ˈtestəmənt] *n.* 确实的证明；遗嘱；（基督教）圣约书

His success is a testament to his skills.

◆ testify [ˈtestɪfaɪ] *v.* [I and T] 作证；声明

The fingerprint expert was asked to testify at the trial.

◆ testimonial [ˌtestɪˈməʊnɪəl] *n.* 证明书 *adj.* 证明的；表扬的

Each individual concerned should provide relevant testimonial material.

◆ testimony [ˈtestɪmənɪ] *n.* 证词；证明，证据；表示，表明

A witness gave testimony that the driver was drunk.

op/opt: eye, sight; choose

◆ optics [ˈɒptɪks] *n.* [U] 光学

◆ optical [ˈɒptɪkl] *adj.* 视觉的，光学的

He has optical trouble.

◆ optician [ɒpˈtɪʃən] *n.* [C] 光学仪器商，眼镜商；验光师

The optician has advised that I wear contact lenses.

◆ myopia [maɪˈəʊpjə] *n.* [U] 近视；缺乏远见

Maybe you have got myopia, or you are just too tired.

◆ option [ˈɒpʃən] *n.* 选择

You will have to pay them; you have no option.

◆ optional [ˈɒpʃənl] *adj.* 可任选的，非强制的

There are many optional courses to choose.

◆ adopt [əˈdɒpt] *v.* [T] 收养，采纳，批准

There are hundreds of people desperate to adopt a child.

leg: read

◆ legible [ˈledʒəbl] *adj.* 易读的

My handwriting isn't very legible.

◆ illegible [ɪˈledʒəbl] *adj.* 难辨认的，字迹模糊的

A former doctor, Che's hand-writing was said to be almost illegible.

◆ legendary [ˈledʒəndərɪ] *adj.* 传奇的；极其著名的

Unicorns are legendary beasts.

◆ elegy [ˈelɪdʒɪ] *n.* 哀歌，挽歌

It's a touching elegy for a lost friend.

gram/graph: draw, write

◆ grammar [ˈgræmə(r)] *n.* 语法

◆ diagram [ˈdaɪəgræm] *n.* [C] 图解，示意图

The engineer drew a diagram of the bridge.

◆ epigram [ˈepɪgræm] *n.* [C] 诙谐短诗；警句

This isn't just an epigram—life is much more successfully looked at from a single window.

◆ program [ˈprəʊgræm] *n.* [C] 程序，计划

This computer program matters very much.

◆ graph [grɑːf] *n.* [C] 曲线图

The graph flattens out gradually after a steep fall.

◆ graphic [ˈgræfɪk] *adj.* 绘画的，文字的，生动的

The book gave a graphic description of the war.

◆ biography [baɪˈɒgrəfɪ] *n.* [C] 传记

After reading a biography of Lincoln, he was able to tell many stories about the President.

◆ autography [ɔːˈtɒgrəfɪ] *n.* 亲笔，笔迹

He was surrounded by the fans who asked for an autography.

◆ bibliography [ˌbɪblɪˈɒgrəfɪ] *n.* 书目；文献，文献学

At the end of this chapter there is a select bibliography of useful books.

◆ calligraphy [kəˈlɪgrəfɪ] *n.* [U] 书法

Her calligraphy was the clearest I'd ever seen.

◆ monograph [ˈmɒnəgrɑːf] *n.* [C] 专题研究，专论

This monograph belongs to the category of serious popular books.

◆ geography [dʒɪˈɒgrəfɪ, ˈdʒɒ-] *n.* 地理学

Geography is the study of the systems and processes involved in the world's weather, mountains, seas, lakes, etc. and of the ways in which countries and people organize life within an area.

◆ photograph [ˈfəʊtəgrɑːf] *n.* [C] 照片

v. [T] 为……照相

We should be glad to photograph the house and its grounds.

◆ phonograph [ˈfəʊnəgrɑːf] *n.* [C] 留声机

Thomas Edison developed the phonograph in 1877, the first device to record music in the world.

◆ polygraph [ˈpɒlɪgrɑːf] *n.* [C] 测谎试验；多种波动描记器

Hill's lawyers announced she had taken and passed a polygraph test.

◆ telegraph [ˈtelɪgrɑːf] *n.* 电报

v. [I and T] 打电报

He telegraphed me to go to the hospital.

liter: letter

◆ literal [ˈlɪtərəl] *adj.* 字面上的，原意的，逐字的

The literal meaning of the word "cat" is an animal.

◆ literary [ˈlɪtərərɪ] *adj.* 文学的，文艺的，书卷气的

His literary and artistic work is loved by the masses.

◆ literate [ˈlɪtərɪt] *adj.* 有读写能力的，博学的

n. 识字的人

Only a few of the nation's peasants are literate.

◆ obliterate [əˈblɪtəreɪt] *v.* [T] 除去（某物）的痕迹；彻底破坏或毁灭

Whole villages were obliterated by fire.

◆ alliteration [əˌlɪtəˈreɪʃn] *n.* 头韵；双声

Below the photo, it said, "ride rough, ride real," a clever alliteration.

◆ literature [ˈlɪtərɪtʃə(r)] *n.* 文学，文学作品；文献

Are you majoring in English Literature?

◆ literacy [ˈlɪtərəsɪ] *n.* [U] 识字，有文化，读写能力

The literacy rate there is the highest in Central America.

◆ illiteracy [ɪˈlɪtərəsɪ] *n.* [U] 文盲，无知

We must do away with illiteracy.

not: mark

◆ note [nəʊt] *n.* 笔记，便条；音符；注意

See the note below.

◆ notary [ˈnəʊtərɪ] *n.* [C] 公证员

The notary looked at the count with astonishment.

◆ notation [nəʊˈteɪʃən] *n.* 有系统的符号；标记法

Music has a special system of notation.

◆ notice [ˈnəʊtɪs] *v.* [I and T] 察觉到

n. 通知

The secretary tacked a meeting notice on the bulletin board.

◆ notify [ˈnəʊtɪfaɪ] *v.* [T] 通知，报告
He didn't notify me of the means of transportation.

◆ notion [ˈnəʊʃən] *n.* 概念；意图
I haven't the faintest notion what you're talking about.

◆ notorious [nə(ʊ)ˈtɔːrɪəs] *adj.* 臭名昭著的
He was notorious as a gambler.

◆ annotate [ˈænə(ʊ)teɪt] *v.* [I and T] 注解
People annotate the history, so does the history annotate people.

◆ annotation [ˌænə(ʊ)ˈteɪʃən] *n.* 注解
This annotation will be discussed in detail in the next section.

◆ connote [kɒˈnəʊt] *v.* [T] 意味着，暗含
The term "organization" often connotes a sense of neatness.

◆ connotation [ˌkɒnə(ʊ)ˈteɪʃən] *n.* [C] 含义，言外之意
A possible connotation of "home" is a place of warmth, comfort and affection.

◆ denote [dɪˈnəʊt] *v.* [T] 意思是，表示
Red eyes denote strain and fatigue.

◆ denotation [ˌdiːnəʊˈteɪʃən] *n.* 直接意义，明示的意义
A good dictionary will give us the connotation of a word as well as its denotation.

sign: mark

◆ signal [ˈsɪgnəl] *n.* [C] 手势，暗号，信号
Send out a distress signal; the ship is sinking.

◆ signature [ˈsɪgnɪtʃə(r)] *n.* [C] 署名，签字
The signature was not genuine.

◆ signet [ˈsɪgnɪt] *n.* 图章，印章
The paper requests signet, not signatures.

◆ signify [ˈsɪgnɪfaɪ] *v.* [T] 意味，表示
v. [I] 具有重要性
What do these marks signify?
It signifies much.

◆ assign [əˈsaɪn] *v.* [T] 分配，指定；派往
I was assigned to Troop A of the 10th Cavalry.

◆ consign [kənˈsaɪn] *v.* [T] 托运；委托
We will consign the goods to him by express.

◆ design [dɪˈzaɪn] *v.* &*n.* 设计，意向
He designed a new plan for the project.

◆ designate [ˈdezɪgneɪt] *v.* [T] 清楚地标出或指出（某事物）；指定
Some of the rooms were designated as offices.

◆ insignia [ɪnˈsɪgnɪə] *n.* [U] 徽章
All officers wear grade insignia on the left side of their caps.

◆ resign [rɪˈzaɪn] *v.* [I and T] 辞职
He chose not to resign to keep his self-respect.

scrib: write

◆ scribe [skraɪb] *v.* [T] 写下，记下
n. [C] 抄写员
These are tools for scribing.

◆ scribble [ˈskrɪbl] *v.* [I and T] 潦草地写，乱画
n. 潦草笔记
She can't write yet, but she loves to scribble with a pencil.
I'm sorry what I wrote was such a scribble.

◆ script [skrɪpt] *n.* 脚本；笔迹
The marvelous acting compensated for the play's weak script.

◆ ascribe [əˈskraɪb] *v.* [T] 认为是某人的作

品；归功于、归咎于某人（某事物）
Scholars ascribe the unsigned painting to Van Gogh.

◆ ascription [ə'skrɪpʃən] *n.* 归因；归属
Israel and Palestine have not yet been in accord on the problem of Jerusalem's ascription.

◆ circumscribe ['sɜːkəmskraɪb] *v.* [T] 受限于；画外接圆
There are laws circumscribing the right of individual citizens to cause bodily harm to others.

◆ describe [dɪ'skraɪb] *v.* [T] 描述，形容
It is very difficult to describe my joy in words.

◆ descriptive [dɪ'skrɪptɪv] *adj.* 描述的，精于描述的
He wrote a book descriptive of the frontier provinces.

◆ inscribe [ɪn'skraɪb] *v.* [T] 雕刻；题写
She and Mark read the words inscribed on the inner walls of the monument.

◆ inscription [ɪn'skrɪpʃn] *n.* [C] 碑文，题字
The medal bears the inscription "For distinguished service."

◆ conscription [kən'skrɪpʃən] *n.* 征兵；征用
All adult males will be liable for conscription.

◆ manuscript ['mænjʊskrɪpt] *n.* [C] 手稿，原稿
None of Shakespeare's plays survives in its original manuscript form.

◆ postscript ['pəʊsskrɪpt, 'pəʊstskrɪpt] *n.* [C] 附言，正文后的补充说明
There was the usual romantic postscript at the end of his letter.

◆ prescribe [prɪ'skraɪb] *v.* [I and T] 明文规定；开处方
Our doctor diagnosed a throat infection and prescribed some antibiotic.

◆ prescription [prɪ'skrɪpʃən] *n.* [C] 药方
The drug is available on prescription only.

◆ subscribe [səb'skraɪb] *v.* [I and T]（在文件下面）签名，同意；订阅
We subscribe to the resolution.

◆ subscription [səb'skrɪpʃən] *n.* 签署；订阅费，会费
You can become a member by paying the yearly subscription.

◆ transcribe [træn'skraɪb] *v.* [T] 誊写，转录
Every telephone conversation will be recorded and transcribed.

◆ transcript ['trænskrɪpt] *n.* [C] 抄写，文字记录
A transcript of the tapes was presented as evidence in court.

◆ transcription [træn'skrɪpʃən] *n.* 抄本；乐曲改编
The transcriptions of the text were available as early as 1960.

verb: word

◆ verb [vɜːb] *n.* [C] 动词

◆ verbal ['vɜːbl] *adj.* 用言语的；用文字的；口头的
We have a verbal agreement with her.

◆ verbalize ['vɜːbəlaɪz] *v.* [T] 用言语表达
I find it difficult to verbalize.

◆ verbose [vɜː'bəʊs] *adj.* 冗长的
His writing is difficult and often verbose.

◆ proverb ['prɒvɜːb] *n.* [C] 谚语，格言
An old Arab proverb says, "The enemy of my enemy is my friend."

Exercises

I. Match the roots with their meanings.

A. spect ( ) 1. write
B. audi ( ) 2. word
C. phon ( ) 3. letter
D. opt ( ) 4. read
E. ora ( ) 5. eye
F. liter ( ) 6. look
G. scrib ( ) 7. sound
H. lingu ( ) 8. tone
I. ton ( ) 9. tongue
J. verb ( ) 10. speak
K. nounc ( ) 11. report
L. leg ( ) 12. hear

II. Fill in the blanks with the words from this theme. The roots are given.

1. The advertisements were all posted in a ________ place. (spic)
2. The West must back up its ________ support with substantial economic aid. (verb)
3. After watching TV, the children went back to their ________ rooms. (spect)
4. Sex education is a sensitive area for some parents, and thus it should remain ________. (opt)
5. ________ stories are passed down from parents to children. (leg)
6. I think that the art of a storyteller is to take the story and ________ on it. (vis)
7. Earlier this year they were ________ that their homes were to be cleared away. (not)
8. When Caroline was five, she loved to ________ on a wall. (scrib)
9. His ________ contradicted that of the preceding witness. (test)
10. We were amazed by the island's ________ scenery. (spect)

III. Finish the words according to the definitions. The first letters are given.

1. b ________ a list of the books and articles that are referred to in a particular book
2. m ________ a book which is a detailed study of only one subject
3. p ________ a record player
4. c ________ the art of producing beautiful handwriting using a brush or a special pen
5. a ________ a name signed by a famous person himself
6. b ________ an account of their life, written by someone else
7. e ________ a short saying or poem which expresses an idea in a very clever or amusing way
8. p ________ a test which is used by the police to try to find out whether someone is telling the truth

IV. Choose among the words with similar roots and fill in the blanks in the right forms.

postscript	describe	inscribe	prescribe	subscribe

1. Words cannot ________ the beauty of my hometown.
2. She ________ her own name on the rock.
3. He failed to notice the ________ at the back of the document.
4. He forgot to ________ his name to the contract, so he had to rush back to the company.
5. The doctor ________ total abstinence from alcoholic drinks.

speculate	despise	circumspect	expect	inspect
introspect	prospect	respect	retrospect	suspect

6. In ________ it's obvious how we went wrong.
7. The ________ for peace in the country's eight-year civil war are becoming brighter.
8. The plants are regularly ________ for disease.
9. To ________ may help a person have a clearer image of oneself.
10. Don't cheat at examination, or your classmates will ________ you.
11. The banks should have been more ________ in their dealings.
12. I want him to ________ me as a career woman.
13. I am ________ several important letters but nothing has arrived.
14. We don't know all the circumstances, so it would be pointless to ________.
15. The police ________ him of having taken the money.

V. Choose the best answers.

1. We cannot agree to ________ the goods by air.
   A. assign B. resign C. consign D. design
2. An ________ is a note that is added to a text, often in order to explain it.
   A. annotation B. denotation C. connotation D. notion
3. Over one-quarter of the adult population are not fully ________.
   A. literal B. literary C. literacy D. literate
4. I can personally ________ that the cold and flu season is here.
   A. protest B. contest C. detest D. attest
5. He was rejected by the ________ office because he was under age.
   A. inscription B. conscription C. manuscript D. transcription
6. He ________ and trained more than 400 volunteers.
   A. revised B. improvised C. devised D. supervised
7. Experts regarded it as a warning ________ of an economic crisis.
   A. signature B. signal C. insignia D. signet

Theme Four

喜恶悲惧

grat/gree: pleasing, agreeable

◆ grateful [ˈgreɪtf(ʊ)l] *adj.* 感谢的；愉快的

I should like to extend my grateful thanks to all the volunteers.

◆ ingrate [ˈɪngreɪt,-ˈ-] *n.* [C] 忘恩负义的人

He's such an ingrate.

◆ gratitude [ˈgrætɪtjuːd] *n.* [U] 感激，感恩

He smiled at them with gratitude.

◆ ingratitude [ɪnˈgrætɪtjuːd] *n.* [U] 忘恩负义

The person always returns ingratitude for kindness.

◆ gratuity [grəˈtjuːətɪ] *n.* 赏钱，小费

The porter expects a gratuity.

◆ gratuitous [grəˈtjuːɪtəs] *adj.* 免费的，无缘无故的，无端的，没必要的

There's too much crime and gratuitous violence on TV.

◆ congratulation [kənˌgrætjʊˈleɪʃən] *n.* 祝贺，恭喜

He has received many letters in congratulation of his birthday.

◆ ingratiate [ɪnˈgreɪʃɪeɪt] *v.* [T] 迎合，讨好

He did his best to ingratiate himself with his employer.

◆ ingratiating [ɪnˈgreɪʃɪeɪtɪŋ] *adj.* 讨好的，谄媚的

He said this with an ingratiating smile.

◆ gratify [ˈgrætɪfaɪ] *v.* [T] 使满足，喜悦

He did that to gratify his girlfriend's vanity.

◆ gratification [ˌgrætɪfɪˈkeɪʃən] *n.* 满足，喜悦

His son's success was a great gratification to him.

◆ grace [greɪs] *n.* 优美，文雅

She is a beautiful girl with the grace and poise.

◆ graceful [ˈgreɪsf(ʊ)l] *adj.* 优雅的，得体的

The ballet dancer is so graceful.

◆ gracious [ˈgreɪʃəs] *adj.* 文雅的，亲切的

She was a gentlewoman of the old school, gracious and mannerly.

◆ disgrace [dɪsˈgreɪs] *n.* 耻辱

v. [T] 使丢脸

This vice president had to resign in disgrace.

I have disgraced my family's name.

◆ agreeable [əˈgriːəbl] *adj.* 愉快的，适意的

It's very agreeable to have you here.

joy: happy

◆ joyful [ˈdʒɔɪf(ʊ)l] *adj.* 高兴的，充满快乐的

Giving birth to a child is both painful and

joyful.

◆ joyous [ˈdʒɔɪəs] *adj.* 充满快乐的，使人高兴的

She had made their childhood so joyous and carefree.

◆ enjoy [ɪnˈdʒɔɪ] *v.* [T] 享受，喜爱

He enjoys swimming.

◆ rejoice [rɪˈdʒɔɪs] *v.* [I and T]（使）感到高兴

We sincerely rejoice over your victories.

◆ jolly [ˈdʒɒlɪ] *adj.* 快活的，兴高采烈的

I was looking forward to a jolly party.

◆ jollify [ˈdʒɒlɪfaɪ] *v.* [I and T]（使）愉快

Children are jollified at the sight of water.

◆ jovial [ˈdʒəʊvjəl] *adj.* 快活的，高兴的

Grandma was plump and jovial.

felic: happy

◆ felicity [fɪˈlɪsɪtɪ] *n.* [U] 幸福；恰当，妥帖

He demonstrated a concern for the felicity of his children.

◆ felicitation [fɪˌlɪsɪˈteɪʃən] *n.* 庆祝，庆贺

Sincere felicitation on your completing the postgraduate course!

◆ infelicitous [ˌɪnfɪˈlɪsɪtəs] *adj.* 不幸的；不恰当的

There are several infelicitous remarks in this article.

joc: joke

◆ jocose [dʒə(ʊ)ˈkəʊs] *adj.* 滑稽的，可笑的

Dr. Daniel was a man of a jocose nature.

◆ jocosity [dʒəʊˈkɒsɪtɪ] *n.* 诙谐，戏谑

His play is characterized as jocosity.

◆ jocular [ˈdʒɒkjʊlə(r)] *adj.* 滑稽的，爱开玩笑的；幽默的

The song was written in a light-hearted jocular way.

◆ jocularity [ˌdʒɒkjʊˈlærɪtɪ] *n.* 滑稽，诙谐

He tried to inject a little jocularity into his voice.

hilar: cheerful

◆ hilarious [hɪˈleərɪəs] *adj.* 十分有趣的，欢闹的

The party got quite hilarious after they brought more wine.

◆ hilarity [hɪˈlærətɪ] *n.* [U] 欢闹，狂欢

Wine gives not light hilarity, but noisy merriment.

◆ exhilarate [ɪgˈzɪləreɪt] *v.* [T] 使愉快

This dangerous task exhilarated his spirits.

◆ exhilarating [ɪgˈzɪləreɪtɪŋ] *adj.* 令人高兴的，令人兴奋的

It was exhilarating to be on the road again and his spirits rose.

plac: please

◆ placate [pləˈkeɪt] *v.* [T] 安慰，抚慰；和解

He smiled, trying to placate me.

◆ placid [ˈplæsɪd] *adj.* 安静的，温和的；满意的

She was a placid child who rarely cried.

◆ placebo [pləˈsiːbəʊ] *n.* 安慰剂；宽心话

Time is the best placebo.

◆ implacable [ɪmˈplækəbl] *adj.* 无法和解的，难以安慰的

His hatred is implacable.

◆ placatory [ˈplækətərɪ, pləˈkeɪtərɪ] *adj.* 抚慰的，安抚的

He raised a placatory hand. "All right, we'll see what we can do."

◆ complacent [kəm'pleɪsnt] *adj.* 自满的，自得的

We must not become complacent about progress.

◆ complacency [kəm'pleɪsnsɪ] *n.* [U] 自满

Be modest in learning, for complacency is the enemy of study.

◆ complaisant [kəm'pleɪzənt] *adj.* 恭敬的；恳切的；讨好的

She was an old-fashioned wife, entirely complaisant to her husband's will.

phil: love

◆ philosophy [fɪ'lɒsəfɪ] *n.* 哲学；哲学体系

Ancient Greece was a fountain of wisdom and philosophy.

◆ philanthropy [fɪ'lænθrəpɪ] *n.* [U] 博爱，慈善

The Red Cross appeals to philanthropy.

◆ philology [fɪ'lɒlədʒɪ] *n.* [U] 语文学；语言学

◆ bibliophilist ['bɪblɪəfɪlɪst] *n.* [C] 书籍收藏家；爱书者

◆ neophilia [ˌniːəʊ'fɪlɪə] *n.* 喜新成癖

amat/amor/am: love

◆ amateur ['æmətə] *n.* [C] 业余爱好者

adj. 业余的，非职业的；外行的

The orchestra is made up entirely of amateurs.

◆ amatory ['æmətərɪ] *adj.* 恋爱的，情人的

He likes to write amatory poem to the lady he loves.

◆ amour [ə'mʊər] *n.* [C] 爱情，奸情

Have you heard about his latest amour?

◆ amorous ['æmərəs] *adj.* 色情的，情爱的

They exchanged amorous glances.

◆ paramour ['pærəmʊə(r)] *n.* [C] 情夫，情妇

She hoped to get a master's degree, great food and an Italian paramour.

◆ amorist ['æmərɪst] *n.* 好色之徒；爱情（尤指色情）小说作家

◆ enamor [ɪ'næmə(r)] *v.* [T] 使倾心，使迷恋

Her beauty enamored the prince.

◆ enamored [ɪ'næməd] *adj.* 迷恋的，倾心的

He became enamored of a girl in New York.

◆ amiable ['eɪmɪəbl] *adj.* 和蔼的，友善的

She was a very kind and amiable old woman.

◆ amicable ['æmɪkəbl] *adj.* 友好的，温和的

Our discussions were amicable and productive.

◆ amity ['æmɪtɪ] *n.* [C] 友好，和睦

He lives in amity with his neighbours.

plaud/plod: clap hands; strike

◆ applaud [ə'plɔːd] *v.* 拍手喝彩

The pupils that had been watching started to applaud.

◆ applause [ə'plɔːz] *n.* [U] 鼓掌

They greeted him with thunderous applause.

◆ plaudit ['plɔːdɪt] *n.* 鼓掌；喝彩；赞美

Her speech won the plaudit of the crowds.

◆ plausible ['plɔːzəbl] *adj.* 似乎有理的；花言巧语的；能说会道的

This explanation fits the facts and is psychologically plausible.

◆ explode [ɪk'spləʊd] *v.* [I and T] 爆炸，爆发；发怒；激增

The population explodes to 40,000 during the tourist season.

◆ explosive [ɪk'spləʊsɪv] *adj.* 爆炸的；突增的
n. 爆炸物，炸药
Race relations are an explosive issue.

rid/ris: laugh

◆ ridicule ['rɪdɪkjuːl] *n.* &*v.* 嘲笑，愚弄
As a heavy child, she became the object of ridicule from classmates.
◆ ridiculous [rɪ'dɪkjʊləs] *adj.* 可笑的，荒谬的
It is ridiculous to predict that the sun will not rise tomorrow.
◆ risible ['rɪzɪbl] *adj.* 可笑的
The entire proposal is risible; it will never be accepted.
◆ deride [dɪ'raɪd] *v.* [T] 嘲笑
This theory is widely derided by conventional scientists.
◆ derision [dɪ'rɪʒən] *n.* 嘲弄
He became an object of universal derision.
◆ derisive [dɪ'raɪsɪv] *adj.* 嘲弄的
She gave a short and derisive laugh.

plaint: lament, strike

◆ plaint [pleɪnt] *n.* 悲叹；抱怨；诉苦
To him I will bring my plaint.
◆ complaint [kəm'pleɪnt] *n.* 抱怨
I'd like to make a complaint about the noise.
◆ plaintive ['pleɪntɪv] *adj.* 痛苦的，伤心的
Her voice was small and plaintive.
◆ plaintiff ['pleɪntɪf] *n.* [C] 原告
The jury found evidence against the plaintiff.

phob/phobia: dislike

◆ phobia ['fəʊbɪə] *n.* 恐惧；十分厌恶
She has a phobia about flying.
◆ hydrophobia [ˌhaɪdrə(ʊ)'fəʊbjə] *n.* 恐水症，狂犬病
Suffering from hydrophobia, he could not even think of water.
◆ acrophobia [ˌækrə(ʊ)'fəʊbjə] *n.* 恐高症
He has acrophobia and always refuses to climb up ladders.
◆ xenophobia [ˌzenə'fəʊbɪə] *n.* 排外
A growing number of refugees and migrants are leading to more intolerance and xenophobia.
◆ Sinophobe ['sinəfəub] *n.* 排华的人

dole: grieve

◆ dole [dəʊl] *n.* 救济物；失业救济金
v. [T] 发放救济
He's been on the dole (= without a job) for a year.
◆ doleful ['dəʊlfəl] *adj.* 沉浸于悲痛中的
Don't look so doleful, girls.
◆ dolorous ['dɒlərəs] *adj.* 悲伤的；痛苦的；阴沉的
With a broken-hearted smile, he lifted a pair of dolorous eyes.
◆ condole [kən'dəʊl] *v.* [I] 安慰，哀悼
We condole with him on his loss.
◆ condolence [kən'dəʊləns] *n.* 慰问，哀悼
Neil sent him a letter of condolence.
◆ indolence ['ɪndələns] *n.* [U] 懒惰，好逸恶劳；无痛
We rode slowly, with pleasant sense of indolence.

plor: cry, weep

◆ deplore [dɪ'plɔː(r)] *v.* [T] 谴责；对……深表痛惜

We deplore what has happened.

◆ deplorable [dɪˈplɔːrəbl] *adj.* 悲惨的；应受谴责的
Many of them live under deplorable conditions.

◆ explore [ɪkˈsplɔː(r)] *v.* [I and T] 探索
Let us explore the possibilities for improvement.

◆ exploration [ˌekspləˈreɪʃən] *n.* 探索
They launched the space exploration.

◆ implore [ɪmˈplɔː(r)] *v.* [I and T] 乞求，恳求
I implore you not to add the bitterness of mine.

hor (r): shudder, dread; bound

◆ horrid [ˈhɒrɪd] *adj.* 可怕的，糟糕的
The winter was horrid.

◆ horrible [ˈhɒrəbl] *adj.* 可怕的
That is the horrible lesson of this week.

◆ horrify [ˈhɒrɪfaɪ] *v.* [T] 使恐怖
When I saw the killings on TV, I was horrified.

◆ abhor [əbˈhɔː(r)] *v.* [T] 憎恨；拒绝；淘汰
He was a man who abhorred violence and loved peace.

◆ abhorrent [əbˈhɒrənt] *adj.* 憎恶的
I am abhorrent of smoking.

◆ aphorism [ˈæfərɪzəm] *n.* [C] 格言，警句
The Olympics have an aphorism, "The most important thing is to participate."

◆ horizon [həˈraɪzn] *n.* 地平线；范围；眼界
By embracing other cultures, we actually broaden our horizons.

terr: frighten

◆ terrible [ˈterəbl] *adj.* 使人苦恼的，很糟的
This terrible event is etched forever in my memory.

◆ terrify [ˈterɪfaɪ] *v.* [T] 使害怕
The thought of dying slowly and painfully terrified me.

◆ terrific [təˈrɪfɪk] *adj.* 极大的，非常好的
You look terrific, Judy. You really do.

◆ terror [ˈterə(r)] *n.* 恐怖；引起恐怖的事
Those rebels are a terror to the entire town.

◆ terrorism [ˈterərɪzəm] *n.* 恐怖主义
Public cooperation is vital in the fight against terrorism.

◆ deter [dɪˈtɜːr] *v.* [I and T] 阻止
Failure did not deter us from trying it again.

◆ deterrent [dɪˈterənt] *adj.* 威慑的（力量）*n.* [C] 制止物；威慑物
Hopefully his punishment will act as a deterrent to others.

tim: fear

◆ timid [ˈtɪmɪd] *adj.* 胆怯的
The rabbit is timid and suspicious.

◆ timidity [tɪˈmɪdɪtɪ] *n.* 胆怯，胆小
His failure is largely due to timidity.

◆ intimidate [ɪnˈtɪmɪdeɪt] *v.* [T] 恐吓，威胁
The gang tried to intimidate the bank manager.

◆ intimidating [ɪnˈtɪmɪdeɪtɪŋ] *adj.* 吓人的，咄咄逼人的
He was a huge and intimidating figure.

◆ timorous [ˈtɪmərəs] *adj.* 胆小的
She is as timorous as a rabbit.

ver: fear

◆ revere [rɪˈvɪə] *v.* [T] 崇敬；敬畏
Today he's still revered as the father of the nation.

◆ reverence [ˈrevərəns] *n.* [U] 尊敬，敬畏
Children are taught to show respect and reverence towards their grandparents.

◆ irreverent [ɪˈrevərənt] *adj.* 不敬的；不虔诚的
It's irreverent for a man not to take his hat off in church.

◆ reverend [ˈrevərənd] *adj.* 可尊敬的
n. 对牧师或神父的尊称，牧师，教士
Our worship today is led by the Reverend John Harris.

trem/trep: fear

◆ tremble [ˈtrembl] *v.* & *n.* 发抖
Gil was white and trembling with anger.

◆ tremendous [trɪˈmendəs] *adj.* 巨大的；可怕的，惊人的
This book was the outcome of a tremendous amount of scientific work.

◆ tremor [ˈtremə(r)] *n.* [C] 轻微地震；震颤；战栗
A slight earth tremor was felt in California.

◆ tremulous [ˈtremjʊləs] *adj.* 颤抖的；敏感的；胆小的
I opened the important letter with tremulous fingers.

◆ trepidation [ˌtrepɪˈdeɪʃən] *n.* [U] 害怕；颤抖
They set off in fear and trepidation.

◆ intrepid [ɪnˈtrepɪd] *adj.* 无畏的
The crowd hailed the intrepid space traveller.

Exercises

I. Match the roots with their meanings.

A. phob	(　) 1. clap hands
B. dole	(　) 2. joke
C. joy	(　) 3. dislike
D. hilar	(　) 4. frighten
E. hor	(　) 5. dread
F. plaud	(　) 6. love
G. joc	(　) 7. happy
H. terr	(　) 8. grieve
I. phil	(　) 9. laugh
J. rid	(　) 10. cheerful

II. Read the clues and complete the crossword.

Across:

1. make somebody decide not to do something or continue doing something
5. someone who does something as a hobby and not as a job
7. inspire with love; captivate
9. the line at which the sky and Earth appear to meet
11. ask for something in an emotional way
12. the practice of giving money and help to people who are poor or in trouble
14. a statement in which you express your dissatisfaction with a particular situation
17. an attractive quality of movement that is smooth, elegant and controlled
18. a very strong irrational fear or hatred of something
19. the feeling of being grateful

Down:

2. shy, nervous, and having no courage or confidence
3. tease or laugh at
4. money paid by the state to unemployed people
6. burst loudly and with great force
8. friendly and easy to like
10. extreme interest in something new
11. frighten or threaten someone into making them do what you want

13. hate very much, especially for moral reasons
15. shake slightly
16. one dedicated to love and lovemaking especially one who writes about love.

III. Complete the sentences with the right forms of the best words.

reverence	derision	plaintive	agreeable	exhilarate
condole	disgrace	amateur	plausible	rejoice
terrific	indolence			

1. There is no ________ in being poor.
2. I ________ that you have recovered so quickly.
3. Jerry is a（n）________ who dances because he feels like it.
4. I regard them as my most ________ companion.
5. His explanation does not sound ________ to me.
6. I ________ with him on his father's death.
7. What a（n）________ idea! Surely we will go.
8. He was a bishop who was held in ________ by all.
9. We could hear the ________ cry of a wounded animal in the woods.
10. The child refused to go to school for he dreaded the ________ of his classmates.
11. He was noted for his ________. Nobody would like to work with him.
12. The children were ________ at the prospect of going to the movies.

IV. Choose the best answers.

1. ________ is the giving of money to the people who need it, without wanting anything in return.
   A. Philosophy B. Philanthropy C. Philology D. Bibliophile
2. Maria's come to ________ the protection of Mr. Tudor.
   A. splore B. explore C. deplore D. implore
3. Taxi drivers don't expect ________, but they won't refuse it.
   A. gratuity B. gratitude C. ingrate D. ingratiate
4. She has ________ and always becomes dizzy in a high-rise elevator.
   A. hydrophobia B. Sinophobe C. acrophobia D. xenophobia
5. We must not become ________ about progress.
   A. placid B. placatory C. complacent D. complaisant
6. It will relieve her of a ________ burden.
   A. tremulous B. tremendous C. timid D. intrepid

Theme Five

心灵世界

memor/men/mne/min: think, mind

◆ memo [ˈmeməʊ] *n.* [C] 备忘录；（美）内部通知

I want this memo to go to all departmental managers.

◆ memorial [mɪˈmɔːrɪəl] *n.* [C] 纪念碑，纪念物；纪念仪式

adj. 纪念的；悼念的

Friends gathered at a memorial for the late statesman.

◆ memorize [ˈmeməraɪz] *v.* [T] 记住，熟记；存储

The boy can memorize the data easily.

◆ commemorate [kəˈmeməreɪt] *v.* [T] 纪念，庆祝；成为……的纪念

This building was built to commemorate the Fire of London.

◆ immemorial [ˌɪmɪˈmɔːrɪəl] *adj.* 无法追忆的，远古的

The Barton family have lived in this village since time immemorial.

◆ amnesia [æmˈniːzjə] *n.* [U]〈医〉遗忘（症），记忆缺失；健忘

The people suffering from amnesia don't forget their general knowledge of objects.

◆ amnesty [ˈæmnɪstɪ] *n.* [C] 大赦，特赦

v. [T] 对……实行大赦；赦免

Some political criminals were favored with amnesty.

◆ mentor [ˈmentə] *n.* [C] 导师

v. [T] 做……的良师；指导

One mentor, one person can change a life forever.

◆ mental [ˈmentl] *adj.* 精神的，思想的

Mental and physical deterioration both occur naturally with age.

◆ mentality [menˈtælɪtɪ] *n.* [C] 心理；智力；思想

He has many years' experience of the criminal mentality.

◆ mentalism [ˈmentəlɪzəm] *n.* 心灵主义

Mentalism is, somehow, what some people might name magic.

◆ memento [mɪˈmentəʊ] *n.* [C] 遗物，纪念品

The photos will be a permanent memento of your wedding.

◆ commentary [ˈkɒmənˌtərɪ] *n.* [C, U] 解说词；评论；个人生平传记

He is giving the commentary on the basketball game.

◆ commentate [ˈkɒmənteɪt] *v.* [T and I] 注释；评论，解说

v. [I] 评论时事；实况报道

A well-known broadcaster has been asked to commentate on the opening ceremony of the national games.

◆ amentia［əˈmenʃə］*n.* 智力缺陷
The handicapped also include deaf-mutes and some amentia.

◆ dementia［dɪˈmenʃ(ɪ)ə］*n.*［U］〈医〉痴呆
Some dementia patients aren't completely out of their minds.

◆ mind［maɪnd］*n.* 精神，心力，智力
v.［I］介意；注意
v.［T］专心于；介意；照顾
Never mind, next time I'm sure you can do better.

◆ remind［rɪˈmaɪnd］*v.*［T］使想起，使记起；提醒
If my father forgets it, I hope you would remind him.

◆ reminiscence［ˌremɪˈnɪsns］*n.* 旧事，回忆；回忆录
The scene aroused the reminiscence of my youth.

put: think

◆ compute［kəmˈpjuːt］*v.*［T］计算，估算；用计算机计算
n. 计算
I compute my losses at 500 dollars.

◆ depute［dɪˈpjuːt］*v.*［T］将（工作、职权等）交给某人；给予（某人）代表行事或发言之权
He deputed the running of the department to an assistant.

◆ deputy［ˈdepjʊtɪ］*n.*［C］副手；代理人；代表
adj. 副的；代理的
John will be my deputy while I am away.

◆ dispute［dɪˈspjuːt］*v.*［T and I］辩论，争论
n. 辩论；争端；（劳资）纠纷
These figures have been disputed.

◆ indisputable［ˌɪndɪˈspjuːtəbl, ɪnˈdɪspjʊ-］*adj.* 无可争辩的；不容置疑的
It's indisputable that we are losing a lot of money.

◆ repute［rɪˈpjuːt］*n.*［U］名气；声望
v.［T］把……称为，认为
He has gained considerable repute.

◆ reputable［ˈrepjʊtəbl］*adj.* 值得尊敬的，声誉好的
Always buy from a reputable dealer.

◆ disreputable［dɪsˈrepjʊtəbl］*adj.* 名誉不好的，不体面的；为人所不齿的
He looked disreputable in his gray beard.

◆ impute［ɪmˈpjuːt］*v.*［T］把（错误等）归咎于
I impute his failure to laziness.

psych: spirit, soul

◆ psychology［saɪˈkɒlədʒɪ］*n.*［U］心理学；心理特点；心理状态

◆ psychotherapy［ˌsaɪkəʊˈθerəpɪ］*n.*［U］精神疗法；心理疗法

◆ psychiatrist［saiˈkaiətrist］*n.* 精神病医生

◆ psychiatry［saɪˈkaɪətrɪ］*n.*［U］精神病学；精神病治疗法
Psychiatry is the medical specialty devoted to the diagnosis, prevention and treatment of mental disorders.

◆ psyche［ˈsaɪkɪ］*n.*［C］灵魂，心灵；心智
She knew, at some deep level of her psyche, that what she was doing was wrong.

◆ psychopath［ˈsaɪkə(ʊ)pæθ］*n.*［C］精神变态者，精神病患者
Diagnosing him as a psychopath was not a simple matter.

soph: wisdom

◆ philosophy [fɪˈlɒsəfɪ] *n.* [C, U] 哲学；哲学思想；生活信条

◆ philosopher [fɪˈlɒsəfə(r)] *n.* 哲学家；豁达的人

He is a teacher by occupation but a philosopher by inclination.

◆ sophomore [ˈsɒfəmɔː(r)] *n.* [C] （中等、专科学校或大学的）二年级学生

He is in his sophomore year.

◆ sophomoric [ˌsɒfəˈmɒrɪk] *adj.* （大学或四年制中学的）二年级的；一知半解的

Do you really believe that sophomoric argument?

◆ sophisticated [səˈfɪstɪkeɪtɪd] *adj.* 复杂的；精致的；富有经验的

She has become very sophisticated since she moved to London.

◆ sophisticate [səˈfɪstɪkeɪt] *v.* [T] 使变得世故，使失去天真

His experience has sophisticated him.

◆ sophist [ˈsɒfɪst] *n.* 诡辩家；博学者；诡辩者

It was basically a selfish act, though no doubt a sophist would argue that it was done for the general good.

◆ sophism [ˈsɒfɪzəm] *n.* 谬论，诡辩

I have done with your foolish sophism!

◆ sophistic [səˈfɪstɪk] *adj.* 诡辩的，强词夺理的

These people are very sophistic.

sens/sent: feel

◆ sensory [ˈsensərɪ] *adj.* 感觉的，感受的，感官的

Now, Carrie began to feel this in various sensory ways.

◆ sensual [ˈsensjʊəl, ˈsenʃʊ-] *adj.* 感觉的；肉欲的；世俗的

Amusements of this kind can only bring some sensual pleasure.

◆ sensate [ˈsenseɪt] *adj.* 感知的，知觉的

Unfortunately, we are carried away by sensate values.

◆ sensation [senˈseɪʃən, sən-, sn-] *n.* [C, U] 感觉；直觉；轰动

The new book has created a great sensation.

◆ sensational [senˈseɪʃənl, sən-] *adj.* 轰动的；耸人听闻的；极好的

Papers of this kind are full of sensational news reports.

◆ sensible [ˈsensəbl, -sɪb-] *adj.* 明智的；合乎情理的；能感觉到的

He was sensible enough to mind his own business.

◆ sensitive [ˈsensɪtɪv] *adj.* 敏感的；感觉的；易受影响的

It's difficult to avoid stepping on her sensitive feelings.

◆ sensibility [ˌsensɪˈbɪlɪtɪ, səˈb-] *n.* [C] 情感；敏感性；识别力

No one with sensibility would buy the book.

◆ sensitivity [ˌsensɪˈtɪvɪtɪ] *n.* 敏感；灵敏性；〈摄〉感光度

Hearing sensitivity declines with age.

◆ sensitiveness [ˈsensɪtɪvnɪs] *n.* 易感知，神经过敏；敏感性

Her sensitiveness on some points was such that it might have been misread as vanity.

◆ sentence [ˈsentəns] *n.* [C] 句子；宣判 *v.* [T] 宣判，判决

His sentence was commuted from death to life imprisonment.

◆ sentient [ˈsenʃənt, -ʃɪənt, -ʃjənt] *adj.* 能感知或感觉事物的

All sentient beings can communicate in one way or another.

◆ sentiment [ˈsentɪmənt] *n.* 感情，情绪；观点；感伤

Should sentiment be controlled by reason?

◆ presentiment [prɪˈzentɪmənt, prɪˈse-] *n.* [C]（对不祥事物的）预感

He had a presentiment of disaster.

◆ sentimental [ˌsentɪˈmentl] *adj.* 伤感的；多愁善感的

She's a sentimental woman who believes marriage comes by destiny.

◆ assent [əˈsent] *v.* [I] 赞成

n. [U] 同意，赞同

The new bill passed by Parliament has received royal assent.

◆ consent [kənˈsent] *n.* [C, U] 准许，赞同；同意

v. [I] 同意；赞成；允许

She was chosen as leader by common consent.

◆ consensus [kənˈsensəs] *n.* 一致；一致同意

Can we reach a consensus on this issue?

◆ dissent [dɪˈsent] *n.* [U] 意见的分歧，异议

v. [I] 不同意，持异议

Only two ministers dissented from the official view.

◆ dissension [dɪˈsenʃən] *n.* [U] 不和，纠纷，争吵

The group were caught in dissension.

◆ resent [rɪˈzent] *v.* [T] 对……感到愤怒；怨恨

I resent all these encroachments on my valuable time.

pass/pat/path: feel, suffer

◆ **passion** [ˈpæʃən] *n.* [C, U] 激情，热情；热恋

In his passion, he tore the letter into pieces.

◆ passionate [ˈpæʃənɪt] *adj.* 热烈的，易怒的；易被情欲所支配的

Joe is passionate about baseball.

◆ dispassionate [dɪsˈpæʃənɪt] *adj.* 不动情感的；平心静气的；公正的

He spoke in the flat and dispassionate tone of a lecturer.

◆ compassion [kəmˈpæʃən] *n.* [C] 怜悯，同情；恻隐之心

She showed no compassion for her patients.

◆ impassion [ɪmˈpæʃən] *v.* [T] 激动，激起热情

He has managed to attract the attention of the audience and impassion their desires to know more.

◆ impassioned [ɪmˈpæʃənd] *adj.* 充满激情的；热烈的；慷慨激昂的

After three hours of impassioned debate the motion was defeated.

◆ passive [ˈpæsɪv] *adj.* 被动的；消极的；冷漠的

n. 动词被动形式，被动语态

In spite of my efforts the boy remained passive.

◆ impassive [ɪmˈpæsɪv] *adj.* 冷漠的；无感情的；无意识的

He was content to stand by as an impassive spectator.

◆ sympathy [ˈsɪmpəθɪ] *n.* [U] 意气相投；同情，同情心

I have absolutely no sympathy for students who get caught cheating in exams.

◆ pathos [ˈpeɪθɒs] *n.* [U] 悲怆，哀婉，伤感

The pathos of the situation brought tears to our eyes.

◆ pathetic [pə'θetɪk] *adj.* 令人同情的，可怜的

How pathetic the little match girl is!

◆ antipathy [æn'tɪpəθɪ] *n.* 反感；憎恶的对象

I feel an antipathy against their behavior.

◆ apathy ['æpəθɪ] *n.* [U] 漠然，冷淡；无动于衷

He was sunk in apathy after his failure.

◆ apathetic [ˌæpə'θetɪk] *adj.* 无感情的；冷淡的；无动于衷的

You won't have any friend if you are so apathetic.

◆ pathology [pə'θɒlədʒɪ] *n.* [U] 病理（学）

Pathology is the study of the way diseases and illnesses develop.

◆ psychopath ['saɪkə(ʊ)pæθ] *n.* [C] 精神变态者，精神病患者

She was endangered as being with a psychopath.

◆ patient ['peɪʃənt] *adj.* 有耐性的；能容忍的

n. [C] 患者；病人

The doctor told the patient that he was in good way.

◆ compatible [kəm'pætəbl] *adj.* 兼容的，相容的；和谐的

The new system will be compatible with existing equipment.

gno/cogn: know

◆ gnosis ['nəʊsɪs] *n.*（诺斯替教）真知，灵知，神秘的直觉

◆ agnostic [æg'nɒstɪk] *n.* [C] 不可知论者

adj. 不可知论（者）的

An agnostic is a doubter.

◆ agnosticism [æg'nɒstɪsɪzəm] *n.* [U] 不可知论

Agnosticism holds that you can neither prove nor disprove God's existence.

◆ diagnose ['daɪəgnəʊz] *v.* [T] 诊断；判断

What more will you want to know to diagnose this problem?

◆ diagnosis [ˌdaɪəg'nəʊsɪs] *n.* [C, U] 诊断；判断；结论

An accurate diagnosis was made after a series of tests.

◆ ignore [ɪg'nɔː(r)] *v.* [T] 忽视，不顾

He's his own man, but he doesn't ignore advice.

◆ ignorance ['ɪgnərəns] *n.* [U] 无知，愚昧

The relation of disease to poverty and ignorance is easy to see.

◆ prognosis [prɒg'nəʊsɪs] *n.* [C] 预测

The prognosis for the economy is uncertain.

◆ prognostic [prɒg'nɒstɪk] *adj.* 预兆的

n. 预兆

He regarded the bad weather as a prognostic of failure.

◆ recognize ['rekəgnaɪz] *v.* [T] 认出；识别；承认

v. [I] 承认，确认

The government does not recognize the legality of this court.

◆ cognition [kɒg'nɪʃən] *n.* [U] 认识，认知

The boy has a big leap in the aspect of cognition.

◆ cognitive ['kɒgnɪtɪv] *adj.* 认知的；认识的

As children grow older, their cognitive processes become sharper.

sci: know

◆ science ['saɪəns] *n.* 科学；技术，学科

He has got interest in biological science since

early days.

◆ conscience［ˈkɒnʃəns］*n.*［C，U］良心；道德心

She was seized by a sudden pang of conscience.

◆ conscientious［ˌkɒnʃɪˈenʃəs］*adj.* 认真负责的；本着良心的

He is a conscientious man and knows his job.

◆ conscious［ˈkɒnʃəs］*adj.* 有意识的，神志清醒的；自觉的

A healthy man is not conscious of his breathing.

◆ nescience［ˈnesɪəns］*n.* 无知

Discussions communicate knowledge and quarrels exchange nescience.

◆ omniscient［ɒmˈnɪsɪənt］*adj.* 无所不知的

In the eyes of believers, God is omniscient and omnipotent.

◆ prescient［ˈpresɪənt］*adj.* 有预知能力的，有先见之明的

It appears that we were prescient, for the result is exactly what we predicted.

vol：will，wish

◆ volunteer［ˌvɒlənˈtɪə(r)］*n.*［C］志愿者，志愿兵

adj. 自愿的，志愿的

v.［T and I］自愿去做；义务服务

She often does volunteer labor during holidays.

◆ voluntary［ˈvɒləntərɪ］*adj.* 自发的；志愿的

Participation in the program would be voluntary.

◆ volition［və(ʊ)ˈlɪʃən］*n.* 意志；意愿；决定

I did not ask him to go; he went of his own volition.

◆ benevolent［bɪˈnevələnt］*adj.* 好心肠的；乐善好施的

He was a benevolent old man. He wouldn't hurt a fly.

◆ benevolence［bɪˈnevələns］*n.* 仁慈；善举

He did it out of pure benevolence.

◆ malevolent［məˈlevələnt］*adj.* 恶毒的；心肠坏的

Why are they so malevolent to me?

sper：hope

◆ desperate［ˈdespərɪt］*adj.* 绝望的；急切的，极度渴望的

They made a desperate attempt to save the company.

◆ despair［dɪˈspeə(r)］*n.*［U］绝望；使人绝望的人（或事物）

v.［I］绝望

If you are in the depths of despair, you are extremely unhappy.

◆ desperado［ˌdespəˈrɑːdəʊ］*n.*［C］亡命徒，暴徒

A desperado is someone who does illegal, violent things without worrying about the danger.

◆ prosper［ˈprɒspə(r)］*v.*［I］繁盛，成功

v.［T］使……成功；使……昌盛

If you want to survive and prosper, there is a price to pay.

◆ prosperity［prɒˈsperɪtɪ］*n.*［U］繁荣；兴旺，成功

The city took on an air of prosperity.

◆ prosperous［ˈprɒspərəs］*adj.* 繁荣的，兴旺的；富裕的

The country is prosperous and the people live in peace.

rat: reckon, reason

◆ ratio [ˈreɪʃɪəʊ] *n.* [C] 比率；比例；系数
v. [T] 求出比值，除，使……成比例
The ratio of pupils to teachers was 30 to 1.

◆ ration [ˈræʃən] *n.* [C] 定量；配给量；口粮
v. [T] 配给供应
They had to ration petrol during the war.

◆ rational [ˈræʃənl] *adj.* 神志清楚的；理智的；合理的
The reasoning seems rational.

◆ irrational [ɪˈræʃənəl] *adj.* 不合理的，荒谬的；〈数〉无理的
A desire cannot, in itself, be either rational or irrational.

◆ ratify [ˈrætəˌfai] *v.* [T] 批准，认可
I heartily ratify your choice of restaurants.

cred: believe, trust

◆ credo [ˈkriːdəʊ] *n.* [C] 信经，信条
To be the first to bear hardship and the last to enjoy comfort is our credo.

◆ creed [kriːd] *n.* [C] （尤指宗教）信条，教义；宗派
Other countries have adopted this political creed enthusiastically.

◆ credit [ˈkredɪt] *n.* 信用；〈金融〉贷款；荣誉；学分
You must pass the examination to get the credit of this course.

◆ creditor [ˈkredɪtər] *n.* 债权人，债主；〈会〉贷方
The boss assigned his car to his creditor.

◆ accredit [əˈkredɪt] *v.* [T] 授权；归因于；委托；相信
The president will accredit you as his assistant.

◆ accredition [ækrəˈdiʃən] *n.* 认可，鉴定

◆ discredit [dɪsˈkredɪt] *v.* [T] 不相信；使不可置信；败坏……的名声
n. 丧失名誉；不信；败坏名声的人或事
They made efforts to discredit the politician.

◆ incredible [ɪnˈkredəbl] *adj.* 难以置信的
The news report is incredible.

◆ credibility [ˌkredɪˈbɪlɪtɪ] *n.* 可靠性，可信性
The recommendations from two previous clients helped to establish her credibility.

◆ credulous [ˈkredjʊləs] *adj.* 轻信的，易受骗的
You must be credulous if she fooled you with that story.

◆ credulity [krɪˈdjuːlɪtɪ] *n.* [U] 轻信，易受骗
The cheat took advantage of the old woman's credulity.

◆ credence [ˈkriːdns] *n.* [U] 相信（传言）；凭证；餐具柜
Don't give credence to all the gossip you hear.

◆ credential [krɪˈdenʃəl] *n.* 外交使节所递的国书，信任状；文凭
You must find a secure way to store the credential.

◆ recreant [ˈrekrɪənt] *adj.* 〈文〉怯懦的
n. [C] 懦夫
He is a recreant knight.

fid: trust, faith

◆ fidelity [fɪˈdelɪtɪ] *n.* [U] 忠诚，忠实；尽责
There is nothing like a dog's fidelity.

◆ infidelity [ˌɪnfɪˈdelətɪ] *n.* 无信仰；不忠实；不贞的行为

He seemed more amazed at his wife's infidelity than angry.

◆ fiduciary［fɪ'duːʃɪərɪ］v. 基于信用的，信托的，受信托的

n. 被信托者，受托人

A company director owes a fiduciary duty to the company.

◆ affidavit［ˌæfɪ'deɪvɪt］n.［C］〈法〉宣誓口供；宣誓书

The affidavit was formally read to the court.

◆ confide［kən'faɪd］v.［T and I］吐露（秘密、心事等）；委托，信赖

It is important to have someone you can confide in.

◆ confidant［ˌkɒnfɪ'dænt，'kɒnfɪdænt］n.［C］心腹朋友，知己

He is a close confidant of the president.

◆ confidence［'kɒnfɪdəns］n. 信心；信任；秘密

I should like to exchange a few words with you in confidence.

◆ confidential［ˌkɒnfɪ'denʃəl］adj. 秘密的；机密的；表示信任的

He refused to allow his secretary to handle confidential letters.

◆ diffident［'dɪfɪdənt］adj. 缺乏自信的，羞怯的；踌躇的

He has a politely diffident manner.

◆ infidel［'ɪnfɪdəl］n.［C］不信宗教的（人），异教徒

◆ perfidy［'pɜːfɪdɪ］n. 背信弃义，背叛，出卖

As devotion unites lovers, perfidy estranges friends.

◆ perfidious［pə'fɪdɪəs］adj. 不诚实的，背信弃义的

Their feet will trample on the dead bodies of their perfidious aggressors.

◆ defy［dɪ'faɪ］v.［T］不服从；公然反抗；蔑视

n. 挑战；对抗

If you defy the law, you may find yourself in prison.

◆ defiant［dɪ'faɪənt］adj. 挑衅的；蔑视的；目中无人的

This made him more defiant and unmanageable than ever.

◆ federal［'fedərəl］adj. 联邦（制）的；同盟的

Switzerland is a federal republic.

◆ confederate［kən'fedərət］［C］adj. 联盟的，同盟的；南北邦联的

n. 同伙，同党；同盟者

v. 联合，结盟

The thief was arrested, but his confederate escaped.

mir: wonder

◆ mirror［'mɪrə(r)］n.［C］镜子；借鉴

v.［T］反映；反射

The surface of the water is as smooth as a mirror.

◆ admire［əd'maɪə(r)］v.［T］赞赏；称赞；欣赏

He is a noble man, so we all admire him.

◆ admirable［'ædmərəbl］adj. 令人钦佩的；极好的；值得赞扬的

She had acted in the ways that he found wholly admirable.

◆ mirage［'mɪrɑːʒ，mɪ'rɑːʒ］n.［C］海市蜃楼，幻景

Perhaps we are all just chasing a mirage.

◆ miracle［'mɪrəkl］n.［C］奇迹；令人惊奇的人（或事）

The PC is a miracle of modern technology.

◆ miraculous［mɪ'rækjʊləs］adj. 奇迹般的；不可思议的

They won a miraculous victory over much stronger enemy.

sur: safe, secure, certain

◆ assure [ə'ʃʊə(r)] *v.* [T] 向……保证；使……确信

He hastened to assure us that the press would not be informed.

◆ ensure [ɪn'ʃʊə(r)] *v.* [T] 确保；担保获得，使安全

Nobody can ensure that he will come.

◆ insure [ɪn'ʃʊə(r)] *v.* [T] 保证；确保；为……保险

He insured his house against fire.

◆ reassure [ˌriːə'ʃʊə(r)] *v.* [T] 使安心；再保证

The doctor reassured the patient that there was nothing seriously wrong.

◆ reassuring [ˌriːə'ʃʊərɪŋ] *adj.* 令人安心的；鼓气的；可靠的

He gave her a reassuring pat on the shoulder.

cert: sure

◆ ascertain [ˌæsə'teɪn] *v.* [T] 弄清，确定，查明

I'm going to ascertain the truth.

◆ certainty ['sɜːtntɪ] *n.* [C, U] 确定性；确定的事

The result is impossible to predict with any degree of certainty.

◆ certify ['sɜːtɪfaɪ] *v.* [T, I] (尤指书面)证明；发证书给……

Can you certify for his ability as a teacher?

◆ certificate [sə'tɪfɪkɪt] *n.* 证明书；文凭，结业证书

v. [T] 发给证明书；用证书证明

He was given a certificate upon the completion of his course of study.

◆ certitude ['sɜːtɪtjuːd] *n.* [C, U] 确信

This is why he could answer with such certitude.

◆ concert ['kɒnsət] *n.* [C, U] 音乐会；一致，和谐

v. [T] 调整，解决

v. [I] 协调一致行动

Britain has to pursue policies in concert with other EU members.

◆ disconcert [ˌdɪskən'sɜːt] *v.* [T] 使不安；使为难；使慌张

I behaved with a politeness which seemed to disconcert him.

Exercises

I. Match the roots with their meanings.

A. rat	( )	1. know
B. psych	( )	2. spirit, soul
C. sent	( )	3. will, wish
D. gno/sci	( )	4. wisdom
E. vol	( )	5. hope
F. soph	( )	6. feel
G. sper	( )	7. reckon, reason
H. fid	( )	8. trust

I. mir ( ) 9. wonder

J. sur ( ) 10. safe, certain

II. Complete the sentences with the right forms of the best words.

commemorate	certificate	mirage	reassure	confederate
fidelity	sentimental	conscience	amnesia	diagnose

1. The airline tried to ________ the customers that the planes were safe.
2. I had to promise ________ to the Queen.
3. In a ________ the desert will mimic a lake.
4. I'm trying not to be ________ about the past.
5. A series of movies will be shown to ________ the 30th anniversary of his death.
6. Doctors use X-rays to study and ________ diseases and injuries within the body.
7. She proudly displayed her degree ________ to her parents.
8. The country agreed to ________ with the neighboring country for mutual security.
9. I'll write and apologize. I've had it on my ________ for weeks.
10. A bump on the head caused her ________.

III. Finish the words according to the definitions. The first letters are given.

1. m ________ a wise and trusted guide and advisor
2. c ________ a spoken description of an event that is given while it is happening, especially on the radio or television
3. d ________ cause to be distrusted or disbelieved
4. p ________ the scientific study of the human mind and the reasons for people's behavior.
5. p ________ a person who studies or writes about philosophy
6. s ________ sharing the feelings of others (especially the feelings of sorrow or anguish)
7. s ________ a student in the second year of college or high school.
8. p ________ deserving or inciting pity
9. p ________ a condition in which a person or community is doing well financially
10. c ________ to be kept secret or private.

IV. Choose among the words with similar roots and fill in the blanks in the right forms.

compute	repute	depute	impute	dispute

1. It is grossly unfair to ________ blame to the United Nations.
2. Another approach is to ________ the gravitational forces involved.
3. Some economists ________ whether consumer spending is as strong as the figures suggest.
4. Chicago has 6 graduate and professional schools of high ________.
5. He ________ the running of the department to an assistant.

sentimental	sensitive	sensational	sensible	sensual

6. Dogs have an extremely ________ sense of smell.
7. Her full-grown ________ appeal is the aspiration of all men.
8. There had been much ________ reporting of his affair in the tabloid press.
9. It's ________ to remain silent and get a lawyer at the moment.
10. The ________ play moved most people to tears and made them recall the past.

Theme Six

自然宇宙

aqua: water

◆ aqueous [ˈeɪkwɪəs] *adj.* 水的

The aqueous phase of margarine contains water and milk or milk products.

◆ aquatic [əˈkwætɪk,-ˈwɒt-] *adj.* 水生的；水上的

Aquatic sports include swimming and rowing.

◆ aquarium [əˈkweərɪəm] *n.* [C] 水族馆

Did you visit Vancouver Aquarium?

◆ aquamarine [ˌækwəməˈriːn] *n.* 海蓝宝石；碧绿色

She wore a large aquamarine ring.

◆ aqueduct [ˈækwɪdʌkt] *n.* [C] 引水渠

In 1913 they completed the 223-mile-long Los Angeles Aqueduct.

◆ aquifer [ˈækwɪfə(r)] *n.* 地下蓄水层

Know the source of your drinking water—the river, lake, or aquifer that supplies your home.

hydr: water

◆ hydrant [ˈhaɪdrənt] *n.* 给水栓，消防龙头

Don't touch the fire hydrant.

◆ hydrate [ˈhaɪdr(e)ɪt] *n.* 水合物

v. [I and T] （使）水合；为（皮肤）补水

After-sun products will cool and hydrate your skin.

◆ dehydrate [diːˈhaɪdreɪt] *v.* [I and T] （使）脱水，（使）干燥

Runners can dehydrate very quickly in this heat.

◆ anhydrous [ænˈhaɪdrəs] *adj.* 无水（尤指结晶水）的

◆ carbohydrate [kɑːbəˈhaidreit] *n.* 碳水化合物

◆ hydrogen [ˈhaɪdrədʒən] *n.* 氢

◆ hydrodynamic [ˌhaɪdrə(ʊ)d(a)ɪˈnæmɪk] *adj.* 水力的

Falling raindrops break up through hydrodynamic effects.

◆ hydrophobia [ˌhaɪdrə(ʊ)ˈfəʊbjə] *n.* 恐水病，狂犬病

mar: water

◆ marine [məˈriːn] *adj.* 海的；海军的

n. [C] 水兵；海军陆战队士兵

Marine creatures are those which live in the sea.

He was a soldier of Marine Corps.

◆ mariner [ˈmærɪnə(r)] *n.* [C] 海员，水手

A smooth sea never made a skillful mariner.

◆ maritime [ˈmærɪtaɪm] *adj.* 海的；海事的

It is the largest maritime museum.

◆ mariculture [ˈmærɪkʌltʃə(r)] *n.* 海水养殖

◆ marsh [mɑːʃ] *n.* 沼泽，湿地
He led them away from a marsh.

◆ morass [məˈræs] *n.* [C] 沼泽；陷阱
I tried to drag myself out of the morass of despair.

◆ submarine [ˈsʌbməriːn] *n.* 潜艇
adj. 水下的，海底的
The submarine at last emerged.
A new submarine cable was laid from England to Netherlands.

◆ transmarine [ˌtrænzməˈriːn] *adj.* 海外的，横越海洋的

◆ ultramarine [ˌʌltrəməˈriːn] *n.* 深蓝色
adj. 群青色的
The horizon beyond is of the deepest ultramarine.

liqu: water

◆ liqueur [lɪˈkjʊə(r)] *n.* 白酒；利口酒（餐后甜酒）
Sangria is typically created from red wine, fruit, soda water, orange liqueur and brandy.

◆ liquor [ˈlɪkə(r)] *n.* 酒
He keeps away from liquor and tobacco.

◆ liquid [ˈlɪkwɪd] *n.* 液体
All substances, whether they are gaseous, liquid or solid, are made of atoms.

◆ liquidity [lɪˈkwɪdɪtɪ] *n.* 流动性
The bank has progressively increased its liquidity.

◆ liquidate [ˈlɪkwɪdeɪt] *v.* [T] 清算；结束
Hitler tried to liquidate the Jews in Germany.

◆ liquidize [ˈlɪkwɪdaɪz] *v.* [T] 把（尤指水果或蔬菜等）榨成汁
Liquidize the mixture and then pass it through a sieve.

◆ liquate [ˈlaɪkweɪt] *v.* [T] 熔解

◆ liquefy [ˈlɪkwɪfaɪ] *v.* [I and T] 液化，溶解
Heat the jam until it liquefies.

lumin/luc/lux/lus: light, bright

◆ luminance [ˈluːmɪnəns] *n.* 亮度

◆ luminary [ˈluːmɪnərɪ] *n.* [C] 发光体；杰出人物
Jung, like his master Freud, became a luminary of the psychoanalytical world.

◆ luminous [ˈluːmɪnəs] *adj.* 发光的；清楚的
My watch has a luminous dial so I can see it in the dark.

◆ luminescent [ˌluːmɪˈnesnt] *adj.* 发冷光的
Most fireflies are winged, which distinguishes them from other luminescent insects of the same family.

◆ illuminate [ɪˈl(j)uːmɪneɪt] *v.* [I and T] 照亮；阐明
No streetlights illuminated the street.

◆ illuminant [ɪˈl(j)uːmɪnənt] *n.* 光源
adj. 发光的
The aircrew of more than ten other airliners flying above Shanghai also reported the illuminant object.

◆ lucent [ˈluːsnt] *adj.* 光亮的，透明的
the lucent moon

◆ translucent [trænzˈluːsnt] *adj.* 半透明的
She had fair hair, blue eyes and translucent skin.

◆ lucid [ˈluːsɪd] *adj.* 清楚的
His explanation was lucid and to the point.

◆ lucifugous [luːˈsɪfjʊgəs] *adj.* 畏光的
Bats are lucifugous.

◆ elucidate [ɪˈluːsɪdeɪt] *v.* [T] 阐明
Please elucidate the reasons for your decision.

◆ luster [ˈlʌstə(r)] *n.* 光泽
v. [I and T]（使）有光泽

These pearls have a beautiful luster.
Winning the Nobel Prize has lustered the poet's name.

◆ lusty [ˈlʌstɪ] *adj.* 生气勃勃的
He has a strong and lusty son.

◆ illustrate [ˈɪləstreɪt] *v.* [I and T] 说明
Here are a few examples to illustrate this principle.

◆ illustrative [ˈɪləstreɪtɪv, -trə-] *adj.* 起说明作用的
The illustrations are strictly illustrative of the text.

◆ illustrious [ɪˈlʌstrɪəs] *adj.* 杰出的；辉煌的
The winners were the most illustrious scientists of the decade.

◆ luxurious [lʌgˈzjʊərɪəs, lʌkˈsjʊ-] *adj.* 奢侈的；豪华的
The millionaire leads a luxurious life.

◆ luxuriant [lʌgˈzjʊərɪənt, lʌkˈsjʊ-] *adj.* 茂盛的
The branches and leaves are luxuriant but well-spaced.

◆ deluxe [dəˈlʌks] *adj.* 高级的；豪华的
I liked the deluxe edition, but I could afford only a second best.

photo: light

◆ photography [fəˈtɒgrəfɪ] *n.* [U] 摄影
Photography is one of his hobbies.

◆ photocopy [ˈfəutəukɔpi] *n.* [C] 复印件 *v.* [T] 复印
I sent him the original document, not a photocopy.

◆ photocopier [ˈfəʊtəˌkɒpɪə] *n.* [C] 影印机
The photocopier isn't printing well.

◆ photophobia [ˌfəʊtəʊˈfəʊbɪə] *n.* 畏光
Most patients report itching, tearing, redness, and photophobia.

◆ photosynthesis [ˌfəʊtəʊˈsɪnθɪsɪs] *n.* 光合作用

cand: white, bright

◆ candle [ˈkændl] *n.* 蜡烛
The candle flickered in the wind.

◆ candid [ˈkændɪd] *adj.* 坦白的
He is quite candid with his friends.

◆ candidate [ˈkændɪdɪt] *n.* [C] 候选人
Voters like a candidate who has the common touch.

◆ incandescent [ˌɪnkænˈdesnt] *adj.* 白炽的
Edison invented incandescent light bulbs.

flam/flagr: fire, burn

◆ flame [fleɪm] *n.* 火焰
The custom of lighting the Olympic flame goes back centuries.

◆ flaming [ˈfleɪmɪŋ] *adj.* 燃烧的
Flaming torches were positioned at intervals.

◆ flamingo [fləˈmɪŋgəʊ] *n.* [C] 火烈鸟

◆ inflame [ɪnˈfleɪm] *v.* [I and T] （使）发怒，（使）过热
Her question seemed to inflame him all the more.

◆ inflammable [ɪnˈflæməbl] *adj.* 易燃的
These gases are highly inflammable.

◆ flagrant [ˈfleɪgrənt] *adj.* 恶名昭著的；公然的
My manager was fired for a flagrant abuse of company funds.

◆ conflagration [ˌkɒnfləˈgreɪʃən] *n.* 大火
A conflagration in 1975 reduced 90 percent of the houses to ashes.

electr: electricity

◆ electric [ɪ'lektrɪk] *adj.* 电的
electric guitar

◆ electrical [ɪ'lektrɪkl] *adj.* 用电的，与电有关的
Franklin's experiments showed that the lightning is an electrical discharge.

◆ electron [ɪ'lektrɒn] *n.* 电子

◆ electrode [ɪ'lektrəʊd] *n.* 电极；电焊条

◆ electrocute [ɪ'lektrəkjuːt] *v.* [T] 触电致死
He accidentally electrocuted himself.

◆ electrolysis [ɪˌlek'trɒlɪsɪs] *n.* 电解
Water can be reduced to oxygen and hydrogen by electrolysis.

geo: earth

◆ geology [dʒɪ'ɒlədʒɪ] *n.* [U] 地质学

◆ geometry [dʒɪ'ɒmətrɪ] *n.* [U] 几何学

◆ geography [dʒɪ'ɒgrəfɪ, 'dʒɒ-] *n.* 地理

◆ geothermal [ˌdʒiːəʊ'θɜːml] *adj.* 地热的

terr: earth, land

◆ territory ['terɪtərɪ] *n.* 领土
Hong Kong became Chinese territory in 1997.

◆ terrain [te'reɪn] *n.* 地形
He knows the terrain of this locality like the back of his hand.

◆ terrestrial [tə'restrɪəl] *adj.* 陆地的；地球的
Forests are home to over 80% of terrestrial biodiversity.

◆ extraterritorial [ˌekstrəterɪ'tɔːrɪəl] *adj.* 在疆界以外的，不受管辖的

◆ extraterrestrial [ˌekstrətɪ'restrɪəl] *adj.* 地球外的
n. [C] (=E. T.) 外星人

◆ Mediterranean [ˌmedɪtə'reɪnjən] *n.* 地中海地区

agri/agro: field

◆ agriculture ['ægrɪkʌltʃə(r)] *n.* [U] 农业

◆ agrarian [ə'greərɪən] *adj.* 农业的；农村的
The center of the U. S. economy shifted from the agrarian areas to the industrial centers in the north.

◆ agronomy [ə'grɒnəmɪ] *n.* [U] 农艺学

◆ agrology [ə'grɒlədʒɪ] *n.* [U] 土壤学

◆ agrestic [ə'grestɪk] *adj.* 乡土的
The fishing village adopts the sea grass as the construction material to keep with its agrestic landscape.

cosm: ornament; universe

◆ cosmetics [kɒz'metɪks] *n.* 化妆品
Cosmetics do not cover up the deficiencies of nature.

◆ cosmetology [ˌkɒzmɪ'tɒlədʒɪ] *n.* 美容学，整容术

◆ cosmos ['kɒzmɒs] *n.* 宇宙
Our world is but a small part of the cosmos.

◆ cosmic ['kɒzmɪk] *adj.* 宇宙的；极广阔的
cosmic explosion

◆ cosmism ['kɒzmɪzəm] *n.* 宇宙论

◆ cosmogony [kɒz'mɒgənɪ] *n.* 宇宙进化论

◆ cosmopolis [kɒz'mɒpəlɪs] *n.* [C] 国际大都市
The World Expo 2010 helps Shanghai become a multi-cultural cosmopolis.

◆ microcosm ['maɪkrə(ʊ)kɒzəm] *n.* 微观世界

Mealtimes are a microcosm of society.

◆ macrocosm [ˈmækrə(ʊ)kɒzəm] *n.* 宏观世界

West medicine is adept at analysis, microcosmic, and fail in macrocosm and synthesis.

sol: sun; alone; comfort

◆ solar [ˈsəʊlə(r)] *adj.* 太阳的

This is a solar calendar.

◆ solarium [sə(ʊ)ˈleərɪəm] *n.* [C] 日光浴室

◆ circumsolar [ˌsɜːkəmˈsəʊlər] *adj.* 围绕太阳的

◆ insolate [ˈɪnsə(ʊ)leɪt] *v.* [T] 暴晒

Plough deeply in 30cm, and insolate in the sun to disinfect.

◆ parasol [ˈpærəsɒl] *n.* [C] 太阳伞

Will you get me a quite plain parasol?

◆ solstice [ˈsɒlstɪs] *n.* [C] 至日

the summer/winter solstice

◆ sole [səʊl] *adj.* 唯一的

The sole survivor of the crash was an infant.

◆ solitary [ˈsɒlɪtərɪ] *adj.* 唯一的；隐居的

I am rather fond of a solitary stroll in the country.

◆ solitude [ˈsɒlɪtjuːd] *n.* 独处；偏僻处

We are always so rushed, without the opportunity for solitude.

◆ solo [ˈsəʊləʊ] *n.* 独唱

adj. 单独的

Cher is currently working on a solo album.

◆ solemn [ˈsɒləm] *adj.* 庄严的，严肃的

The mourning hall was filled with a solemn silence.

◆ soliloquy [səˈlɪləkwɪ] *n.* 独白

Hamlet's soliloquy is probably the most famous in English drama.

◆ desolate [ˈdesəlɪt] *adj.* 荒凉的；孤独的

He has been desolate since his wife died.

◆ isolate [ˈaɪsəleɪt] *v.* [I and T]（使）隔离

Do not isolate yourself from others.

◆ console [kənˈsəʊl] *v.* [T] 安慰

Nothing could console him when his wife died.

◆ solicit [səˈlɪsɪt] *v.* [I and T] 恳求；征求

May I solicit your advice on a matter of some importance?

◆ solicitous [səˈlɪsɪtəs] *adj.* 关心的

He was so solicitous of his guests.

◆ solace [ˈsɒlɪs] *n.* 安慰，安慰物

They sought the solace in religion from the harshness of their everyday lives.

luna: moon

◆ lunar [ˈluːnə(r)] *adj.* 月球的

The Spring Festival is the lunar New Year.

◆ lunatic [ˈluːnətɪk] *adj.* 精神错乱的

n. 精神失常者

Her son thinks she's an absolute lunatic.

◆ lunacy [ˈluːnəsɪ] *n.* 精神失常

She saw that he stood on the verge of lunacy, if he had not already stepped across it.

astr/stell: star

◆ astronomy [əˈstrɒnəmɪ, -trɑ-] *n.* [U] 天文学

◆ astrology [əˈstrɒlədʒɪ, -trɑ-] *n.* [U] 占星术

◆ astral [ˈæstrəl] *adj.* 星形的；星际的

She was amazed at the number of astral bodies the new telescope revealed.

◆ asterisk [ˈæstərɪsk] *n.* 星号

v. [T] 用星号标出

All the required fields are marked by a red

asterisk.

◆ asteroid [ˈæstərɔɪd] *n.* 小行星
adj. 星状的

◆ disaster [dɪˈzɑːstə(r)] *n.* 灾难
The news of the disaster soon got abroad.

◆ stellar [ˈstelər] *adj.* 星的
A stellar wind streams outward from the star.

◆ stellate [ˈsteleɪt,-lɪt] *adj.* 星形的

◆ constellation [ˌkɒnstəˈleɪʃən] *n.* 星座；一群杰出人物
The star sits in the southern constellation of Fornax.

◆ interstellar [ˌɪntəˈstelər] *adj.* 星际的
In any event we will likely undertake interstellar travel in the next century.

aer/air: air

◆ aerospace [ˈeərəspeɪs] *n.* 航空航天（工业）
He's an aerospace engineer.

◆ aerobatics [ˌeərəʊˈbætɪks] *n.* 特技飞行

◆ aerobics [eəˈrəʊbɪks] *n.* [U] 有氧健身法

◆ aerology [eəˈrɒlədʒɪ] *n.* [U] 高空气象学

◆ aerolite [ˈeərəlaɪt] *n.* 陨石

◆ aerosphere [ˈeərəsfɪər] *n.* 大气层

◆ aerodynamics [ˌeərəʊdaɪˈnæmɪks] *n.* [U] 空气动力学

◆ aeromechanics [ˌeərəʊmɪˈkænɪks] *n.* 航空力学

◆ aeronautics [ˌeərəˈnɔːtɪks] *n.* [U] 航空学

◆ aircraft [ˈeəkrɑːft] *n.* [C] 飞机，航空器
All aircraft at London Airport were grounded by fog yesterday.

◆ airtight [ˈeətaɪt] *adj.* 密封的
Store the cookies in an airtight tin.

◆ airy [ˈeərɪ] *adj.* 通风的；轻浮的
Hang it in an airy place.

ann/enn: year

◆ annals [ˈænlz] *n.* 史册
He has become a legend in the annals of military history.

◆ annual [ˈænjʊəl] *adj.* 每年的
The annual rainfall in this area is less than 50mm.

◆ annuity [əˈnjuːɪtɪ] *n.* [C] 年金
Alexander receives a small annuity.

◆ anniversary [ˌænɪˈvɜːsərɪ] *n.* 周年纪念日
Today is my parents' 30th wedding anniversary.

◆ perennial [pəˈrenɪəl] *adj.* 终年的
n. 多年生植物
There's a perennial shortage of teachers with science qualifications.

◆ biennial [baɪˈenɪəl] *adj.* 两年一次的
The workers were strongly against the biennial election.

◆ biannual [baɪˈænjʊəl] *adj.* 一年两次的

◆ millennium [mɪˈlenɪəm] *n.* 一千年；千禧年
The whole world was counting down to the new millennium.

jour: day

◆ journey [ˈdʒɜːnɪ] *n.* [C] 旅行
Journey to the West is one of the four masterpieces of China.

◆ journal [ˈdʒɜːnl] *n.* [C] 日志；期刊
The finding appears in the journal Science.

◆ journalism [ˈdʒɜːnəlɪzəm] *n.* 新闻业
He was the head of the department of journalism.

◆ adjourn [əˈdʒɜːn] *v.* [I and T]（使）休会
The court may not adjourn until three or even later.

chron: time

◆ chronic [ˈkrɒnɪk] *adj.* 慢性的；长期的
His mother's illness is acute rather than chronic.

◆ chronicle [ˈkrɒnɪkl] *n.* [C] 编年史；记录
Her latest novel is a chronicle of life in a Devon village.

◆ chronological [ˌkrɒnəˈlɒdʒɪkl] *adj.* 按时间的前后顺序排列的
The paintings are exhibited in chronological sequence.

◆ synchronize [ˈsɪŋkrənaɪz] *v.* [I and T] （使）同时发生
The sound on a film must synchronize with the action.

◆ synchronic [sɪnˈkrɒnɪk] *adj.* 限于一时的，同时的
I try to re-examine the question from a synchronic and a diachronic viewpoint.

◆ diachronic [ˌdaiəˈkrɔnik] *adj.* 历时的，历经时间长河的

tempo: time

◆ temporary [ˈtempərərɪ] *adj.* 临时的，暂时的
His job here is only temporary.

◆ temporal [ˈtempərəl] *adj.* 时间的；世俗的
The Church has no temporal power in the modern state.

◆ temporize [ˈtempəraɪz] *v.* [I] 拖延
They are still temporizing in the face of a disaster.

◆ extemporary [ɪkˈstempərərɪ] *adj.* 无准备的，随口说的
an extemporary lecture

◆ extemporaneous [ɪkˌstempəˈreɪnɪəs] *adj.* 毫无准备的；即席的
He made an extemporaneous speech on the ceremony.

◆ tempo [ˈtempəu] *n.* 速度；拍子，节奏
Both teams played with a lot of qualities, paces and tempi.

◆ temper [ˈtempə] *n.* [C] 脾气；怒气，火气
He must learn to control his temper.
v. [T] 调和，使缓和
The heat in this coastal toum is tempered by cool sea breezes.

◆ temperament [ˈtempərəmənt] *n.* 气质，性格；急躁
He has an artistic temperament.

◆ tempest [ˈtempɪst] *n.* [C] 暴风雨
He won a tempest of applause when he ended his speech.

◆ tempestuous [temˈpestjʊəs] *adj.* 暴风雨的；激烈的，冲突不断的
She burst into a tempestuous fit of anger.

ev: age, time

◆ longevity [lɒnˈdʒevɪtɪ] *n.* [U] 长寿
Good habits promote longevity.

◆ medieval [ˌmedɪˈiːvl] *adj.* 中古的，中世纪的
The museum has a fine collection of medieval ivories.

◆ primeval [praɪˈmiːvl] *adj.* 原始的；太古的
The railway cuts through a primeval forest.

◆ coeval [kəʊˈiːvl] *adj.* 同年代的
The industry is coeval with the construction of the first railways.

hor: hour, time

◆ horary [ˈhɔːrəri] *adj.* 每小时的

◆ horology [ˌhɔˈrɔlədʒi] *n.* 钟表学，测时法

◆ horoscope [ˈhɔrəskəup] *n.* 占星术；十二宫图

Exercises

I. Match the words with their meanings.

Group 1

( ) 1. aerobatics	A. the scientific study of the universe and its origin and development
( ) 2. conflagration	B. the scientific study of the stars, planets, and other natural objects in space
( ) 3. cosmetology	C. the study of the movements of the planets, sun, moon, and stars in the belief that these movements can have an influence on people's lives
( ) 4. aerobics	D. the study of the way in which objects move through the air
( ) 5. constellation	E. skillful displays of flying, usually to entertain the people watching from the ground
( ) 6. astrology	F. exercise that increases the need for oxygen
( ) 7. solarium	G. a group of stars that form a shape in the sky and have a name
( ) 8. solstice	H. a very large fire that destroys a lot of land or buildings
( ) 9. aerodynamics	I. a room enclosed largely with glass and affording exposure to the sun
( ) 10. astronomy	J. either of the two times of the year when the sun is at its greatest distance from the celestial equator

Group 2

( ) 1. photosynthesis	A. a written record of events in the order in which they happened
( ) 2. millennium	B. a span of 1, 000 years
( ) 3. incandescence	C. brightness
( ) 4. chronicle	D. the way that green plants make their food using sunlight
( ) 5. luminance	E. the phenomenon of giving out a lot of light when heated

Group 3

( ) 1. agronomy	A. the scientific study of the earth, including the origin and history of the rocks and soil
( ) 2. agrology	B. the branch of mathematics that deals with the measurements and relationships of lines, angles, surfaces and solids
( ) 3. geology	C. the application of soil and plant sciences to land management and crop production
( ) 4. mariculture	D. the science of soils in relation to crops
( ) 5. geometry	E. the cultivation of sea organisms for food and other products

II. Finish the words according to the synonyms. The first letters are given.

1. d ________ lonely
2. s ________ only
3. c ________ frank
4. l ________ crazy
5. c ________ contemporary
6. l ________ transparent
7. i ________ outstanding
8. l ________ lush
9. d ________ luxurious
10. t ________ disposition

III. Complete the sentences with the right forms of the best words.

dehydrate	illustrate	inflame	flagrant	isolate
adjourn	synchronize	temporize	console	solicit

1. Let's ________ our watches before setting out.
2. The organization decided to ________ the funds from overseas investors.
3. Normally specimens have to be ________.
4. The speaker ________ in order to delay the vote.
5. All the patients known to have been in contact with the virus were immediately ________.
6. The attack on civilians is a ________ violation of the peace agreement.
7. These remarks have only served to ________ an already dangerous situation.
8. The judge announced that the case was ________ until Friday.
9. The company's bank statements ________ its success.
10. Brian was crying and she could do nothing to ________ him.

IV. Choose the best answers.

1. The company closed down operations and began ________ its assets in January.
   A. liquidizing B. liquidating C. liquefying D. liquating
2. The exhibition is organized in ________ order.
   A. chronic B. synchronic C. diachronic D chronological
3. The old man was very ________ about his descendants.
   A. solicitous B. solitary C. solemn D. desolate
4. The first time I saw seals was in an ________.
   A. aquamarine B. aqueduct C. aquarium D. aquifer
5. For years, the couple's ________ relationship made the headlines.
   A. tempest B. tempestuous C. extemporaneous D. extemporary

Theme Seven

战争之束

mar: war

◆ Mars [mɑːz] *n.* 火星；战神

◆ Martian [ˈmɑːʃ(ɪ)ən] *n.* [C] 火星人

◆ mar [mɑː(r)] *v.* [T] 破坏

That election was marred by massive cheating.

◆ martial [ˈmɑːʃəl] *adj.* 军事的；战争的；尚武的

He is expert at martial arts.

bell: war; beautiful

◆ rebel [ˈrebl] *n.* 反叛者

[riˈbel] *v.* [I] 反抗权威

Rebels are people who are fighting against their own country's army in order to change the political system there.

He excited the people to rebel against the king.

◆ rebellion [rɪˈbeljən] *n.* 叛乱

The troops suppressed the rebellion by firing on the mob.

◆ rebellious [rɪˈbeljəs] *adj.* 反叛的

As a rebellious teenager, he moved out of his home.

◆ antebellum [ˌæntɪˈbeləm] *adj.* (美国南北)战争前的

There are many antebellum houses in the area.

◆ bellicose [ˈbelɪkəʊs] *adj.* 好战的

The animal was studying him with bellicose curiosity.

◆ belligerent [bɪˈlɪdʒərənt] *adj.* 好战的；交战的

Our government has forbidden exporting petroleum to the belligerent countries.

◆ belligerency [bɪˈlɪdʒərənsɪ] *n.* 交战状态

She was always in belligerency when others belittled her.

◆ belle [bel] *n.* [C] 美女

She was the belle of her Sunday school class.

◆ embellish [ɪmˈbelɪʃ] *v.* [I and T] 装饰；润色

The stern was embellished with carvings in red and blue.

arm: weapon

◆ army [ˈɑːmɪ] *n.* [C] 军队

the Chinese Red Army

◆ arms [ɑːmz] *n.* 武器

In case of need, we must bear arms.

◆ armament [ˈɑːməmənt] *n.* 武器，军械

The unit has insufficient armament to fight with.

◆ disarmament [dɪsˈɑːməmənt] *n.* [U] 裁军；缴械

They did not reach agreement on nuclear

disarmament.

◆ disarm [dɪs'ɑːm] *v.* [I and T]（使）缴械
Most of the rebels were captured and disarmed.

◆ disarming [dɪs'ɑːmɪŋ] *adj.* 消除敌意的
Leonard approached with a disarming smile.

◆ armistice ['ɑːmɪstɪs] *n.* 停战
An armistice is an agreement between countries who are at war with one another to stop fighting and to discuss ways of making peace.

◆ armor ['ɑːmə(r)] *n.* [U] 盔甲；装甲
Knights fought in armor.

◆ armada [ɑː'mɑːdə] *n.* [C] 舰队
The vast armada comprised 3,000 merchant vessels and 700 warships.

◆ alarm [ə'lɑːm] *n.* 惊恐；警报；闹铃
She sat up in alarm.

pot: powerful, capable of

◆ potent ['pəʊtənt] *adj.* 强有力的
The drug is extremely potent, but causes unpleasant side effects.

◆ omnipotent [ɒm'nɪpətənt] *adj.* 全能的
When we are omnipotent, we shall have no more need of science.

◆ impotent ['ɪmpətənt] *adj.* 无力的
We felt quite impotent to resist the will of the dictator.

◆ potentate ['pəʊtənteɪt] *n.* [C] 有权势的人
A potentate is a ruler who has complete power over his people.

◆ potential [pə'tenʃəl] *adj.* 潜在的
n. 潜力；潜在性
It's important to draw out a child's potential capacities.
The potential for conflict is great.

vict/vinc: conquer

◆ victim ['vɪktɪm] *n.* [C] 受害者
Not all the victims survived.

◆ victory ['vɪktərɪ] *n.* 胜利
We have absolute confidence in victory.

◆ victorious [vɪk'tɔːrɪəs] *adj.* 胜利的
The victorious army returned in triumph.

◆ convict [kən'vɪkt] *v.* [T] 宣判有罪；证明……有罪
n. [C] 罪犯
He was convicted of murder.

◆ conviction [kən'vɪkʃən] *n.* 定罪；说服；确信
She has six previous convictions for theft.

◆ convince [kən'vɪns] *v.* [T] 使相信，说服
I tried to convince her to see a doctor.

◆ convincing [kən'vɪnsɪŋ] *adj.* 令人相信的；有说服力的
There is no convincing evidence that this substance has anything to do with cancer.

◆ evince [ɪ'vɪns] *v.* [T] 表明，标示
The new president has so far evinced no such sense of direction.

◆ evincible [ɪ'vɪnsəbl] *adj.* 可证明的
That's an evincible hypothesis.

◆ invincible [in'vinsibl] *adj.* 不可战胜的
Weapons that would have been invincible 20 years before are now vulnerable and obsolete.

pugn: fight

◆ pugnacious [pʌg'neɪʃəs] *adj.* 好战的
My normally easygoing personality turned pugnacious.

◆ expugnable [eks'pʌgnəbl] *adj.* 可突击的，可攻克的

◆ impugn [ɪm'pjuːn] *v.* [T] 非难，指摘

The good name of the Bank will be impugned in some way.

◆ repugnant [rɪˈpʌgnənt] *adj.* 令人厌恶的
All food was repugnant to me during my illness.

milit: fight

◆ militant [ˈmɪlɪtənt] *adj.* 激进的，好战的；战斗中的
He is a militant reformer.

◆ military [ˈmɪlɪtərɪ] *adj.* 军事的；军用的
n. 军人；军队
Military action may become necessary.
Did you serve in the military?

◆ militia [mɪˈlɪʃə] *n.* 民兵组织，民兵
The building was guarded by the local militia.

◆ militarize [ˈmɪlɪtəraɪz] *v.* [T] 军事化
The new policy permitted the government to militarize the country's air towers.

◆ demilitarize [ˌdiːˈmɪlɪtəraɪz] *v.* [T] 解除武装；使非军事化
The area could be turned into a demilitarized zone.

veng: avenge, punish

◆ avenge [əˈvendʒ] *v.* [I and T] 报仇
He wanted to avenge his brother's death.

◆ revenge [rɪˈvendʒ] *n.* [U] 报仇
v. [T] 为……报仇
The attack was in revenge for the deaths of two delegates.

◆ revengeful [rɪˈvendʒf(ʊ)l] *adj.* 报复的，深藏仇恨的
Her pride was hurt and she felt revengeful.

◆ vengeance [ˈvendʒəns] *n.* [U] 报仇，复仇
He swore vengeance on everyone involved in the murder.

bat: beat

◆ bat [bæt] *n.* [C] 球棒；球拍
v. 击球
He bought a baseball bat.

◆ baton [ˈbætən,-tɒn] *n.* [C] 警棍；指挥棒；接力棒
The conductor beat time with a baton.

◆ battlement [ˈbætlmənt] *n.* 城垛
The battlement is very strong.

◆ battery [ˈbætərɪ] *n.* [C] 电池；炮台，炮位；殴打罪
Assault and battery is the crime of attacking someone and causing them physical harm.

◆ abate [əˈbeɪt] *v.* [I] 减轻
We waited for the storm to abate.

◆ combat [ˈkɒmbæt,kəmˈbæt] *n.* 战斗
v. [T] 与……战斗
He was killed in combat.
The new government took measures to combat crime.

◆ combatant [ˈkɒmbətənt] *adj.* 好斗的
n. [C] 斗士；参战国
They come from the combatant nations.
UN forces could physically separate the combatants in the region.

◆ debate [diˈbeit] *v.* [T and I] 辩论，争论
n. [C and U]
The new drug has become the subject of heated debate.

◆ debatable [dɪˈbeɪtəbl] *adj.* 可争辩的
That's a debatable point. Not everyone would agree.

fend/fest: strike

◆ fend [fend] *v.* [I and T] 照料；防御；闪

避，挡开

The old couple have no one to help do housework; they have to fend for themselves.

He raised his hand to fend off the blow.

◆ fender［ˈfendər］n.［C］挡泥板；防御物

Their car dented my car's fender.

◆ defend［dɪˈfend］v.［I and T］辩护；保卫

It is impossible to defend against an all-out attack.

◆ fence［fens］n.［C］篱笆；围墙

v.［I and T］用篱笆围住；防护

The first task was to fence the wood to exclude sheep.

◆ defense［dɪˈfens］n. 辩护；防御

He told the police that he had acted in self-defense.

◆ offend［əˈfend］v.［I and T］犯规，触犯

I never meant to offend you.

◆ offensive［əˈfensɪv］adj. 无礼的，冒犯的

He apologized for the offensive remarks made by his son.

◆ infest［ɪnˈfest］v.［T］骚扰；成群出现

The prison is infested with rats.

◆ manifest［ˈmænɪfest］v.［T］证明；使显现

adj. 明白的，明显的

He doesn't manifest much interest in his studies.

Fear was manifest on her face.

flict: strike

◆ inflict［ɪnˈflɪkt］v.［T］把……强加给，使承受

Don't inflict your ideas on me.

◆ conflict［kənˈflɪkt］n. &v. 冲突；战斗

The conflict between two cultures lasted a century.

These results conflict with earlier findings.

◆ conflicting［kənˈflɪktɪŋ］adj. 相矛盾的，冲突的

Another team of scientists has come up with conflicting evidence.

◆ afflict［əˈflikt］V.［T］折磨，使受痛苦

The country is afflicted by famine.

◆ affliction［əˈflɪkʃən］n. 苦恼，痛苦；灾难

His deafness is a great affliction to him.

damn/demn/dam: curse, harm

◆ damned［dæmd］adj. 该死的；该谴责的

The damned meeting seemed endless.

◆ damnation［dæmˈneɪʃən］n. 罚入地狱，遭天谴

They believe he will suffer damnation for his sins.

◆ condemn［kənˈdem］v.［T］谴责；宣判

He was condemned to death for murder.

◆ indemnity［ɪnˈdemnɪtɪ］n. 赔偿；保障

They paid an indemnity to the victim after the accident.

◆ damage［ˈdæmɪdʒ］n. &v. 损害，毁坏

They suffered severe/extensive/permanent/minor damage.

divid: separate

◆ dividend［ˈdɪvɪdend］n.［C］红利，股息，利息

If one owned 100 shares, the dividend would be ＄200.

◆ divider［dɪˈvaɪdə(r)］n. 间隔物；分配器；圆规

A curtain acted as a divider between the bedroom and the living room.

◆ division［dɪˈvɪʒən］n. 分开，分隔；除法；部门

The division between the rich and the poor became wider and wider.

He worked in the sales division.

◆ individualism [ˌɪndɪˈvɪdjʊəlɪzəm, -dʒʊəl-] *n.* 个人主义，利己主义；个性，特立独行

Individualism refers to the behaviours of someone who likes to think and do things in his own way, rather than imitating other people.

◆ individualize [ˌɪndɪˈvɪdjʊəlaɪz, -dʒʊəl-] *v.* [T] 赋予个性，使具有自己的特色

Prisoners try to individualize their cells by hanging up pictures.

◆ indivisible [ˌɪndɪˈvɪzəbl] *adj.* 不可分的，不能除尽的

Small as atoms are, they are not indivisible.

◆ subdivide [ˌsʌbdɪˈvaɪd] *v.* [T and I] 细分；再分

The company has subdivided markets into regions.

cret/cern: observe, separate

◆ secrecy [ˈsiːkrɪsɪ] *n.* [U] 保密；保密能力

The plan was made in secrecy.

◆ secretion [sɪˈkriːʃ(ə)n] *n.* 分泌，分泌物

Is there much secretion from your eyes?

◆ discreet [dɪˈskriːt] *adj.* 谨慎的，考虑周到的

He followed at a discreet distance.

◆ discretion [dɪˈskreʃən] *n.* [U] （处理权）决断能力；慎重；考虑周到

Promotions are left to the discretion of the superior.

◆ discretionary [dɪˈskreʃənərɪ] *adj.* 自由决定的；酌情行事的

Judges were given wider discretionary powers.

◆ excrement [ˈekskrɪmənt] *n.* [U] 排泄物

The cage smelled of excrement.

◆ decree [dɪˈkriː] *n.* &*v.* 命令；裁定

It was decreed that the Mid-autumn Festival would be a holiday.

◆ concern [kənˈsɜːn] *v.* [T] 涉及，关系到；使关心

n. 关心；关系

The book is concerned with European history.

The spread of the disease became public concern.

◆ discern [dɪˈsɜːn] *v.* [T] 看出；理解，了解；识别

v. [I] 辨明，分清

Some people find it difficult to discern blue from green.

band/bond/bind: something that binds

◆ band [bænd] *n.* 乐队；衣带

v. [I and T] 聚集，联合

He was a drummer in a rock band.

We must band together to fight the common enemy.

◆ bandage [ˈbændɪdʒ] *n.* [C] 绷带

v. [T] 用绷带绑扎

Apply a dressing to the wound and bandage it.

◆ bandwagon [ˈbændwæɡən] *n.* [C] 时尚，浪潮

What is really happening as the information bandwagon starts to roll?

◆ bandwidth [ˈbændwɪtθ, ˈbændwɪdθ] *n.* 带宽

You pay for capacity, storage, and bandwidth as you use them.

◆ bond [bɒnd] *n.* 绳，带；捆绑物；结合

v. [T and I] （使）结合

A bond of friendship had been forged

between them.

◆ bind［baɪnd］v.［T］约束；装订；捆绑

v.［I and T］（使）结合

It will loose if you don't bind it fast.

◆ binding［ˈbaɪndɪŋ］n. 捆绑，（书籍的）封面

adj. 捆绑的；（书面材料）有约束力的

Its books are noted for the quality of their paper and bindings.

The agreement will be legally binding on both parties.

fix：fasten

◆ affix［əˈfɪks］v.［T］附加；粘贴

［ˈæfɪks］n. 附加物；词缀

Affix the stamp to the upper right corner of the envelope.

◆ infix［ɪnˈfɪks］v.［T］使……钻进

Infix a nail here.

［ˈɪnfɪks］n. 插入词，中缀

◆ prefix［ˈpriːfɪks］n.［C］前缀

◆ suffix［ˈsʌfɪks］n.［C］后缀

◆ transfix［trænsˈfɪks］v.［T］刺穿；钉住；使惊恐

We were all transfixed by the images of the war.

◆ fixate［ˈfɪkseɪt］v.［I and T］注视；使固定

An infant with normal vision will fixate on a light held before him.

◆ fixture［ˈfɪkstʃə(r)］n.［C］固定装置；常客

She was a fixture in New York's nightclubs.

her/hes：stick；heir

◆ adhere［ədˈhɪə(r)，æd-］v.［I and T］（使）黏附；遵循，坚持

All members must adhere to a strict code of practice.

◆ coherent［kəʊˈhɪərənt］adj. 一致的；连贯的

The government policy is perfectly coherent.

◆ inherent［ɪnˈhɪərənt］adj. 固有的，内在的；天生的

The desire for freedom is inherent in us all.

◆ heir［eə(r)］n.［C］继承人；后嗣

The King's eldest son is the heir to the throne.

◆ heirloom［ˈeəluːm］n.［C］传家宝

She treasured the brooch because it was an heirloom.

◆ heirship［ˈeəʃɪp］n. 继承权

Male or female can both have the heirship to the throne.

◆ heredity［hɪˈredətɪ］n.［U］遗传；遗传性

Do heredity and environment determine a man's character?

◆ heritage［ˈherɪtɪdʒ］n. 遗产；传统

The ancient buildings are part of the national heritage.

◆ heritable［ˈherɪtəbl］adj. 可遗传的，可继承的

These plant characteristics are heritable.

◆ inherit［ɪnˈherɪt］v.［I and T］继承；遗传

Her children have inherited her love of sport.

◆ hesitant［ˈhezɪtənt］adj. 踌躇的；犹豫的

He took a hesitant step towards her.

◆ adhesive［ədˈhisiv］n. 黏合剂

adj. 粘的，附着的

waterproof adhesive

◆ cohesive［kəuˈhisiv］adj. 团结的，有聚合力的

This is a cohesive community.

◆ cohesion［kəuˈhiʒən］n. 团结，凝聚力

The work at present lacks cohesion.

lig/li/leag/ly：bind，tie

◆ oblige［ə'blaɪdʒ］*v.* 强制，强迫；使感激；施惠于
I am much obliged for your assistance.

◆ obligate［'ɒblɪgeɪt］*v.*［T］强迫
He was obligated to pay his ex-wife £ 50,000 a year.

◆ ligament［'lɪgəmənt］*n.*［C］韧带
The runner pulled a ligament in his leg.

◆ religious［rɪ'lɪdʒəs］*adj.* 宗教的
She has strong religious belief.

◆ alliance［ə'laɪəns］*n.*［C］结盟，同盟，联合
What will be the effect of the alliance between IBM and Apple?

◆ liaison［lɪ'eɪzn，-zɒn］*n.*［U］联络；联系；沟通
She is responsible for the liaison with the researchers at other universities.

◆ liability［ˌlaɪə'bɪlɪtɪ］*n.*［C］累赘；负债
The company had assets of ＄138 million and liabilities of ＄120.5 million.

◆ reliance［rɪ'laɪəns］*n.*［U］依赖
A child has reliance on his or her mother.

◆ league［liːg］*n.*［C］联盟；社团
Barcelona looks likely a winner of the Spanish League.

◆ colleague［'kɒliːg］*n.*［C］同事

◆ rally［'rælɪ］*n.*［C］群众大会；集会
v.［I and T］集合
About three thousand people held a rally in support of the strike.

nect/nex：bind

◆ connective［kə'nektɪv］*adj.* 起连接作用的
n. 连接词
connective word

◆ disconnect［ˌdɪskə'nekt］*v.*［T］切断；断开
If you don't pay your bills, they'll disconnect your electricity/gas.

◆ annex［ə'neks］*v.*［T］附加，追加；吞并
Hitler was determined to annex Austria to Germany.

◆ annexation［ˌænek'seɪʃən］*n.* 合并，附加
He mentioned the Japanese annexation of Korea in 1910.

join/jug/junct：join，bind

◆ adjoin［ə'dʒɔɪn］*v.*［I and T］邻近，毗连
The two houses adjoin.

◆ conjoin［kən'dʒɔɪn］*v.*［I and T］结合，联合
America's rise in rates was conjoined with higher rates elsewhere.

◆ enjoin［ɪn'dʒɔɪn］*v.*［T］命令
She enjoined me strictly not to tell anyone else.

◆ joint［'dʒɔint］*n.* 关节；接合处
adj. 共同的，连接的
The report was a joint effort.

◆ disjointed［dɪs'dʒɔɪntɪd］*adj.* 脱离开的，不连贯的
John was drunken, and talked in a wild disjointed way.

◆ jointure［'dʒɔɪntʃə(r)］*n.* 寡妇所得遗产
She has only her jointure, which will descend to her children.

◆ subjugate［'sʌbdʒʊgeɪt］*v.*［T］征服，降伏
They attempted to subjugate the Afghans.

◆ conjugate［'kɒndʒʊgeɪt］*v.*［I and T］（使）结合；（根据数、人称、时态等）列举（动词）的变化形式

The child can conjugate Latin verbs at four.

◆ junction [ˈdʒʌŋkʃən] *n.* [C] 连接，接合；会合点，接合点
There's a bridge at the junction of the two rivers.

◆ juncture [ˈdʒʌŋktʃə(r)] *n.* [C] 关键时刻；接合点
We're at a critical juncture in terms of this domestic program.

◆ conjunction [kənˈdʒʌŋkʃən] *n.* [C] 连词；（事件的）同时发生，同地发生
The conjunction of heavy rains and strong winds caused flooding.

◆ disjunctive [dɪsˈdʒʌŋktɪv] *adj.* 分离（性）的；（指连词）转折的
The play consists of a series of brief, disjunctive scenes.

◆ subjunctive [səbˈdʒʌŋktɪv] *n.* 虚拟语气

◆ adjunct [ˈædʒʌŋkt] *n.* [C] 附属品；辅助物
Physical therapy is an important adjunct to drug treatments.

strain/stric/string/stress: bind, tie, draw tight

◆ strain [streɪn] *v.* [I and T] 拉紧，拉伤；（使）紧张
n. 压力；负担
Resources will be further strained by new demands for housing.
The prison service is already under considerable strain.

◆ unstrained [ʌnˈstreɪnd] *adj.* 不勉强的，未拉紧的
His preference of bold and unstrained style shows his personality.

◆ constrain [kənˈstreɪn] *v.* [T] 强迫；（客观条件）限制
Women are too often constrained by family commitments.

◆ distrain [dɪˈstreɪn] *v.* [I] 扣押（人、财物等）
If he does not pay, will the court distrain upon his car?

◆ restrain [rɪˈstreɪn] *v.* [T] 压抑（情感、情绪等）；阻止；限制
If you can't restrain your dog, you must lock it up.

◆ constrict [kənˈstrɪkt] *v.* [I and T]（使）收紧，收缩；限制，束缚
Men and women alike have been constricted by traditional sexual roles.

◆ restrict [rɪˈstrɪkt] *v.* [T] 限制
Don't restrict her proper activities.

◆ strait [streɪt] *n.* [C] 海峡；困境
The Bering Strait parts North America from Asia.

◆ strangle [ˈstræŋgl] *v.* [T] 使……窒息；抑制；压制
His creative drive has been strangled.

◆ stringent [ˈstrɪndʒənt] *adj.* 严格的；迫切的；（货币）紧缩的
There would be more stringent controls on the possession of weapons.

◆ astringent [əˈstrɪndʒənt] *adj.* 严厉的；收敛的；止血的
An astringent substance causes the skin or other tissue to tighten.

◆ stringy [ˈstrɪŋɪ] *adj.* 多纤维的，柴的；线状的
The meat was stringy.

greg: group, flock

◆ aggregate [ˈægrɪgɪt, -geɪt] *n.* [C] 合计，集合
v. 总计

Our team scored the most goals on aggregate.

◆ congregate [ˈkɒŋgrɪgeɪt] *v.* [I and T] (使) 集合

Young people often congregate in the main square in the evenings.

◆ segregate [ˈsegrɪgeɪt] *v.* [T] 隔离

They segregated blacks from the white.

◆ egregious [ɪˈgriːdʒəs, -dʒɪəs] *adj.* 异乎寻常的

The case is the most egregious abuses of human rights.

◆ gregarious [grɪˈgeərɪəs] *adj.* 合群的，群居的

She is such a gregarious and outgoing person.

soci: companion, associate

◆ sociable [ˈsəʊʃəbl] *adj.* 喜欢交际的

He is very sociable and makes friends easily.

◆ social [ˈsəʊʃəl] *adj.* 社会的

He is fond of social activities.

◆ sociology [ˌsəʊsɪˈɒlədʒɪ] *n.* 社会学

◆ associate [əˈsəʊʃɪeɪt, -sɪ-] *v.* [I and T] 联系 *n.* 同事

I always associate the smell of those flowers with my childhood.

◆ consociate [kənˈsəʊʃɪɪt] *v.* [I and T] (使) 结合 *n.* 同事，同僚，合伙人

The churches consociated to fight their dissolution.

◆ dissociate [dɪˈsəʊʃɪeɪt] *v.* [I and T] (使) 分离

They are learning to dissociate emotion from reason.

Exercises

I. Match the roots in the left column with the meanings in the right.

A. mar	( )	1. group
B. pugn	( )	2. fasten
C. pot	( )	3. strike
D. veng	( )	4. war
E. damn	( )	5. separate
F. divid	( )	6. curse
G. fix	( )	7. avenge
H. greg	( )	8. stick
I. her	( )	9. powerful
J. fend	( )	10. fight

II. Finish the words according to the contexts. The roots are given.

1. Just tell the truth and don't ________ the story by any means. (bell)
2. After four years of bitter war, a (n) ________ was signed. (arm)
3. The medicine is ________ enough to produce the desired effect. (pot)
4. The huge influx of ________ and civilian personnel created a problem. (mil)

5. The soldiers were engaged in hand-to-hand ________ with the enemy. (bat)

6. Some children have more ________ personalities than others. (soc)

7. They are ________ birds and feed in flocks. (gre)

8. The police are working in ________ with tax officers on the investigation. (junct)

9. The Act imposes more ________ regulations on atmospheric pollution. (string)

10. The government paid the family an ________ for the missing pictures. (damn)

III. Complete the sentences with the right forms of the best words.

vanquish	inherit	abate	adhere	infest
convict	conflict	inflict	mar	fixate
obligate	impugn	offend	annex	revenge

1. The rule ________ airlines to release information about their flight delays.
2. He has no son to ________ his land.
3. The doctor gave him some medicine to ________ the powerful pain.
4. The villagers seemed certain to take ________ on the enemies.
5. Crime and drugs are ________ the inner cities.
6. Such policies would ________ severe hardship and suffering.
7. The violence was the result of political and ethnic ________.
8. Mexico was once ________ by Spain.
9. We must strictly ________ to the terms of the contract.
10. She seems ________ on losing weight.
11. That election was ________ by massive cheating.
12. There was insufficient evidence to ________ him.
13. If I stayed on an island lonely, I absolutely couldn't ________ my fear.
14. You are not in a position to question my integrity and to ________ my motives.
15. They avoided saying anything that might ________ their audience.

IV. Choose among the words with similar roots and fill in the blanks in the right forms.

strain	restrain	constrict	constrain	distrain

1. His confidence cracked under the ________.
2. Research has been ________ by a lack of funds.
3. If he doesn't pay, will the court ________ upon him?
4. She was unable to ________ her desperate anger.
5. Her throat ________ and she swallowed hard.

concern	discern	decree	discreet	discretion

6. He ________ a certain coldness in their welcome.
7. In July the president issued a ________ ordering all unofficial armed groups in the country

to disband.

8. Where our children's education is ________, no compromise is acceptable.
9. He was always very ________ about his love affairs.
10. This is confidential, but I know that I can rely on your ________.

V. Choose the best answers.

1. The army has decided not to ________ men and women during training.
   A. aggregate B. congregate C. segregate D. desegregate
2. She put a finger to her lips to ________ silence.
   A. disjoin B. conjoin C. adjoin D. enjoin
3. What was once a vote-catching policy is now a political ________.
   A. liaison B. liability C. reliance D. rally
4. Diet and exercise can influence a person's weight, but ________ is also a factor.
   a. heirloom B. heirship C. heredity D. heritage
5. U. S. Army troops and ________ blocked the access to the main palace grounds.
   A. armada B. armament C. arms D. armor

Theme Eight

法治社会

leg/legis: law

◆ legal [ˈliːgl] *adj.* 法律的；合法的

This is partly a political and partly a legal question.

◆ legalize [ˈliːgəlaɪz] *v.* [T] 使合法化

Divorce was legalized in 1960.

◆ legislate [ˈledʒɪsleɪt] *v.* [I and T] 立法，制定法律

It has been proved necessary to legislate against gambling.

◆ legist [ˈliːdʒɪst] *n.*（尤指精通罗马法或民法的）法学家，（中国古代的）法家人物

◆ legitimate [lɪˈdʒɪtɪmɪt] *adj.* 合法的，合理的；合法婚姻所生的

They only married in order that the child should be legitimate.

◆ allege [əˈledʒ] *v.* [T] 断言，声称；指控；提出……作为理由

The accused is alleged to have killed a man.

◆ allegiance [əˈliːdʒəns] *n.* 忠诚，拥护

FBI demands its employees' absolute allegiance to the bureau.

◆ privilege [ˈprɪvɪlɪdʒ] *n.* 特权

v. [T] 给予……特权

No other country has the privilege of fishing in our coastal water.

just/jur: law; right; swear

◆ justice [ˈdʒʌstɪs] *n.* [U] 正义；公正

He stood for the cause of liberty and justice.

◆ justify [ˈdʒʌstɪfaɪ] *v.* [I and T] 证明有理

No argument can justify a war.

◆ justifiable [ˈdʒʌstɪfaɪəbl, ˌ--ˈ---] *adj.* 有理由的；正当的

Whether mercy killing is justifiable is still an open question.

◆ adjust [əˈdʒʌst] *v.* [I and T] 适应，调整；校正

It is difficult to adjust one's habits to someone else.

◆ unjust [ʌnˈdʒʌst] *adj.* 不公平的

It was unjust of them not to hear my side.

◆ jury [ˈdʒʊərɪ] *n.* [C] 陪审团

The jury did not believe the witness' cock and bull story.

◆ jurist [ˈdʒʊərɪst] *n.* [C] 法理学家

◆ juror [ˈdʒʊərə(r)] *n.* [C] 陪审员

The attorney for the defense challenged the juror.

◆ juridical [dʒʊəˈrɪdɪkəl] *adj.* 裁判的，司法的

The juridical reform was a doomed failure.

◆ jurisprudence [ˌdʒʊərɪsˈpruːdəns] *n.* [U] 法学，法理学

◆ perjury [ˈpɜːdʒərɪ] *n.* [U] 假誓，伪证

I think there is perjury; people do tell lies in court.

◆ abjure [æb'dʒʊər, əb-] *v.* & *n.* 发誓放弃

They were compelled to abjure their faith.

◆ adjure [ə'dʒʊə(r)] *v.* [T] 命令要求；祈求

I adjure you to tell the truth before this court.

◆ conjure ['kʌndʒə(r)] *v.* [I and T] 变魔术；使（某事）突然出现

They managed to conjure a victory.

jud: judge

◆ prejudge [ˌpriː'dʒʌdʒ] *v.* 预先判断

It is hard to prejudge the final result of this matter based on the present situation.

◆ judgment ['dʒʌdʒmənt] *n.* 判断，鉴定

His judgment carries weight.

◆ judicial [dʒuː'dɪʃl] *adj.* 司法的；法庭的

Previous judicial interpretations are of great weight.

◆ judiciary [dʒuː'dɪʃ(ɪ)ərɪ] *n.* 司法部；（总称）法官，审判官

The independence of the judiciary in France is guaranteed by law.

◆ judicious [dʒuː'dɪʃəs] *adj.* 明智的；判断正确的

A judicious parent encourages his children to make their own decisions.

◆ injudicious [ˌɪndʒuː'dɪʃəs, -dʒʊ-] *adj.* 判断不当的，不聪明的

Unfortunately, injudicious management can cause serious performance problems.

◆ adjudicate [ə'dʒuːdɪkeɪt] *v.* & *n.* 判决，宣判

Which court system should properly adjudicate this case?

◆ prejudice ['predʒʊdɪs] *n.* & *v.* 偏见，歧视

There is widespread prejudice against workers over 45.

◆ unprejudiced [ʌn'predʒʊdɪst] *adj.* 无偏见的，公正的

We must be honest and unprejudiced as we attempt to analyze it.

pen/pun: punish

◆ penal ['piːnl] *adj.* 刑法上的；刑罚的

penal law

◆ penalty ['penltɪ] *n.* [C] 惩罚；刑罚

One of those arrested could face the death penalty.

◆ penance ['penəns] *n.* （赎罪的）苦行，苦修

Are you willing to do penance for your sins?

◆ penitent ['penɪtənt] *adj.* 悔罪的

They all appeared very penitent, and begged hard for their lives.

◆ impenitent [ɪm'penɪtənt] *adj.* 不悔悟的

His impenitent attitude is really annoying.

◆ repent [rɪ'pent] *v.* [I and T] 感到懊悔或忏悔

Those who refuse to repent will be punished.

◆ repentant [rɪ'pentənt] *adj.* 悔改的

I'll be repentant of my evil ways.

◆ punitive ['pjuːnɪtɪv] *adj.* 处罚的

The US could impose punitive tariffs on some countries' exports.

◆ impunity [ɪm'pjuːnɪtɪ] *n.* 不受惩罚，无罪

If laws are not enforced, crimes are committed with impunity.

arch: rule; chief; old

◆ autarchy ['ɔːtɑːkɪ] *n.* 闭关政策，实行闭关政策的国家；独裁，专制

◆ monarchy ['mɒnəkɪ] *n.* 君主政体

◆ monarch ['mɒnək] *n.* [C] 君主

Solomon was a wasteful and oppressive monarch.

◆ oligarchy [ˈɒlɪɡɑːkɪ] *n.* 寡头统治的政府

◆ matriarchy [ˈmeɪtrɪɑːkɪ] *n.* 母系氏族制

◆ patriarchy [ˈpeɪtrɪɑːkɪ] *n.* 父权制

◆ archbishop [ˌɑːtʃˈbɪʃəp] *n.* [C]（基督教会的）大主教

the Archbishop of Canterbury

◆ archenemy [ˌɑːtʃˈenɪmɪ] *n.* [C] 主要敌人

Sunburn is the archenemy of skin care.

◆ archetype [ˈɑːkɪtaɪp] *n.* [C] 典型；原型

An archetype is something that is considered to be a perfect or typical example of a particular kind of person or thing, because it has all their most important characteristics.

◆ archipelago [ˌɑːkɪˈpelɪɡəʊ] *n.* [C] 群岛，列岛

Zhoushan Archipelago

◆ architect [ˈɑːkɪtekt] *n.* [C] 建筑师；〈喻〉缔造者

You are the architect of your own fortunes.

◆ archaeology [ˌɑːkɪˈɒlədʒɪ] *n.* 考古学

◆ archaic [ɑːˈkeɪɪk] *adj.* 古代的；过时的

In fact, the rules were as unrealistic as they were archaic.

◆ archive [ˈɑːkaɪv] *n.* [C] 档案文件；档案室

dom: lord, master; house

◆ dominant [ˈdɒmɪnənt] *adj.* 占优势的；统治的

The British were formerly dominant in India.

◆ dominate [ˈdɒmɪneɪt] *v.* [I and T] 控制

As a child he was dominated by his father.

◆ dominion [dəˈmɪnjən] *n.* 统治权；领土

Our country's dominion is very vast.

◆ domineer [ˌdɒmɪˈnɪər] *v.* [T and I] 压制；盛气凌人

He tried to domineer over everyone.

◆ domain [də(ʊ)ˈmeɪn] *n.* [C] 范围；领土

The Arctic remains the domain of the polar bear.

◆ predominate [prɪˈdɒmɪneɪt] *v.* [I and T] 占优势；支配，统治

In older age groups women predominate, because men tend to die younger.

◆ predominant [prɪˈdɒmɪnənt] *adj.* 主要的；占优势的

The love of peace is the predominant feeling of many people today.

◆ dome [dəʊm] *n.* [C] 圆屋顶；半球形

The dome of St. Paul's Cathedral is well-known.

◆ domical [ˈdəʊmɪkl, ˈdɒ-] *adj.* 圆屋顶的

The White House is not domical.

◆ domestic [dəˈmestɪk] *adj.* 国内的；家的

domestic flights

domestic appliances

◆ domicile [ˈdɒmɪsaɪl] *n.* [C] 住处

Domicile is the place where a person lives.

crac/reig: rule, govern

◆ autocracy [ɔːˈtɒkrəsɪ] *n.* 独裁

◆ autocrat [ˈɔːtəˌkræt] *n.* [C] 独裁统治者

The last monarch was replaced by another autocrat.

◆ autocratic [ˌɔːtəˈkrætɪk] *adj.* 独裁的；专制的

◆ aristocracy [ˌærɪsˈtɒkrəsɪ] *n.* 贵族（阶层）

◆ aristocratic [ˌærɪstəˈkrætɪk] *adj.* 贵族的

After he graduated, he entered the service of an aristocratic family.

◆ aristocrat [əˈrɪstəkræt, ˈærɪs-] *n.* [C] 贵族

He was an aristocrat descendent.

◆ bureaucracy [bjʊəˈrɒkrəsɪ] *n.* 官僚主义；官僚机构

◆ democracy [dɪˈmɒkrəsɪ] *n.* 民主

◆ monocracy [mɒˈnɒkrəsɪ] *n.* 独裁政治

reg/reig: rule

◆ regal [ˈriːgəl] *adj.* 君主的，皇家的；豪华的

The regal lady is her mother.

◆ regicide [ˈredʒɪsaɪd] *n.* 弑君者，弑君

◆ regent [ˈriːdʒənt] *n.* [C] 摄政者

◆ regime [reɪˈʒiːm] *n.* [C] 政体

◆ regiment [ˈredʒɪmənt] *n.* [C]（军队的）团

He deserted from his regiment.

◆ regimental [ˌredʒɪˈmentl] *adj.* 团的，团队的

The man over there was the regimental commander.

◆ regimen [ˈredʒɪmen, -ən] *n.* [C] 养生法

◆ region [ˈriːdʒən] *n.* [C] 地区

The region abounds in coal.

◆ regulate [ˈregjʊleɪt] *v.* [T] 调节；控制，管理

This system can regulate the temperature of the room.

◆ reign [reɪn] *v.* &*n.* 统治

Better to reign in hell than serve in heaven.

◆ sovereign [ˈsɒvrɪn] *n.* [C] 君主；最高统治者

adj. 具有独立主权的

For a brief time Texas was a sovereign nation.

ord/ordin: order

◆ orderly [ˈɔːdəlɪ] *adj.* 整齐的，有序的

When there is a fire, it is important that people file out of the building in an orderly way.

◆ disorder [dɪsˈɔːdə(r)] *n.* 混乱，凌乱

v. [T] 使失调；扰乱

The room was disordered when they arrived at the scene of the burglary.

◆ ordinal [ˈɔːdɪnəl] *n.* 序数；比较 *adj.* 序数的

◆ ordinance [ˈɔːdɪnəns] *n.* [C] 条例，法令

The ordinance is another attempt by city officials to target the homeless.

◆ coordinate [kəʊˈɔːdɪnɪt] *v.* [I and T]（使）协调，（使）调和

You must coordinate what you said with what you did.

◆ inordinate [ɪˈnɔːdɪnɪt] *adj.* 无节制的

They spend an inordinate amount of time talking.

◆ subordinate [səˈbɔːdɪnət] *adj.* 下级的

n. [C] 下级

v. [T] 使从属

Nearly all her subordinates adored her.

In the army, lieutenants are subordinate to captains.

◆ superordinate [ˌsjuːpəˈɔdinət] *adj.* 上级的

n. 上级

mand/mend: order

◆ command [kəˈmɑːnd] *n.* &*v.* 命令

He commanded the soldiers to shut the gate.

◆ commandeer [ˌkɒmənˈdɪər] *v.* [T] 征用；强占

The soldiers commandeered the vehicles in the town.

◆ commandment [kəˈmɑːndmənt] *n.* [C] 戒条

The Ten Commandments are the ten rules of behaviour which, according to the Old Testament of the Bible, people should obey.

◆ demanding [dɪˈmɑːndɪŋ] *adj.* 要求高的

The work is physically demanding.

◆ mandatory［ˈmændətərɪ］*adj.* 强制的；命令的

The mandatory retirement age is 60.

◆ remand［rɪˈmɑːnd］*n.* & *v.* 遣回，送还；还押候审

He was remanded on theft charges.

◆ reprimand［ˈreprɪmɑːnd］*n.* & *v.* 训斥；惩戒；谴责

His boss gave him a reprimand for being late.

◆ commend［kəˈmend］*v.*［T］推荐；表扬

The reports commend her bravery.

◆ recommend［ˌrekəˈmend］*v.*［I and T］推荐

She recommended us another restaurant.

liber: free

◆ liberal［ˈlɪbərəl］*adj.* 自由的

n. 自由主义者

She is known to have liberal views on divorce and contraception.

◆ liberalize［ˈlɪbərəlaɪz］*v.*［I and T］（使）自由化

The government has decided to liberalize travel restrictions.

◆ liberate［ˈlɪbəreɪt］*v.*［T］解放；释放

They planned to march on and liberate the city.

◆ liberty［ˈlɪbətɪ］*n.* 自由

The Statue of Liberty is the landmark of America.

◆ libertine［ˈlɪbətiːn,-taɪn］*n.*［C］放荡不羁的人

◆ libertarian［ˌlɪbəˈteərɪən］*n.*［C］自由论者

solv/solu: loosen, free

◆ solvent［ˈsɒlvənt］*n.* 溶剂；解释；解决方法

adj. 有清偿能力的

Water is the universal solvent.

A bankrupt firm is not solvent.

◆ soluble［ˈsɒljʊbl］*adj.* 能溶解的

◆ solvable［ˈsɒlvəbl］*adj.* 可以解决的

One has to wonder if this is even a solvable problem.

◆ absolve［əbˈzɒlv］*v.*［T］宣告……无罪，赦免……的罪行

A police investigation yesterday absolved the police of all blame in the incident.

◆ dissolve［dɪˈzɒlv］*v.*［I and T］（使）溶解

Salt dissolves in water.

◆ resolve［rɪˈzɒlv］*v.*［I and T］决定；决心；使分解

They hoped the crisis could be resolved peacefully.

◆ resolution［ˌrezəˈl(j)uːʃən］*n.* 决心；解决；决议

The UN had passed two major resolutions calling for peaceful solution.

◆ irresolute［ɪˈrezəl(j)uːt］*adj.* 犹豫不定的

Irresolute persons make poor victors.

◆ dissolute［ˈdɪsəluːt］*adj.* 放荡的，淫乱的

He leads a dissolute lifestyle.

◆ absolute［ˈæbsəluːt］*adj.* 绝对的；不受任何约束的

The absolute perfection in a dictionary is rare.

lax/lyse/lyze: loose, break down

◆ lax［læks］*adj.* 松弛的

Lax security allowed the thieves to enter.

◆ laxative［ˈlæksətɪv］*n.* 泻药

◆ relax［rɪˈlæks］*v.*［I and T］（使）轻松

I need a cup of tea to relax myself.

◆ analyze［ˈænəlaɪz］*v.*［T］分析

How do you analyze this change?

◆ analytical［ænəˈlɪtɪkl］*adj.* 分析的

During the course, students will develop their

analytical skills.

◆ paralyze [ˈpærəlaɪz] *v.* [T] 使瘫痪

A stroke paralyzed half his face.

equ: equal

◆ adequate [ˈædɪkwɪt] *adj.* 足够的

The city's water supply is no longer adequate for its need.

◆ equable [ˈekwəbl] *adj.* 宁静的；温和的；稳定的

He was a man of the most equable temper.

◆ equality [ɪˈkwɒlɪtɪ] *n.* [U] 平等

The new law provided for the equality of human rights.

◆ equalize [ˈiːkwəlaɪz] *v.* [I and T] (使) 相等

A small adjustment will equalize the temperature in the two rooms.

◆ equation [ɪˈkweɪʒn,-ʃən] *n.* [C] 等式

One side of an equation must balance the other.

◆ equilateral [ˌiːkwɪˈlætərəl] *adj.* 等边的

an equilateral triangle

◆ equitable [ˈekwɪtəbl] *adj.* 公正的，公平的

Each person must have an equitable share.

◆ equity [ˈekwɪtɪ] *n.* [U] 公平

They shared the work of the house with equity.

◆ equivalent [ɪˈkwɪvələnt] *adj.* 相等的，相当的

n. 对应物

One kilometer is equivalent to two li.

This word has no satisfactory equivalent in English.

◆ equivocate [ɪˈkwɪvəkeɪt] *v.* [I] 使用模棱两可的话隐瞒真相；含糊其词

Don't equivocate with me. I want a straight answer.

◆ unequalled [ʌnˈiːkwəld] *adj.* 无双的；出类拔萃的

This record was unequalled for 13 years.

par: equal; arrange

◆ parity [ˈpærɪtɪ] *n.* [U] 价值对等；平等

The two currencies have now reached parity.

◆ imparity [ɪmˈpærɪtɪ] *n.* 不平等

Imparity is closely connected with poverty.

◆ compare [kəmˈpeə(r)] *v.* [I and T] 比较，对照

How does your bike compare with mine?

◆ disparate [ˈdɪspərɪt] *adj.* 完全不同的

These countries are immensely disparate in size, culture and wealth.

◆ disparage [dɪˈspærɪdʒ] *v.* [T] 轻视；贬低

The actor's work for charity has recently been disparaged in the press as an attempt to get publicity.

◆ disparity [dɪˈspærɪtɪ] *n.* 不同

The wide disparity between the rich and the poor is so obvious.

◆ apparel [əˈpærəl] *n.* [U] (商店出售的) 衣服；外观

This shop sells sports apparel.

◆ apparatus [ˌæpəˈreɪtəs] *n.* 仪器；机器；机构

One of the boys had to be rescued by the firemen wearing breathing apparatus.

◆ parade [pəˈreɪd] *v.* &*n.* 检阅；游行

Traffic was tied up for three hours because of the parade.

◆ pare [peə(r)] *v.* [T] 削皮；修剪 (指甲等)

Pare the rind from the lemons.

◆ prepare [prɪˈpeə(r)] *v.* [I and T] 准备

◆ separate [ˈsepəreit] *v.* [I and T] 分离，分开 *adj.* 独立的；不相关的

◆ repair [rɪˈpeə(r)] *v.* &*n.* 修理；补救

◆ impair [ɪm'peə(r)] *v.* [T] 损害，削弱
The blast permanently impaired his hearing.
◆ impairment [ɪm'peəmənt] *n.* 损害，损伤
He has a visual impairment in the right eye.

salv/sav: safe

◆ salvage ['sælvɪdʒ] *n.* & *v.* 营救
The team's first task was to decide what equipment could be salvaged.
◆ salvation [sæl'veɪʃən] *n.* [U] 拯救，救助
Their marriage was beyond salvation.
◆ salve [sælv] *n.* 药膏
v. [T] 使良心得到宽慰
She bought a soothing salve for sore and dry lips.
◆ savior ['seɪvjə(r)] *n.* 救星
They regarded him as the savior of their country.

peas/pac: peace

◆ peace [piːs] *n.* [U] 和平
I believe this treaty will pave the way to the peace in Europe.
◆ appease [ə'piːz] *v.* [T] 安抚，缓和
He tried to appease the crying child by giving him candy.
◆ pacify ['pæsɪfaɪ] *v.* [T] 使平静；安抚；平定
The government tried to pacify the rebels.
◆ pacific [pə'sɪfɪk] *adj.* 爱好和平的；太平的
The Liberals were traditionally seen as the more pacific party.
◆ pacifist ['pæsɪfɪst] *n.* [C] 和平主义者

Exercises

I. Match the words in the left column with the meanings in the right.

( ) 1. bureaucracy
( ) 2. patriarchy
( ) 3. democracy
( ) 4. matriarchy
( ) 5. autocracy
( ) 6. monarchy
( ) 7. aristocracy
( ) 8. oligarchy

A. government controlled by one person who has complete power
B. a class of people in some countries who have a high rank and special titles
C. a system in which power or property is passed from mother to daughter
D. a small group of people who control and run a particular country
E. an autocracy governed by a monarch who usually inherits the authority
F. a system in which men (not women) have all or most of the power
G. an administrative system operated by a large number of officials
H. a system of government in which all the people of a country can vote to elect their representatives

II. Read the clues and complete the crossword.

Across:

3. relating to the punishment of criminals
5. related to law
6. a government that controls a country, especially in a strict or unfair way
10. the group of people who have been chosen from the general public to listen to the facts about a crime and to decide whether the person accused is guilty or not
11. to control someone or something or to have more importance than other people or things
13. more important or noticeable than anything else in a set of people or things
18. something that is considered to be a perfect or typical example of particular kind of person or thing
19. an unreasonable dislike and distrust of people who are different from you in some way, especially because of their race, sex, religion etc.
20. criminal offense of making false statements under oath
21. a person in authority who has complete power

Down:

1. regret

2. not careful or strict about maintaining high standards
4. an expert in law in ancient time
6. find a solution to; make a definite decision to do something
7. imposed on one by authority or required by law
8. unfair
9. the king, queen, emperor, or empress
12. a special right or advantage
14. a person or thing equal to another in value or measure or force
15. extremely old or extremely old-fashioned
16. a round roof
17. very sorry for something wrong

III. Complete the sentences with the right forms of the best words.

disparage	legislate	liberate	paralyze	dominate
absolve	impair	coordinate	allege	salvage

1. All attempts to ________ the wrecked ship failed.
2. Fatigue can seriously ________ your ability to drive.
3. The government will ________ against the discrimination in the workplace.
4. It was ________ that the restaurant discriminated against black customers.
5. The report ________ the pilot from any blame for the crash.
6. The book is expected to ________ the best-seller lists.
7. I don't mean to ________ your achievements.
8. They appointed a new manager to ________ the work of the team.
9. They did their best to ________ slaves.
10. The electricity failure ________ the train service.

IV. Finish the words according to the context. The first letters are given.

1. There was a deep-rooted racial p________ long before the two countries went to war.
2. The r________ of Queen Elizabeth lapped over into the seventeenth century.
3. Some people want to l________ homosexual marriage.
4. In many societies women are s________ to men.
5. His grandfather had a collection of paintings u________ anywhere in the world.
6. He tried to j________ his absence with lame excuses.
7. The government tried to a________ discontented workers.
8. If you are i________ too long, you will miss the opportunity and spend much of your life regretting.
9. As a housewife, she does the d________ affairs every day.
10. At a key moment in his life, he made a j________ investment that laid the foundation of his success.

Part III Vocabulary in Context

Topic One

Weather

A. Cold weather

Read the following news and pay attention to the words in bold.

A Little Snow and a Lot of Chaos: Airports and Roads Are Hit

✓ Southern England, the Midlands, the North East, Wales and Scotland were hit by brief **snow shower** (1) early yesterday.

✓ More than 40 flights cancelled in brief closures at five major airports and delays are up to three hours.

✓ Rain becomes **sleet** (2) and then snow, at first turning to **slush** (3) in the streets, but soon **settling** (4).

✓ Severe **blizzards** (5) and **snowdrifts** (6) caused traffic chaos with ten-car pile-up on the London-bound A299 in Whitstable, Kent.

✓ Disruption on trains with rail replacement buses in operation and services cancelled and delayed.

✓ Last night council bosses admitted they had been caught out by the winter weather.

(1) snow in short duration; (2) rain and snow mixed; (3) dirty, brownish, half-snow, half-water; (4) staying as a white covering; (5) snow blown by high winds; (6) deep banks of snow against walls, etc.

B. Warm/hot weather

close [warm and uncomfortable] *The weather that night was hot and close, with a hint of thunder in the distance.*

stifling [hot, uncomfortable, you can hardly breathe] *a stifling, crowded train*

humid [hot and damp, makes you sweat a lot] *humid air*

scorching [very hot, often used in positive contexts] *scorching desert heat*

boiling [very hot, often used in negative contexts] *Can I open a window? It's boiling in here.*

torrid [extremely hot and dry] *the torrid desert sun*

sweltering [extremely hot] *sweltering August days*

stuffy [unpleasantly warm, no enough fresh air] *The hotel room was hot and stuffy.*

sultry [hot and damp] *a hot and sultry day*

We had a **heatwave** last month. [very hot, dry period]

Note:

➢ heatwave: 酷暑期(夏季间歇出现的持续数日或数周的异常高温现象)

C. Wet weather

This wet weather scale gets stronger from left to right.

overcast→damp→sprinkle/drizzle→shower→downpour→cloudburst, torrential rain, thunderstorm→flood

The sky's a bit **overcast**; I think it's going to rain. [very cloudy]

The cottage was cold and **damp**.

If it is **sprinkling**, it is raining very lightly.

This rain won't last long; it's only a **shower**. [short duration]

A **downpour** is a sudden and unexpected heavy fall of rain.

A cloudburst is a sudden and very heavy fall of rain.

The **torrential rain** may **flood** the low-lying land out.

A **thunderstorm** is a storm in which there is thunder and lightning and a lot of heavy rain.

Hailstones were battering the roof of our car.

Hail consists of small balls of ice that fall like rain from the sky.

D. Mist and fog

Nouns and adjectives:

haze/hazy [light mist, usually caused by heat]

✓ E.g. They vanished into the **haze** near the horizon.

mist/misty [light fog, often on the sea, or caused by drizzle]

✓ E.g. The hills were hidden in the **mist**.

fog/foggy [quite thick, associated with cold weather]

✓ E.g. The ships cast anchor because of the heavy **fog**.

smog/smoggy [mixture of fog and pollution (**sm**oke + **fog**)]

✓ E.g. Black **smog** reduced visibility to about fifty yards.

E. Wind

There was a gentle **breeze** on the beach, just enough to cool us.

We got our roof blown off in the **gale** last night.

It's a very **blustery** day; the umbrella will just blow away.

The **typhoon** sank a ferry, drowning over 200 people.

The **hurricane** blew with such force that trees were uprooted.

A tropical **cyclone** brought heavy rain to the country last week.

Note:

➢ typhoon/hurricane/cyclone：台风/飓风/旋风（都指热带低压气旋。台风源于西北太平洋，飓风源于北大西洋、加勒比海、墨西哥湾等地，旋风起源于印度洋、阿拉伯海等）

F. Climate

continental climate, oceanic climate, desert climate, subtropical climate, tropical climate, temperate climate, monsoon climate, highland climate, subarctic climate, polar climate

Exercises

I. Match each word with its opposite word from the box.

1. drizzle   2. gale   3. damp   4. overcast   5. scorching

dry	freezing	breeze	downpour	sunny

II. Choose the proper words to fill in the blanks.

Torrential rain is any amount of rain that is considered especially ________ (1. heavy/light). There is not a formal definition of torrential rain as recognized by the National Weather Service. The proclamation that rain is torrential simply means the amount of rain is abundant, had a ________(2. slow/fast) on-set, or lasts for a long period of time.

Hazards associated with torrential rain include flash floods, stream flooding, and landslides. Heavy rain events can also be accompanied by ________ (3. low/high) winds and lightning. If it rains over an area for a (4. short/long) period of time, secondary damages can also result as the ground becomes saturated with precipitation. This can cause problems in watersheds and building stability. In addition, if temperatures are ________ (5. low/high) enough, freeze-thaw cycles can cause problems for other structures including roadways.

III. Fill in the blanks with the proper words.

1. Cars cause pollution, both ________ and acid rain.
2. The ________ heat of the little room was beginning to make me nauseous.
3. ________ Betty is now approaching the coast of Florida.
4. As the ________ melt, the flood waters rise.
5. The game was cancelled owing to ________ rain.
6. The moisture in the air makes it ________ today.
7. The rain isn't too bad; it's only ________ .

8. There'll be bright or sunny spells and scattered ________ this afternoon.

9. More than 70 people were killed in the ________, caused when a dam burst.

10. Last night's ________ nearly took the roof off!

IV. What types of weather are bad and good for doing these things?

Example: Skiing

bad: mild weather which makes the snow melt; good: cold, clear days

1. Planting
2. Barbecue
3. Sailing
4. Sightseeing
5. Camping
6. Backpacking

V. Read the following passages and answer the following questions. Please pay special attention to the underlined words.

Passage A

The English Weather

"Other countries have a climate; in England we have weather." This statement, often made by Englishmen to describe the strange weather conditions of their country, is both revealing and true. It is revealing because in it we see the Englishman insisting once again that what happens in England is not the same as what happens elsewhere; its truth can be proved by any foreigner who stays in the country for longer than a few days.

In no country other than England, it has been said, can one experience four seasons in the course of a single day! Day may break as a warm spring morning; an hour or so later black clouds may have appeared from nowhere and the rain may be pouring down. At midday it may be really winter with the temperature down by about eight degrees or more centigrade. And then, in the late afternoon the sky will clear, the sun will begin to shine, and for an hour or two before darkness falls, it will be summer.

In England one can experience almost every kind of weather except the most extreme. (Some foreigners seem to be under the impression that for ten months of the year the country is covered by a dense blanket of fog; this is not true.)

The problem is that we can never be sure when the different types of weather will occur. Not only do we get several different sorts of weather in one day, but we may very well get a spell of winter in summer and a spell of summer in winter.

The uncertainty about the weather has had a definite effect upon the Englishman's character; it tends to make him cautious, for example. The foreigner may laugh when he sees the Englishman setting forth on a brilliantly sunny morning wearing a raincoat and carrying an umbrella, but he may well regret his laughter later in the day!

And, of course, the weather's variety provides a constant topic of conversation. Even the most taciturn (沉默寡言的) Englishman is always prepared to discuss the weather. And, though he sometimes complains bitterly of it, he would not, even if he could, exchange it for the more predictable climate of other lands.

Questions:

1. The English weather is always ________.

   A. pleasant B. changeable C. foggy D. predictable

2. The weather uncertainty has a/an ________ influence on the Englishmen's character.

   A. negligible B. infinite C. definite D. unidentified

3. According to the passage, Englishmen are good at ________.

   A. predicting weather B. complaining about weather

   C. talking about weather D. communicating

Passage B

A **weather station** is a facility, either on land or sea, with instruments and equipment for observing atmospheric conditions to provide information for weather forecasts and to study the weather and climate. The measurements taken include temperature, barometric temperature (大气温度), barometric pressure, humidity, wind speed, wind direction, and precipitation amounts (降雨量). Wind measurements are taken as free of other obstructions as possible, while temperature and humidity measurements are kept free from direct solar radiation, or insolation. Manual observations are taken at least once daily, while automated observations are taken at least once an hour. Weather conditions out at sea are taken by ships and buoys, which measure slightly different meteorological (气象的) quantities such as sea surface temperature (海面水温), wave height (浪高), and wave period (波浪周期). Drifting weather buoys outnumber their moored versions by a significant amount.

Questions:

1. What's the function of a weather station?
2. Is the temperature measured under the direct solar radiation?
3. In a weather station, how often are manual observations conducted every day?

Passage C

A **storm** is any disturbed state of an astronomical body's atmosphere, especially affecting its surface, and strongly implying severe weather. It may be marked by strong wind, hail, thunder and/or lightning (a thunderstorm), heavy precipitation, heavy freezing rain (ice storm), strong winds (tropical cyclone and windstorm) or wind transporting some substance through the atmosphere (as in a dust storm, blizzard, sandstorm, etc). Storms generally lead to negative impacts to lives and property, such as storm surge, heavy rain or snow (causing flooding or road impassibility), lightning, wildfires, and vertical **wind shear**; however, the systems with significant rainfall can alleviate drought in the places they move through. Heavy snowfall can allow special recreational activities to take place which would not be possible otherwise, such as skiing and snowmobiling.

Note：

➢ wind shear：风切（变）（风切变是一种大气现象，是风速在水平和垂直方向的突然变化。风切变是导致飞行事故的大敌，特别是低空风切变。国际航空界公认低空风切变是飞机起飞和着陆阶段的一个重要危险因素。）

Questions：

1. What could be the negative impacts of a storm?
2. What could be the positive impacts of a storm?

Topic Two

Health

A. How do you feel?

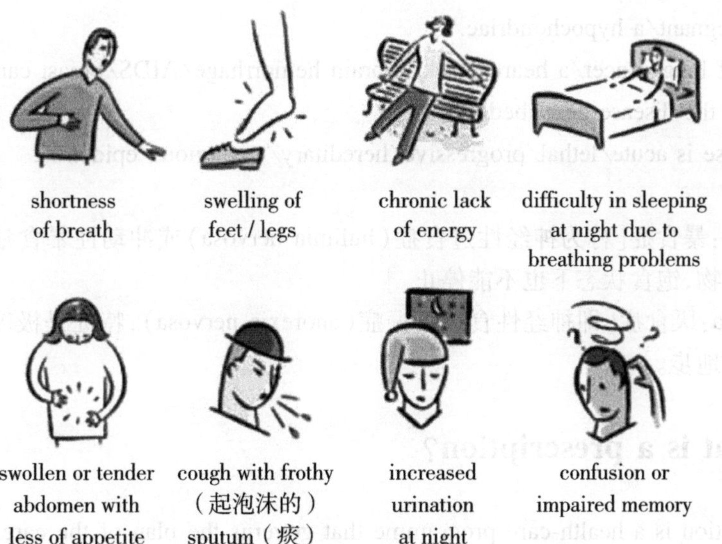

I've got a weak appetite/excessive fatigue/a weight loss/a cough/a sore throat/a temperature/fever and chills/a stomachache/chest pain/earache/a pain in my side/a rash on my chest/spots/a bruise on my leg/a black eye/a lump on my arm/indigestion/diarrhoea/painful joints/blisters/sunburn.

I feel sick/drowsy/nauseated/dizzy/breathless/shivery/faint/particularly bad at night.

I am depressed/constipated/tired all the time.

I've lost my appetite/voice; I can't sleep; my nose itches and my leg hurts.

I have some pain and itching around my eyes.

B. What do doctors do?

Doctors see patients, run and interpret tests. They take your temperature, listen to your chest, look in your ears, examine you, take your blood pressure, ask you some questions and prescribe medicine or treatments. They may also talk to you about how to stay healthy, respond to emergencies, and regularly read books and medical journals or take classes to keep their knowledge up-to-date!

C. What's the diagnosis?

a. What's the disease?

You've got flu/chickenpox/mumps/pneumonia/rheumatism/a virus/a bug/heart attack/high blood pressure/influenza/a sore throat/asthma/tuberculosis/diabetes/gastric ulcer/hepatitis/arthritis/neuralgia/bruise/measles/polio/cataract/hyperopia/athlete's foot/insomnia/phobia/obsession/neurosis/**bulimia**/**anorexia**/depression/manic depression.

You've broken your wrist and sprained/dislocated your ankle.

You're pregnant/a hypochondriac.

He died of lung cancer/a heart attack/a brain hemorrhage/AIDS/breast cancer/leukemia.

b. How is the disease described?

This disease is acute/lethal/progressive/hereditary/contagious/epidemic.

Notes:

- bulimia：暴食症［称为神经性过食症（bulimia nervosa）或冲动性暴食症，即一次性大量摄入食物，饱食状态下也不能停止。］
- anorexia：厌食症［即神经性食欲不振症（anorexia nervosa），特征是极度拒食，达到威胁生命的地步。］

D. What is a prescription?

A prescription is a health-care programme that governs the plan of the care for an individual patient and is implemented by a qualified **practitioner**. A qualified practitioner might be a physician, dentist, nurse practitioner, **pharmacist**, psychologist, or other health care providers. Prescriptions may include the orders to be performed by a patient, caretaker, nurse, pharmacist, physician, other **therapist**, or by automated equipment, such as an intravenous infusion pump（静脉注射器）.

Formerly, prescriptions often included the detailed instructions regarding compounding of medications, but as medications have increasingly become pre-packaged manufactured products, the term "prescription" now usually refers to an order that a pharmacist dispenses（配药）and that a patient takes certain medications. Prescriptions have legal implications, as they may indicate that the prescriber takes responsibility for the clinical care of the patient and in particular for monitoring efficacy and safety. As medical practice has become increasingly complex, the scope of the meaning of the term "prescription" has broadened to also include clinical assessments, laboratory tests, and imaging studies relevant to optimizing the safety or efficacy of a medical treatment.

Notes:

- practitioner：从业者（常用 medical practitioner 表示医生，general practitioner 表示全科医生。）
- pharmacist：药剂师（或称药师，是负责提供药物知识及药事服务的专业人员。）
- therapist：（某治疗法的）治疗专家（如 physical therapist 表示理疗师，提供康复理疗指导或帮助的人。）

Exercises

I. Discuss the picture with your partner. Try to tell how much you know about your body. If necessary, use a dictionary.

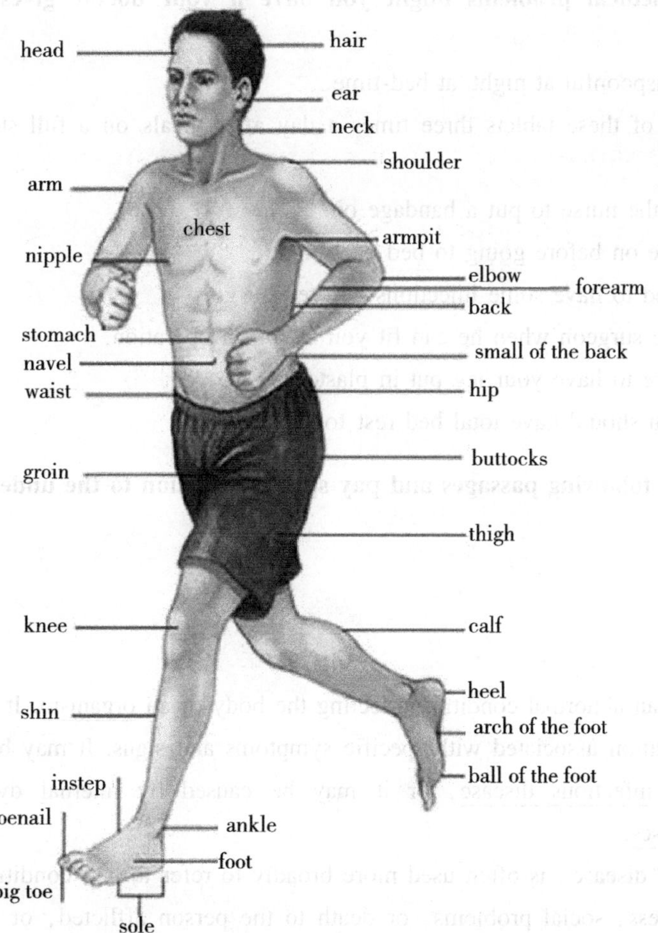

II. Match the diseases with their symptoms.

1. flu — A. swollen glands in front of ear, earache or pain on eating
2. pneumonia — B. burning pain in abdomen, pain or nausea after eating
3. rheumatism — C. rash starting on body, slightly raised temperature
4. chickenpox — D. dry cough, high fever, chest pain, rapid breathing
5. mumps — E. headache, aching muscles, fever, cough, sneezing
6. an ulcer — F. swollen, painful joints, stiffness, limited movement

III. What are the following things used for?

Example: The stethoscope *is used for listening to a patient's chest.*

1. thermometer
2. disposable venous infusion needle（一次性注射针）
3. anesthetic equipment（麻醉机）
4. scalpel

IV. What medical problems might you have if your doctor gives you the following prescriptions?

1. Take a teaspoonful at night/at bed-time.
2. Take one of these tablets three times a day after meals/on a full stomach/on an empty stomach.
3. We'll get the nurse to put a bandage on.
4. Rub a little on before going to bed each night.
5. You'll need to have some injections before you go.
6. I'll ask the surgeon when he can fit you in for an operation.
7. You'll have to have your leg put in plaster.
8. I think you should have total bed rest for a week.

V. Read the following passages and pay special attention to the underlined words.

Passage A

Disease

A **disease** is an abnormal condition affecting the body of an organism. It is often construed to be a medical condition associated with specific symptoms and signs. It may be caused by external factors, such as infectious disease, or it may be caused by internal dysfunctions, such as autoimmune diseases.

In humans, "disease" is often used more broadly to refer to any condition that causes pain, dysfunction, distress, social problems, or death to the person afflicted, or similar problems for those in contact with the person. In this broader sense, it sometimes includes injuries, disabilities, disorders, syndromes, infections, isolated symptoms, deviant（不正常的）behaviors, and a typical variation of structure and function, while in other contexts and for other purposes these may be considered distinguishable categories. Diseases usually affect people not only physically, but also emotionally, as living with many diseases can alter one's perspective on life, and his personality.

The death due to diseases is called death by natural causes. There are four main types of diseases: pathogenic (引起疾病的) diseases, deficiency diseases, hereditary diseases, and physiological diseases.

Question:

Please explain the underlined words.

Passage B

7 Signs Your Work Life Is Affecting Your Health

Work is important, but definitely not at the cost of your health. Many a time, women ignore their health due to work related stress. Ignoring health because of work can cause trouble in the long run. Listed below are some signs that your work life is affecting your health.

Sleep disorders

It is important to maintain a normal work life balance. Set a definite time frame for work. Working at odd hours can cause sleeping disorders. If possible, do not work at home. All the official work should be done in the office only. This will ensure a normal sleeping pattern. Working at odd hours can also cause stress.

Exhaustion

Work life imbalance can cause exhaustion. Working for prolonged hours can cause physical and mental exhaustion in most cases. It is important to work for definite hours. Working all the time can cause stress. And, stress causes physical burnout.

Negative thinking

Working for long hours can also cause inefficiency. Inefficiency can cause loss of productivity. You might be physically present in the office, but might not be able to give one hundred percent to your work. Long working hours can also cause negative thinking.

Stress

Work life imbalance can trigger the condition of stress. Meeting deadlines and working at odd hours can result in mental stress. Mental stress can cause physical problems in the body. To relieve stress, it is important to set fixed hours for working. Practise some stress relief tricks to maintain your health.

Change in behavior

There may be a possible change in your behavior due to work life imbalance. There is a feeling of frustration. Many women also experience mood swings because of this reason.

Change in physical appearance

Work life imbalance also causes a change in physical appearance. There may be a sudden weight gain or weight loss because of this. As working for long hours causes stress, there might be appearance of wrinkles on the face. It is important to take care of your health and reduce the stress related to work.

Physical ailments

If you work for long hours, it can cause stress in the body. Stress causes various physical ailments like high cholesterol(胆固醇) and blood pressure. The increase in cholesterol levels and blood pressure can cause heart related problems. Therefore, it is important to keep work related stress in control.

Stressful work life can cause many problems related to health. It is important to maintain a proper balance to stay active and fit.

Questions:

1. Working at odd hours can cause ________.
   A. stress　　B. sleeping disorders
   C. work life imbalance　　D. all the above
2. Work life imbalance can cause ________.
   A. stress　　B. mood swings
   C. physical appearance changes　　D. all the above
3. All the following statements are true EXCEPT ________.
   A. work life imbalance might cause wrinkles
   B. work life imbalance might cause high cholesterol
   C. work life imbalance might cause heart attack
   D. work life imbalance might help control stress

Passage C

6 Tips for Staying Healthy and Happy in Your Golden Years

There are a number of myths regarding aging. Some people may mistakenly believe that aging inevitably involves getting sick or disabled, while others may think that all adults face memory loss in their later years. Even more people may think that once you reach a certain age, there is less that you can contribute to society and that you are done learning. All of these beliefs are absolutely false. In fact, many people find that the years following retirement are filled with health, vitality, and meaning. Since we are all going to get to those golden years eventually, here are a few tips to consider that may help to make that stage of life some of the best years you'll ever have.

Keep your mind sharp

Your mind is like any muscle in your body; the more you exercise it, the stronger it will be. In earlier years, it may have been easy to keep your mind active while problem-solving at work or at home, but as you age, though, you may need to plan specific activities to engage the mind. Some of the best ways to exercise the mind is by learning a new skill or hobby. Consider learning a foreign language. If you've always regretted never learning to play the piano, take a class. Reading is also a great way to keep the mind growing and learning, so either join or form a book club in your area to allow yourself the opportunity to discuss ideas and thoughts regarding the books you are reading.

Volunteer

Volunteering is one of the best ways to give your life meaning and purpose. As you help others, you can feel a greater gratitude for the things that you have and a greater connection to the people around you. No matter where you live, there are sure to be boundless volunteer opportunities. Visit a local elementary school for opportunities to reach out to the children in your community and help them to learn and succeed. Local government and nonprofit agencies are also often in great need of help. Contact the hospitals in your area for more ideas on how you can serve.

Eat well

A body needs proper fuel to remain strong and active. As you age, your digestive system tends to slow down, and as a result, the foods that are high in fiber are of special importance. At the same time, older adults are more susceptible to dehydration (脱水), so it is important that you drink a lot of water every day. In addition, don't let meal times become boring or lonely—make an effort to make your food look and taste good even if you are only cooking for one or two. Seek out other adults to spend meal time with so that you can enjoy social interaction while you are enjoying your food.

Stay in touch with loved ones and friends

For some, aging equals loneliness and isolation. As children leave home and move away, you leave the workforce and the relationships you built there, and friends and loved ones pass away, it may become easy to feel lost or forgotten. It is vital that you continue to stay in touch with those you care about — your role in their lives may be different, but it can be equally important. Learn to use technology to stay connected. Spend time e-mailing friends, children, and grandchildren. Resurrect the lost art of letter-writing by regularly writing to the loved ones who have moved away.

Exercise

Even if you have never participated in regular exercise, it's never too late to start. Before beginning a new exercise program, however, it is important that you get your doctor's permission. After visiting your doctor, find some form of activity that interests you and that you like to participate in. Look for the health clubs that have classes especially for older adults. Exercising does not have to be overly strenuous(费力的) either; going for a brisk walk every day could be a great way to stay healthy and active.

Stay positive

So much of how we feel is dependent upon our thoughts. Sometimes the best way to fight discouragement and loneliness is by reminding yourself of all of the things that you have to be grateful for every day. Moreover, try to find something to laugh about as you go about your day. If you find yourself facing severe discouragement or depression, seek out professional help right away to assess whether or not you may be facing senior depression.

The possibilities and adventures that await you as you enter your golden years are endless. Seek out new experiences and enjoy the opportunities that you never had time to pursue before. By doing so, you can make the later years of your life some of the most exciting, meaningful years you have ever experienced.

Questions:

1. Who are the target readers of this article?

   A. Youngsters. B. Seniors.

   C. Adults. D. Middle-aged persons.

2. The more you practice your mind, the ________ it is.

   A. sharper B. worse C. slower D. happier

3. According to the passage, the retirement life can be very ________ if the retired person holds positive attitudes.

   A. dynamic B. exciting C. meaningful D. all the above

Topic Three
Character

A. Intellectual ability

Ability: brainy, bright, clever, smart, able, shrewd, intelligent, gifted, talented

Lacking ability: stupid, foolish, half-witted, silly, brainless, daft, dumb, dim (The last four are predominantly colloquial words.)

In a negative way, using brains to trick or deceive: cunning, crafty, sly, plotting, scheming, calculating

B. Attitudes towards life

Looking on the bright side of things: optimistic, hopeful

Looking on the dark side of things: pessimistic, cynical, despairing

Outward-looking: extroverted, gregarious, outgoing, social, sociable

Inward-looking: introverted, shy, introspective, inner-directed, self-contained, withdrawn

Calm or not calm with regard to the attitude to life: relaxed, tense

Practical, not dreamy in the approach to life: sensible, down-to-earth, rational

Feeling things very intensely: sensitive, susceptive

C. Attitudes towards other people

Enjoying others' company: sociable, gregarious

Disagreeing with others: quarrelsome, argumentative

Taking pleasure in others' pain: cruel, sadistic

Relaxed in attitude to self and others: easy-going, even-tempered

Not polite to others: impolite, rude, ill-mannered, discourteous

Telling the truth to others: honest, trustworthy, reliable, sincere

Unhappy if others have what one does not have oneself: jealous, envious

D. One person's meat is another one's poison

Some characteristics can be either positive or negative depending on your point of view. The words in the right-hand column mean roughly the same as the words in the left-hand column except that they have negative rather than positive connotations.

innocent	naive
generous	extravagant
ambitious	pushy (colloquial)
determined	obstinate, stubborn, pig-headed
thrifty/economical	miserly, mean, tight-fisted
frank/direct/open	blunt, abrupt, brusque, curt
assertive	aggressive, bossy (colloquial)
broad-minded	unprincipled, permissive
original	peculiar, weird, eccentric, odd
self-assured	arrogant, full of oneself (colloquial)
inquiring	inquisitive, nosy (colloquial)

Exercises

I. Match these words with their opposites.

1. clever	A. introverted
2. outgoing	B. tight-fisted
3. rude	C. good-mannered
4. cruel	D. gregarious
5. generous	E. kind-hearted
6. inward-looking	F. brainless

II. Do you think that the speaker likes or dislikes the people she/he is talking about?

1. Wang's very thrifty.
2. Lisa's usually frank.
3. Andy's quite broad-minded.
4. Sam can be aggressive.
5. Mark's quite bossy.
6. I find Kate self-important.
7. Don't you think Tim's nosy?
8. Jimmy is very original.

III. Reword the sentences above to give the opposite impression.

Example: Wang's very stingy.

IV. Find a partner and interview each other with the following questions. When the interview is finished, describe your partner's character with the help of the words you have just learned.

1. What is your normal daily routine?
2. How do you feel and react when this routine is interrupted for some reason?
3. What are your hobbies?
4. What would you do if you had insomnia and had to find something to do to amuse yourself?
5. What do you do for relaxation? What things do you do for enjoyment? What interests do you have?
6. Do you, or did you, have any role models? Do you have any heroes or idols, either contemporary or from legend?

V. Please use the words you have learned to describe your character.

VI. Read the following passages and pay special attention to the underlined words.

Passage A

Personality

Personality style has been defined as "an individual's relatively consistent inclinations and preferences across contexts."

Personality can be defined as a dynamic and organized set of personal traits and patterns of behavior. "Personality includes attitudes, the modes of thought, feeling, impulses, strivings, actions, the responses to opportunity and stress and everyday modes of interacting with others." Personality style is apparent "when these elements of personality are expressed in a characteristically repeated and dynamic combination."

According to Oldham and Morris, "Your personality style is your organizing principle. It propels you on your life path. It represents the orderly arrangement of all your attributes, thoughts, feelings, attitudes, behaviors, and coping mechanisms. It is the distinctive pattern of your psychological functioning—the way you think, feel, and behave—that makes you definitely you."

The origin of personality style is in some combination of genetic inheritance and environmental influence.

Mark each of the following statements with T (for True) or F (for False).

1. Personality can decide how someone takes the chances in his or her life.
2. According to Oldham and Morris, personality functions in someone's whole life.
3. A person's personality is decided by his or her genes.

Passage B

Blood Type and Character, Do You Think It Matches Yours?

Type A

Speaking broadly, it is said that the people with Type A Blood are calm, composed（沉着的）, and very level-headed and serious. They have a firm character, and are reliable, trustworthy and hardheaded. They think things over and make plans deliberately, and they plug away at（坚持不懈地干）things steadily and assiduously（勤勉地）. They try to make themselves more like their own ideal of what they should be. A Types may look aloof（孤傲）or distant to others. They try to suppress their own emotions, and because they have continual practice in doing this, this makes them appear strong. But, actually, they have a fragile（脆弱的）, nervous side as well. They tend to be hard on the people who are not of the same type, and so they consequently tend to be surrounded with the people of the same temperament.

Type B

The people with Type B Blood are curious about and interested in everything. That's maybe good, but they also tend to have too many interests and hobbies, and they tend to get all excited about something suddenly and then later drop it again just as quickly. But they do manage to know which of their many interests or loved ones are the ones that are really important, the ones they should hold on to. B Types tend to excel in things rather than just be average. But they tend to be so involved in their own world or become so carried away with something that they neglect other things. They have the image of being bright and cheerful, full of energy and enthusiasm, but some people think that they are really quite different on the inside. And it can also be said about them that they don't really want to have much real contact with others.

Type O

Type O Blood people are said to set the mood for a group and to take on the role of creating harmony among its members. Their image is one of taking it easy, of being peaceful and carefree. They are also thought to be big-hearted and benevolent（好心肠的）, and they tend to spend money on others generously. O Types are generally "loved by all." But, they also, surprisingly, have a stubborn and strong-willed side as well, and tend to secretly have their own opinions on things. On the other hand, they have the flexible, adaptable side of readily accepting new things. They are easily influenced by other people or by what they see on TV. They seem to appear level-headed and trustworthy, but they often slip and make big blunders（失误）inadvertently（不注意地）. But that is also the point that makes O Types lovable.

Type AB

The people with Type AB Blood are said to have a delicate sensitivity. They are considerate of other people's feelings and deal with them with care and caution. On the other hand, though, they are strict with themselves and those close to them. They, therefore, seem to have two personalities: one for those "outside," and another for the people on the "inside." They often become sentimental（伤感的）, and they tend to think too deeply about things. AB Types have a lot of friends, but they need time to be alone and think things through.

Questions:

1. Discuss with your partner about the above information. Have you found any agreement between your actual character and the listed ones?

2. According to the passage, what's the character for Type A, B, O and AB persons respectively?

3. Which blood type person can easily win the popularity among others?

Topic Four

Crime

A. What's crime?

Crime is the breaking of rules or laws for which some governing authority (via mechanisms such as legal systems) can ultimately prescribe a conviction(定罪). Crimes may also result in cautions (警告), rehabilitation (改造) or be unenforced (未实施的). Individual human societies may each define crime and crimes differently, in different localities (state, local, and international), at different time stages of the so-called "crime", from planning, disclosure, supposedly intended, supposedly prepared, incomplete, complete or future proclaimed after the "crime".

B. The following is the U.S. Federal Court System Structure. Read it and tell how the different courts interrelate with each other.

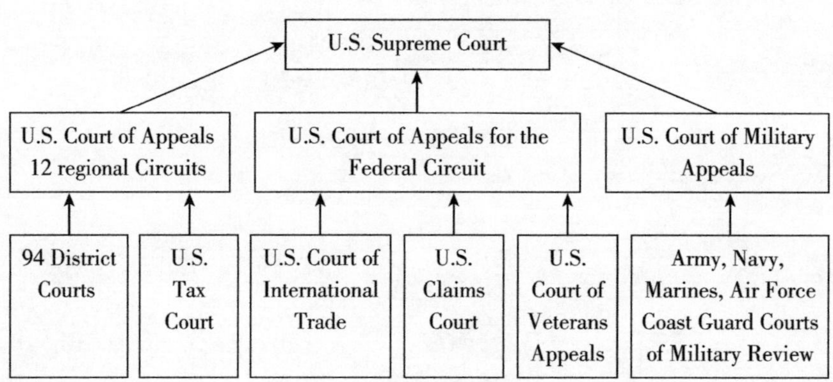

Notes:

➢ district court: <美>(美国每个地区的)联邦地方法院
➢ circuit court of appeal: 巡回上诉法院
➢ federal court of appeal: 美国联邦巡回上诉法院

C. The table below gives the names of some types of crimes together with their associated verbs and the names of the persons who commit the crimes.

Crime	Definition	Criminal	Verb
forgery	trying to pass off a copy as the real thing	forger	forge
hijacking	robbery of a traveller or vehicle in transit or seizing control of a vehicle by the use of force	hijacker	hijack
burglary	stealing from someone's home	burglar	burgle
smuggling	taking something illegally into another country	smuggler	smuggle
arson	setting fire to something in a criminal way	arsonist	set fire to
kidnapping	taking a person hostage in exchange for money or other favors, etc.	kidnapper	kidnap

D. Here are some more useful verbs connected with crime and law. Note that many of them have particular prepositions associated with them.

to **commit** a crime or an offence: to do something illegal

to **accuse** someone **of** a crime: to say someone is guilty

to **charge** someone **with** (murder): to bring someone to court

to **plead guilty** or **not guilty**: to swear in court that one is guilty or otherwise

to **defend/prosecute** someone in court: to argue for or against someone in a trial

to **be tried**: to have a case judged in court

to **pass verdict on** an accused person: to decide whether the accused person is guilty or not

to **sentence** someone to a punishment: what the judge does after a verdict of guilty

to **acquit** an accused person of a charge: to decide in court that someone is not guilty (the opposite of to **convict** someone)

to **fine** someone a sum of money: to punish someone by making them pay

to **send** someone **to prison**: to punish someone by putting them in prison

to **release** someone **from prison/jail**: to set someone free after a prison sentence

E. Here are some useful nouns.

case: a crime that is being investigated

verdict: the decision: guilty or not guilty

judge: the person who leads a trial and decides on the sentence

proof: the evidence that shows conclusively whether something is a fact or not

jury: a group of twelve citizens who decide whether the accused is guilty or not

evidence: the information used in a court of law to decide whether the accused is guilty or not

trial: the legal process in court whereby an accused person is investigated, or tried, and then found guilty or not guilty

Exercises

I. Here are some more crimes. Complete the table.

Crime	Criminal	Verb	Definition
shoplifting			
blackmail			
drug-trafficking			
assault		assault	
pickpocketing			

II. Fill the blanks in the paragraph with proper words.

One of the two (1) ____________ men were convicted at yesterday's trial. Although his (2) ________ defended him very well, he was still found guilty by the (3) ____________. The (4) ________ sentenced him to two years in prison. He'll probably be released after eighteen months. The other accused man was luckier. He (5) ________ and left the courtroom smiling broadly.

III. Categorize the following crimes based on the different principles of classification.

offence against the person, indictable offence, felony or misdemeanor, sexual offence, indictable-only offence, violent offence, treason, hybrid offence, summary offence, offence against property

Type: ____________________

Seriousness of the offence: ____________________

Mode of trial: ____________________

IV. Here are some words related to criminals and crimes. If necessary, use a dictionary to help you check so that you understand what they all mean. Then divide them into two groups in the most logical way.

rape	suspect	sexual harassment	outlaw	blackmail
ex-convict	robbery	fraud	accessory	principal

Notes:

➢ principal: 主犯（根据法律，依个人意志而触犯法律的人被称作“主犯”，也叫作

"原犯"。)

➢ accessory：同谋者（根据法律，帮助他人犯罪的人被称为"同谋"，也被称为"从犯"。)

V. Read the following passages and answer the following questions. Please pay special attention to the underlined words.

Passage A

Law and Crime

What happens in a court case: At the beginning of the trial, the person who is accused pleads guilty or not guilty to the charge against him/her. The lawyers for the prosecution try to prove that the defendant is guilty, and the lawyers for the defence try to prove that their client is innocent. The judge and the jury examine the evidence and listen to the testimony of the witnesses. At the end of the trial, the judge then sums up the case, and the jury then gives their verdict. If the person is found guilty, the judge sentences him/her to a period of time in prison, or orders him/her to pay a fine. If the person is found not guilty, he/she is released.

Note: **lawyer** is a general word for someone who has professional training in legal work or who is an expert in law. In American English, the word **attorney** is often used instead, especially in legal or official language and especially to refer to a lawyer who represents people in court. In British English, there is a difference between a **solicitor**, who gives legal advice and prepares legal documents, and a **barrister**, who represents people in court. In both American and British English, someone's counsel is the lawyer or group of lawyers who represent him/her in court.

Questions:

1. What is the relationship between prosecution and defence in the court?
2. In the court, who provide/provides the testimony?
3. Who has the right to sentence the charged one in the court?

Passage B

Types of Trials

There are many kinds of trials that take place in the United States courtrooms every day. All trial types, however, can be categorized into 4 different case types: civil, criminal, juvenile and traffic.

Civil Case — A trial that consists of a disagreement between two or more people or businesses. Examples: The disputes between a landlord and tenant, divorce actions, small claims cases and a case where one person is suing another for damages.

Criminal Case — A trial involving a person who has been accused of committing either a misdemeanor or a felony offense.

Juvenile Case — A trial that usually involves a minor who is under the age of seventeen. Juvenile cases are heard by the family division of the circuit court. There are three types of juvenile cases: juvenile delinquency, child protective hearings and traffic cases.

Traffic Case — This is the most common type of trial, related to a traffic violation. A traffic violation can be considered either a civil infraction or a misdemeanor.

Questions:

1. Try to give two more examples to illustrate what is "civil case."
2. Try to guess the meanings of the underlined words based on the contexts.
3. Which is the most common one among the above-mentioned case classifications?

Topic Five
At Home

A. Places in the home

utility room: usually just for washing machine/freezer, etc.
study: a room for reading/writing/studying in
attic: a room in the roof space of a house (could be lived in)
loft: the space in the roof of a house usually used only for storage
cellar: a room below ground level, used for storage
basement: a room below ground level, for living/working
landing: the flat area at the top of a staircase
hall: an open area as you come into a house
porch: the covered area before an entrance-door
pantry or larder: a large cupboard (usually big enough to walk into) for storing food
terrace or patio: the paved area between the house and garden for sitting and eating, etc.
shed: a small building separated from the house usually for storing garden tools

B. Small objects at home

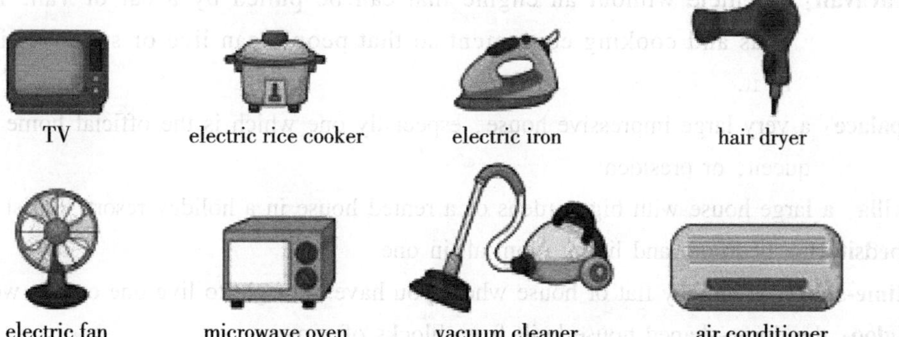

TV   electric rice cooker   electric iron   hair dryer

electric fan   microwave oven   vacuum cleaner   air conditioner

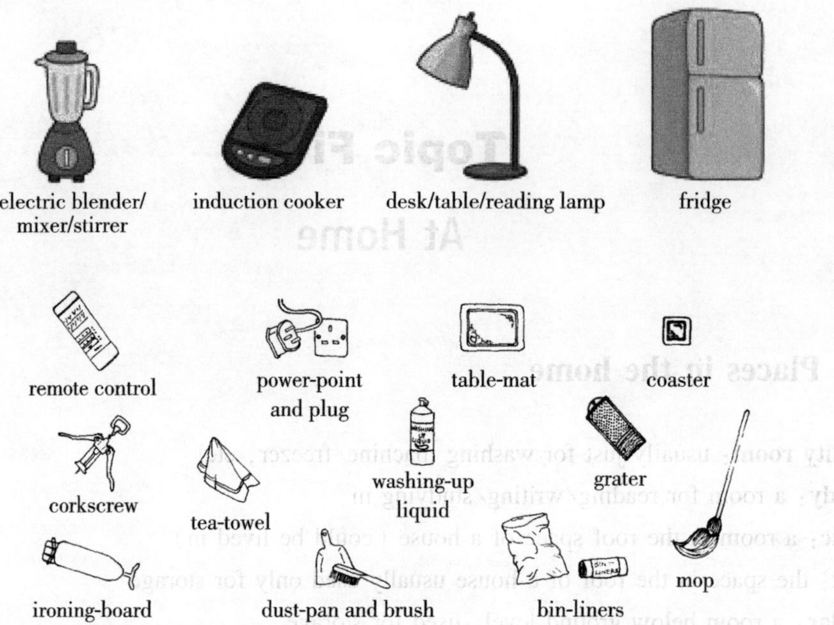

C. Types of houses/places people live

flat: usually on one floor and part of a larger building

skyscraper: a very tall building in a city

detached house: not joined to any other house

semi-detached house: joined to one other house

terraced house: joined to several houses to form a row

cottage: a small house in the country or in a village

bungalow: a house with only one story (no upstairs)

farmhouse: usually where the farmer lives

caravan: a vehicle without an engine that can be pulled by a car or van. It contains beds and cooking equipment so that people can live or spend their holidays in it.

palace: a very large impressive house, especially one which is the official home of a king, queen, or president

villa: a large house with big gardens or a rented house in a holiday resort/tourist area

bedsit: the bedroom and living room all in one

time-share: a holiday flat or house where you have the right to live one or two weeks a year

igloo: the dome-shaped house built from blocks of snow

D. Parts of a house and different types of houses

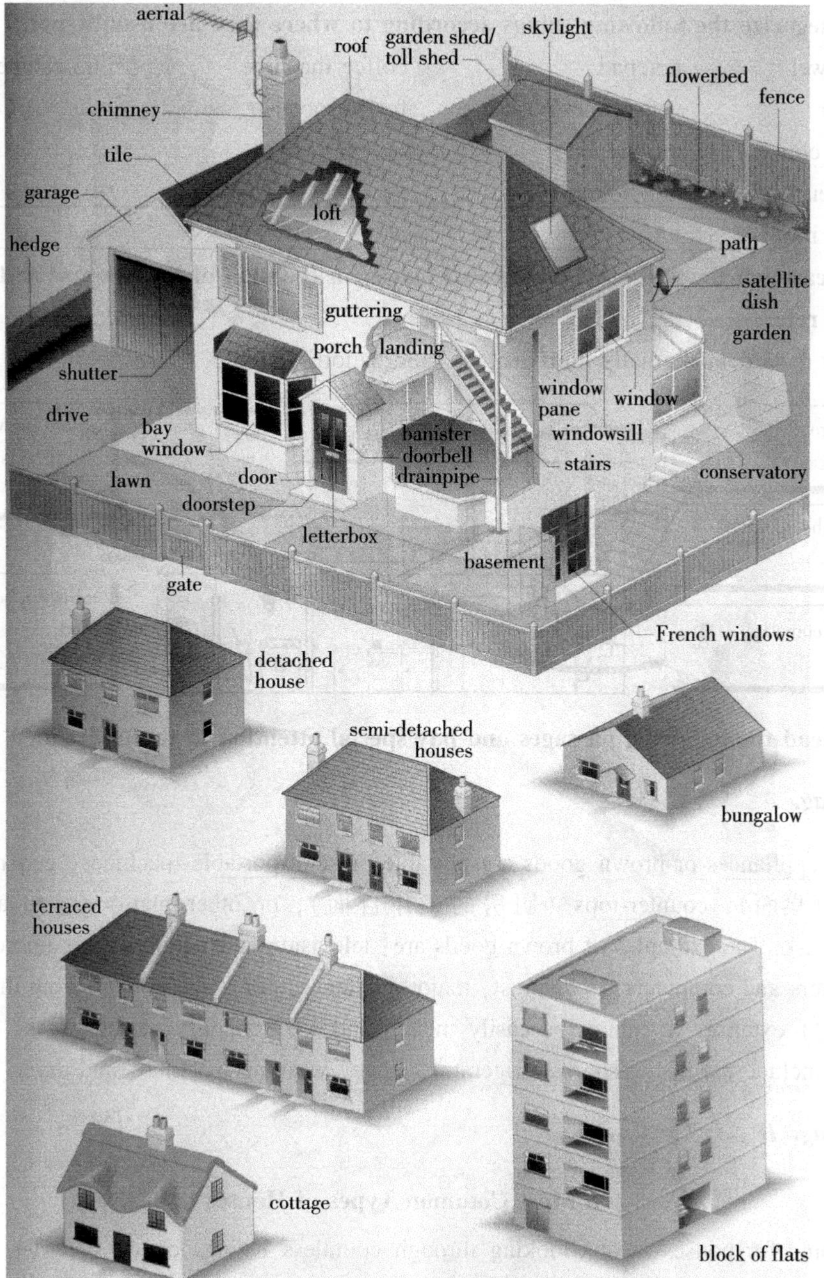

From *Macmillan English Dictionary*

Exercises

I. Categorize the following things according to where they are usually put.

tea towel	notepad	coffee machine	filing cabinet
printer	wastepaper basket	food processor	kettle
paper clip	microwave		

Kitchen: ________________________________

Study room: ________________________________

II. Please tell the names of the labeled places on the plan of the house. Use the provided names for reference.

pantry or larder; the hall; utility room; attic or loft; landing

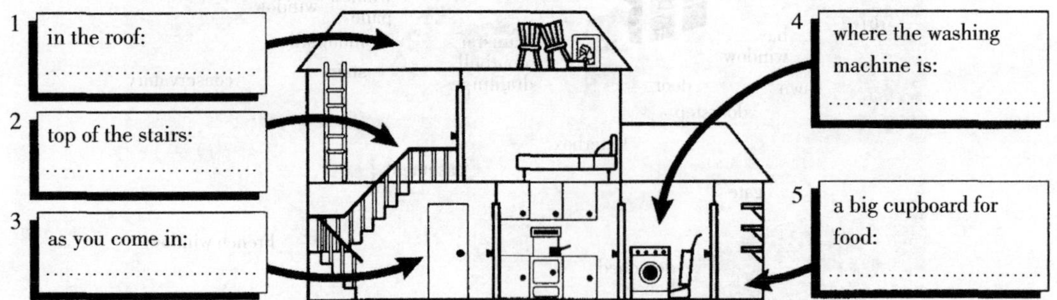

III. Read the following passages and pay special attention to the underlined words.

Passage A

Small appliances or brown goods are portable or semi-portable machines, generally used on table-tops（桌面）, counter-tops（厨房的工作台面）, or other platforms, to accomplish a household task. The examples of brown goods are: television and wireless sets; microwave oven; coffee makers and computers. In contrast, major appliances, or white goods [from their enameled（涂瓷漆的）exteriors], cannot be easily moved and are generally placed on the floor. Major appliances include the dishwasher, refrigerator, stove, washing machine, and dryer.

Passage B

8 Most Common Types of Houses

Shopping for houses means looking through countless listings on the Internet. Many times these lists don't come with pictures, so you have to simply imagine how the house looks like through the written description alone.

Most descriptions come with key words such as, a spacious bungalow, a cozy villa, or a practical row house.

In order to eliminate the confusion, below are the eight most common types of houses. Before you buy your house, check out some things your broker won't tell you.

Bungalow — A bungalow is classically defined as a one-story house, cottage, or cabin. Traditionally, bungalow style houses are associated with small square footage, though you can also find larger, generally newer bungalows. Bungalows generally do not have basements, and they were originally designed to provide affordable housing to the working class.

Single detached — A single detached is actually any house that stands on its own, and its four walls are not attached to another house. It is structurally separated from the neighboring houses and is surrounded by open land. Basically, a bungalow, cottage, or even mansion can be termed as a single detached house, as long as it is not connected to any other property through the same wall or tenement.

Duplex — The term itself refers to a two-fold apartment or condominium（公寓楼）where there are separate entrances for the dwelling units. Usually a duplex comes in the form of a two story house where a common wall separates the two areas. A duplex can then be extended to make three units or more, and then it would be termed as a "three-plex, four-plex, five-plex" and so on. This is also referred to as a semi-detached home.

Row house — Row houses are modern type of homes that are located in the same area and have the same architectural design and appearance. They are situated side by side, and the units share a common wall. These houses are usually priced less than single detached households in closed subdivisions.

Colonial house — This type of house features the designs that are related to the United States colonial period. Several types of colonial houses exist such as the French colonial, Spanish colonial, Dutch colonial, Georgian and German colonial. The houses that are built in the colonial style take their designs from the houses, government offices, and churches that were built sometime during the 16th to the 19th century.

Farm house — No particular design is associated with the style "farm house," but it is a term that describes the main house that is situated on a farm land. These houses are more practical than aesthetic（美学的）, but they are often well equipped in terms of insulation（隔热）and food storage.

Villa — A villa was once used to refer to as the upper class country homes of ancient Romans. Today, the term villa has evolved to refer to a beautiful, tasteful, upper class country home. The term villa can refer to the houses of the elite, and the properties with the description of villas are usually larger homes with landscaped gardens and perhaps a view of the sea or the countryside.

Mansion — A mansion is the word used to describe a very large house. In the US, real estate brokers define mansions as the houses with an area of 8,000 square feet or 740 square meters or more. Traditionally, mansions are characterized by having a large ballroom and numerous bedrooms. Today, however, there is no particular requirement as to what makes a mansion, aside from the fact that it should be a large and well-endowed（设施完善的）home.

These are only some of the most common types of houses that can usually be found in real estate listings. Some of the many other types of houses include the end of terrace（一排房屋中最

靠边的），deck houses，log cabins（小木屋），gambrels（复斜屋顶），and so on.

However, many of these terms are not as popular or as common as they once were (like castles for example). Whatever the purpose may be, learning about different types of houses gives us insight into different architectural viewpoints. It also helps us decide which type of house would be most suitable for our personal use.

Topic Six
Money

A. Personal finance

Sometimes in a shop they ask you: "How do you want to pay?" You can answer: "**Cash/ By cheque/By credit card.**"

In a bank you usually have a **current account**, which is one where you **pay in your salary** and then withdraw money to **pay your everyday bills**. The bank sends you a regular **bank statement** telling you how much money is in your account. You may also have a **savings account** where you **deposit** any extra money that you have and only **take money out** when you want to spend it on something special. You usually try to avoid having an **overdraft** or you end up paying a lot of **interests**. If your account is overdrawn, you can be said to be **in the red** (as opposed to **in the black** or **in credit**).

Sometimes the bank may lend you money — This is called a **bank loan**. If the bank (or **building society**) lends you money to buy a house, that money is called a **mortgage**.

When you buy (or, more formally, **purchase**) something in a shop, you usually pay for it **outright** but sometimes you buy **on credit**. Sometimes you may be offered a **discount** or a **reduction** on something you buy at a shop. This means that you get, say, £ 10 off perhaps because you are a student. You are often offered a discount if you buy **in bulk**. It is not usual to **haggle** about prices in a British shop, as it is in, say, a Turkish market. If you want to return something which you have bought to a shop, you may be given a **refund**, i. e. your money will be returned, provided you have a **receipt**.

The money that you pay for services, e. g. to a school or a lawyer, is usually called **tuition** or **fees**; the money paid for a journey is a **fare**.

If you buy something that you feel was very **good value**, it's a **bargain**. If you feel that it is definitely **not worth** what you paid for it, then you can call it a **rip-off** (very colloquial).

B. Public finance

The government collects money from citizens through **taxes**. **Income tax** is the tax collected on **wages** and **salaries**. **Inheritance tax** is collected on what people inherit from others.

Customs or **excise duties** have to be paid on the goods imported from other countries. **VAT**

or **Value Added Tax** is a tax paid on most goods and services when they are bought or purchased. Companies pay **corporation tax** on their profits. If you pay too much tax, you should be given some money back, a **tax rebate**.

The government also sometimes pays out money to the people in need, e. g. **unemployment benefit** (also known informally as **the dole**), **disability allowances** and student grants (to help pay for studying). Recipients draw a **pension**, **unemployment benefit** or are **on the dole** or **on social security**.

Every country has its own special **currency**. Every day the **rates of exchange** are published and you can discover, for example, how many dollars there are currently to the pound sterling.

A company may sell shares to the members of the public who are then said to have invested in that company. They should be paid a regular **dividend** on their investment, depending on the **profit** or **loss** made by the company.

Exercises

I. Circle the statements that best describe you. Count the number of circles under each type. The type with the most circles is your primary money personality type.

Type 1

1. I love spending money.
2. I feel emotionally satisfied when I spend money.
3. I cannot turn down a good sale, even if I have no need for the item.
4. I cannot control myself in stores.
5. I buy a lot of things that I don't need or don't use (for example, I don't cook, but I own many cookbooks and fancy kitchen appliances).
6. I am very impulsive when it comes to shopping. I will act and buy something before I have a chance to think about it.
7. I have a lot of debt, but I cannot or will not stop shopping.

Type 2

1. I only buy things on sale.
2. I actively clip coupons and make an event out of it.
3. I conserve energy — I like the concept of "going green."
4. I check my online bank account on a daily basis.
5. I do not use credit cards, but if I do, the balance is always paid off in full every month.
6. I do not have to "keep up with the Joneses" (buy every new and fad item) — really, I could care less.
7. I reduce, reuse and recycle.

Type 3

1. I have a purpose-filled life. I feel rewarded in what I do.
2. I work for myself and that has proven to be financially rewarding.

3. I always have ideas and I often put action to those ideas.

4. I understand that entrepreneurship (running my own business) is one of the main ways to get wealth.

5. I am comfortable with taking risks with money.

6. I don't depend on an employer for my financial well-being.

7. I am empowered by choice.

Type 4

1. I know what is going on with my money at all times.

2. I make my money work for me.

3. I am confident about my money choices.

4. I actively participate in the stock market. I believe in creating passive streams of income (income I do not have to work at to earn).

5. I like a balance between financial security and spending money.

6. I enjoy making budgets and being an active participant in planning what to do with my money.

7. I am empowered by money.

Your Money Personality-RESULTS

Please keep in mind; the results of this questionnaire ARE NOT CONCLUSIVE. It just gives you a look into what your current and major money habits are. Your money personality will change over time.

Type 1: Spenders

Spenders love to spend money. They feel satisfied emotionally when they spend money.

Spenders tend to be very compulsive shoppers. They will often buy things they do not need just for the sake of buying something. They are expert bargain shoppers and are pleased when they feel they have found a good deal. Some spenders may be controlled, while others may have a shopping addiction. Spenders are usually aware of their need to buy things and even worry about the debt that it creates. Sometimes that is still not enough to stop them from spending money.

Type 2: Savers

Savers tend to be the opposite of spenders. Many savers are very aware of how much they buy, spend, and use items. They clip coupons, keep up with sales, and are always trying to figure out how to save more money. Savers also tend to watch their carbon footprint (碳排放). This may not be out of concern for the environment, but because they want to save money on utility bills. They turn off the lights when leaving a room, close the refrigerator door quickly to keep in the cold, shop only when needed, and rarely use credit cards. On the extreme, they can be viewed as frugal or cheap. Savers avoid trends and like to see their money (and interest) grow in their many bank accounts.

Type 3: Entrepreneurs

Entrepreneurs (the people who run their own business) are driven by a passion to live a purposeful life. They do this while solving a business need. They know that running their own business is a sure way to get wealth. Despite being the highest income earners, they can be workaholics who are not motivated by money alone. Money is used as a way to measure their achievements. They enjoy the power and status that hard work and money bring. They are proud and reward themselves with the best cars, home, wines, etc. Entrepreneurs like to make the most out of every dollar that they can. They often favor investing in business ventures, real estate or the stock markets. This is a way for them to create passive income (the money that is earned without working for it).

Type 4: Planners/Investors

Planners are very aware of money. They understand their financial situation and try to put their money to work. Regardless of their current finances, they seek a day when passive investments (the money they earn without working) will give them enough money to cover all of their bills. The actions of Planners/Investors are carefully chosen. Their investments show the need to take some risk in pursuit of their goals.

II. Fill in the table below for your own country.

Rate of inflation	________
Exchange rate (against the US dollar)	________
Interest rate	________
Basic level of income tax	________
Rate of VAT	________
Monthly state pension	________

Note:

➢ VAT: Value Added Tax，增值税（是对销售货物或者提供加工、修理修配劳务以及进口货物的单位和个人，就其实现的增值额征收的一个税种。）

III. Read the following passages and answer the following questions. Please pay special attention to the underlined words.

Passage A

Money

Money is any object or record that is generally accepted as payment for goods and services and the repayment of debts in a given socio-economic context or country. The main functions of money are distinguished as: a medium of exchange; a unit of account; a store of value; and, occasionally in the past, a standard of deferred（推迟）payment. Any kind of object or secure verifiable record that fulfills these functions can serve as money.

Money is historically an emergent market phenomenon establishing a commodity money, but nearly all contemporary money systems are based on **fiat money**. Fiat money is without intrinsic use value as a physical commodity, and derives its value by being declared by a government to be legal tender（法定货币）; that is, it must be accepted as a form of payment within the boundaries of the country, for "all debts, public and private."

The money supply of a country consists of currency (banknotes and coins) and bank money (the balance held in checking accounts and savings accounts). Bank money usually forms by far the largest part of the money supply.

Questions:

1. What are the major functions of money?
2. What is fiat money?
3. As for the money supply of a country, which part is the larger one?

Note:

➢ commodity money/metal money/fiat money/bank money:（按货币的形态，大致可以分为）实物货币、金属货币、纸币和存款货币

Passage B

Commercial Bank Money

Commercial bank money or demand deposits are the claims against financial institutions that can be used for the purchase of goods and services. A demand deposit account is an account from which funds can be withdrawn at any time by check or cash withdrawal without giving the bank or financial institution any prior notice. Banks have the legal obligation to return funds held in demand deposits immediately upon demand (or "at call"). Demand deposit withdrawals can be performed in person, via checks or bank drafts, using automatic teller machines (ATMs), or through online banking.

Commercial bank money is created through fractional-reserve banking（部分准备金银行制度）, the banking practice where banks keep only a fraction of their deposits in reserve (as cash and other highly liquid assets) and lend out the remainder, while maintaining the simultaneous obligation to redeem all these deposits upon demand. Commercial bank money differs from commodity and fiat money in two ways. Firstly, it is non-physical, as its existence is only reflected in the account ledgers（分类账）of banks and other financial institutions, and secondly, there is some element of risk that the claim will not be fulfilled if the financial institution becomes insolvent（破产的）. The process of fractional-reserve banking has a cumulative effect of money creation by commercial banks, as it expands money supply (cash and demand deposits) beyond what it would otherwise be. Because of the prevalence of fractional reserve banking, the broad money supply of most countries is a multiple larger than the amount of base money（基准货币）created by the country's central bank. The money multiplier（货币增长倍数）is determined by the reserve requirement（准备金要求）or other financial ratio（财务比率）requirements imposed by financial regulators.

The money supply of a country is usually held to be the total amount of currency in circulation plus the total amount of checking and savings deposits in the commercial banks in the country. In modern economies, relatively little of the money supply is in physical currency. For example, in December 2010 in the U. S., of the $ 8853. 4 billion in broad money supply (M2), only $ 915. 7 billion (about 10%) consisted of physical coins and paper money.

Questions:

1. Try to guess the Chinese meaning of "demand deposits."

2. How does commercial bank money differ from commodity and fiat money?

3. What are the major components of the money supply of a country?

Note:

➢ central bank：中央银行（指代表政府经济利益的银行，多与其他银行交易而不直接与普通人民交易。）

Passage C

Financial Management for a New Year

Here are five ideas to help you get a good start—not just for a new year, but the start of a new decade.

1. Set up a savings plan.

Ever since the financial tsunami（金融海啸）swept all before it in September 2008, many people have saved furiously. That's a good thing, but there's a temptation to lose that discipline（自制力）once the storm clouds start to break.

While the economy remains fragile and many people are still out of work, the signs of recovery are becoming more and more apparent. Among your New Year's resolutions include a savings goal that is a function of your regular income, even if it's not a large amount of money. Maintaining the discipline is crucial. The amount of savings can grow over time.

2. Build a rainy-day fund.

A rainy-day fund（应急基金）, which your savings plan can feed, should cover about six months of income. It's a form of personal insurance valuable in these rapidly changing times.

This fund should be kept in safe and easy-to-tap assets. Laddering certificates of deposit out six months（存入6个月的阶梯式定期存款）is one way.

That means buying CDs (Current Deposit, 活期存款) of one month, two months, etc. to six months. As each CD matures, you buy another six-month CD to keep the ladder in place.

3. Migrate to a debit card or to the plastic that must be paid each month.

Cutting up credit cards makes a lot of sense and eliminating all credit-card debt makes even more sense. The interest rates associated with credit-card debt can easily overwhelm the returns you can get elsewhere.

But the world is moving away from cash at a rapid clip. The notion of having no plastic is barely feasible. Try buying a plane ticket with cash and see what that sparks in the government computers.

Second best are charge cards（签账卡）that require payment in full each month. Ever since I paid off my last credit-card debt in 1996, I have only used a charge card or a debit card. It gets tough, especially around big events such as Christmas. But it's nice to not have a tempting and expensive option in the wallet.

4. Rebalance your investments.

Last year, rebalancing meant adding to stock exposure after a year of steep stock losses. That notion felt mildly crazy at the time, but it proved wise.

That's because stocks rallied from the March lows and put in a remarkably strong year. Now, most of us are probably too heavy on the stock side of the equation. Moving some of the money into bonds or even cash to regain balance would be prudent (谨慎的).

5. Plan to reward yourself.

New Year's resolutions usually don't stick and a big reason is that it's all like eating sawdust (木屑). Go on a diet, save money, and don't spend. We start the year like ascetic monks and by February we discover that the monastic (修士的) life isn't for us.

Therefore, it's important to have one resolution that is fun.

Questions:

1. The underlined word "discipline" in Para. 2 refers to ________.

   A. spending money wisely　　B. spending less money

   C. saving money regularly　　D. making more money

2. A rainy-day fund should cover about ________ months of income.

   A. 4　　B. 5　　C. 6　　D. 7

3. "Adding to stock exposure after a year of steep stock losses" proved ________.

   A. stupid　　B. useless　　C. wise　　D. meaningful

Topic Seven

Arts

A. What are arts?

The arts are a vast subdivision of culture, composed of many endeavors (or art forms) united by their employment of the human creative impulse. The term implies a broader range of disciplines than "art," which in modern usage usually refers only to the **visual arts**. The other major constituents of the arts are the **literary arts**, more often called **literature**—including **poetry**, **novels** and **short stories**, among others—and the **performing arts**, including **music**, **dance**, **magic**, **theatre** and **film**. Literary arts and creative writing are interchangeable terms. These divisions are by no means absolute as there are art forms which combine a visual element with performance (e. g. film) and the written word (e. g. **comics**).

B. What are specific art forms?

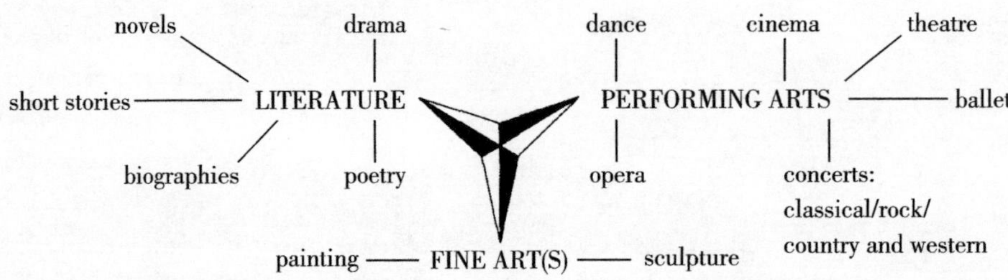

✓ **Poetry**: epic 叙事诗, lyric 抒情诗, ode 颂诗, elegy 悲歌 (挽歌), sonnet 十四行诗, anthology 诗集, verse 韵文。

✓ **Story**: fiction 小说, narrative 故事, folklore 民间故事, fairy tale 童话, anecdote 轶事, fable 寓言。

✓ We often also include **architecture** and **ceramics** (陶艺) within the arts.

✓ **The arts** (plural) covers everything in the network. **Art** (singular, uncountable) usually means **fine art**, but can also refer to technique and creativity.

✓ **Dance** usually refers to modern artistic dance forms; **ballet** usually has a more traditional feel, unless we say **modern ballet**.

Notes：

➢ ode：颂诗（以特殊的主题歌颂人物或事物的抒情诗。）

➢ verse：韵文（与散文相对，语言的排列具有一定的规律，诗歌为其代表形式。）

C. Describing a performance

Tonight we did the "Vegas Thing", and went to see a show. Specifically, we saw **Zumanity** at New York, one of seven cirque shows currently running in Vegas. How would I describe the show Modern Dance, superb athleticism, a touch of **comedy**, audience participation, combined with lots of sex? It was a beautiful show—I don't know how typical it was of Cirque shows—and one that I enjoyed. But it wasn't a show in the theatre sense—there was no **plot** or **through line**.

Note：

➢ Zumanity：人类动物园秀（是拉斯维加斯太阳马戏团的巨作，就像处于充满声光效应的万花筒里观赏超出人类体能极限的马戏表演。）

D. Words connected with events in the arts

There is an **exhibition** of work by contemporary British artists.

He acted in radio **dramas**.

We need volunteers to help build and print the **set**.

The Festival of Asian Arts & Music will include two days of live **performances**.

The venue for the **show** is Birmingham's National Exhibition Centre Hall.

What's **on** at the cinema/theatre, etc. recently?

Exercises

I. Which branch of the arts do you think these people are talking about?

Example: "It was a strong cast but the play itself is weak." *Theatre*

1. "Animation doesn't have to be just *Disney*, you know."
2. "It's called Peace. It stands in the main square."
3. "It was just pure movement, with very exciting rhythms."
4. "I was falling asleep by the second act."
5. "Oils to me don't have the delicacy of water-colours."
6. "I read them and imagine what they'd be like on stage."
7. "Her design for the new shopping centre won an award."
8. "The first chapter was boring but it got better later."
9. "It doesn't have to rhyme to be good."

II. Discuss how much you know about the following people.

1. Leonardo da Vinci

2. Vincent Willem Van Gogh
3. William Shakespeare
4. Charles John Huffam Dickens
5. Ernest Miller Hemingway

III. Each one of these sentences contains a mistake of the usage of the words connected with the arts. Find the mistake and correct it. You may need a dictionary.

Example: The scene at this theatre projects right out into the audience.

Not "scene" but "stage" (the place where the actors perform).

1. "I wandered lonely as a cloud" is my favourite verse of English poetry.
2. What's the name of the editorial of that book you recommended? Was it Cambridge University Press?
3. Most of the novels in this collection are only five or six pages long. They're great for reading on short journeys.
4. He's a very famous sculpture; he did that statue in the park, you know, the one with the soldiers.
5. The sceneries are excellent in that new production of *Macbeth*, so dark and mysterious.
6. There's an exposition of ceramics at the museum next week.
7. What's in at the Opera House next week? Anything interesting?

IV. Read the following passages and pay special attention to the underlined words.

Passage A

William Shakespeare (baptised 26 April, 1564; died 23 April, 1616) was an English poet and playwright, widely regarded as the greatest writer in the English language and the world's pre-eminent <u>dramatist</u>. He is often called England's national poet and the "Bard of Avon" (艾冯诗人，莎士比亚的别称，因莎士比亚出生并安葬于艾冯河畔的斯特拉特福). His surviving <u>works</u>, including some collaborations, consist of about 38 plays, 154 <u>sonnets</u>, two long narrative <u>poems</u>, and several other poems. His plays have been translated into every major living language and are performed more often than those of any other playwright.

Shakespearean representative works have 4 big *tragedies—Hamlet*, *Othello*, *King Lear* and *Macbeth*; 4 big comedies—*A Midsummer Night's Dream*, *The Merchant of Venice*, *Twelfth Night*, *As You Like It*; historical plays: *King Henry the Fourth Part 1*, *King Henry the Fifth*, *King Richard II* and so on. He had written 154 sonnets, two leading poems. Jonson says he is "the time's soul"; Max says he and Helladic Aisiku Ross are "the greatest human being drama genius." Although Shakespeare uses English writing only, he is a famous writer of the world. Most works of his have already been translated into various languages, whose plays perform also in a lot of countries.

Shakespeare was born and raised in Stratford-upon-Avon. At the age of 18, he married Anne Hathaway, with whom he had three children: Susanna, and twins Hamnet and Judith. Between 1585 and 1592, he began a successful career in London as an actor, writer, and part owner of a playing company called the Lord Chamberlain's Men, later known as the King's Men. He appears to have retired to Stratford around 1613, where he died three years later. Few records of Shakespeare's private life survive, and there has been considerable speculation about such matters as his physical appearance, sexuality, religious beliefs, and whether the works attributed to him were written by others.

Shakespeare produced most of his known works between 1589 and 1613. His early plays were mainly comedies and histories, genres（体裁）he raised to the peak of sophistication and artistry by the end of the sixteenth century. He then wrote mainly tragedies until about 1608, including *Hamlet*, *King Lear*, and *Macbeth*, considered as some of the finest works in the English language. In his last phase, he wrote tragicomedies, also known as romances, and collaborated with other playwrights.

Many of his plays were published in the editions of varying quality and accuracy during his lifetime. In 1623, two of his former theatrical colleagues published the First Folio, a collected edition of his dramatic works that included all but two of the plays now recognized as Shakespeare's.

Shakespeare was a respected poet and playwright in his own day, but his reputation did not rise to its present heights until the nineteenth century. The Romantics, in particular, acclaimed Shakespeare's genius, and the Victorians worshipped Shakespeare with a reverence（尊敬）that George Bernard Shaw called "bardolatry（莎士比亚崇拜）". In the twentieth century, his works were repeatedly adopted and rediscovered by new movements in scholarship and performance. His plays remain highly popular today and are constantly studied, performed and reinterpreted in diverse cultural and political contexts throughout the world.

Questions:

1. *King Lear* is a ________.

   A. comedy　　B. tragedy

   C. romance　　D. tragicomedy

2. Stratford is the place where Shakespeare ________.

   A. was born　　B. was raised　　C. died　　D. all the above

3. Shakespeare's reputation in his life time was ________ its present heights.

   A. better than　　B. as good as

   C. no better than　　D. unknown compared to

Passage B

Papercuts

Chinese papercuts are rich in content. The auspicious（吉利的）designs symbolize good luck and the avoidance of evil. The child, lotus and bottle gourd designs suggest a family with a large number of children and grandchildren. Domestic birds, livestock, fruit, fish and worms are also familiar objects depicted by Chinese farmers in papercuts.

Papercuts are mainly used as decorations and patterns for religious and ornamental purposes. Papercuts can also be used as ornaments on gates, windows, walls, columns, mirrors, lamps and lanterns. They are still widely used today at important festivals, especially during the New Year. It is very important to put papercuts on the entrance gates for good luck for the family. Papercuts can also serve as presents or as decorations or gifts and sacrificial offerings（祭品）to the ancestors or gods.

Paper and scissors are the usual materials used for making papercuts, but sometimes an engraving knife（雕刻刀）is also used.

The papercuts made in different areas have different characteristics. Shanxi window papercuts are simple and bold. Guangling papercuts from Shanxi Province are painted with many colors and portray opera figures. The Nanjing papercuts of Jiangsu Province are simple, robust and skillful. The Yixing papercuts of Jiangxi Province are magnificent and neat. The Nantong papercuts of Jiangsu Province are delicate and beautiful. The Fuoshan papercuts of Guangdong Province are colorful and decorative and utilize a variety of production techniques. The Gaomi papercuts of Shandong Province are delicate and fine.

Topic Eight
Education

A. Stages in UK education system

Here are different stages of education in Britain.

School	Stage	Content
play-school nursery school	pre-school (2–5 years old)	some early learning playing
infant school junior school	primary (5/6–12/13 years old)	basic reading, writing. arithmetic, art, etc
comprehensive school or grammar school	secondary (12/13—16–18)	wide range of subjects in arts and sciences and technical areas
college or polytechnic or university	further/higher (18+)	degrees/diplomas in specialised academic areas

Note: **Comprehensive schools** in the UK are for all abilities, but **grammar** schools are usually by competitive entry. **The Public schools** in the UK are very famous private schools. **Polytechnics** are similar to **universities**, but the courses tend to be more practically-oriented. **Colleges** include **teacher-training colleges**, **technical colleges** and general **colleges of further education**.

B. Exams and qualifications

take/do/sit/resit an exam

pass/do well in/put up a good show in/improve one's grade in an exam

fail/do badly in an exam

✓ Before an exam it's a good idea to **revise** for it.

✓ If you **skip classes/lectures**, you'll feel difficult to keep up with other students.

✓ If you play **truant**, **to play hooky**, your **exam results** will be disappointing.

✓ If you study all the semester, you won't need to **cram for** the examination.

✓ The **school-leaving exams** are held in May/June. In some schools, colleges and universities, instead of tests and exams, there is **continuous assessment**, with **marks**, e. g. 65%, or grades, e. g. A, B+, for essays and projects during the term.

✓ If you pass your university exams, you **graduate** (get a degree), then you're a **graduate.**

C. Talking about education

Discuss with your partner about your country's education system.

How much do you know about **single-sex education** and **coeducation** school?

How is the **continuing education** provided for adults?

Is **homeschooling** common in your country?

How's the **scholarship policy** in your university?

Have you ever gone to **preparatory school**?

Note: Mixed-sex education, also known as coeducation (American English) or mixed-gender education, is the integrated education of male and female students in the same environment. This and single-sex education are alternatives.

Exercises

I. Use the information of the UK's education system listed in the previous section, and make a table to illustrate the education system in your country.

II. Fill in the blanks with proper words.

The term (1) ________ refers to a school for the children who are not old enough to attend kindergarten. It is a nursery school. During this education period, children will be taught the alphabet, counting, shapes and colors, etc.

(2) ________ (or elementary) education consists of the first 5 – 7 years of formal, structured education. In general, it consists of six or eight years of schooling starting at the age of five or six. The division between primary and (3) ________ education is somewhat arbitrary, but it generally occurs at about eleven or twelve years of age. Some education systems have separate middle schools, with the transition to the final stage of secondary education taking place at around the age of fourteen.

(4) ________, also called tertiary, third stage, or post secondary education, is the non-compulsory educational level that follows the completion of a school providing a (5) ________ education, such as a high school or secondary school.

III. Here are some words connected with education. If necessary, use a dictionary to help you check that you understand what they all mean. Then divide them into three groups.

college	freshman	sophomore	university	junior	credit
repeater	syllabus	term paper	grade	graduate	school
GPA	curriculum	diploma	undergraduate	senior	

Students: ____________________

Academic affairs management: ____________________

Educational institution: ____________________

Notes:

➢ GPA: Grade Point Average（即学生获得的学分的平均值。）

IV. Read the following passages and answer the following questions. Please pay special attention to the underlined words.

Passage A

Education

American children start their education in elementary school. Most youngsters enter first grade at around six years of age. Children can prepare for this step by attending preschool and kindergarten from ages three to five. Young learners finish elementary school in fifth or sixth grade. From there, students go on to junior high school until eighth or ninth grade. Americans complete their required education in high school. They graduate and receive a diploma after twelfth grade.

Beyond high school, Americans have many chances for further education. In contrast to other countries, the U. S. has no national college entrance exam. Instead, private companies give exams to students. Universities decide which tests students must take. In addition to test scores, university officials also consider applicants' high school grades and other activities. Universities give scholarships and financial aid to help many who cannot afford the high tuition costs. The students with less academic goals may enroll in vocational schools or community colleges.

Questions:

1. When do American children start their elementary school life?
2. Is there any national college entrance exams in America?
3. How do American universities help those students with tuition paying problems?

Passage B

American Grading System

The academic grading in the United States most commonly takes on the form of five letter grades. Historically, the grades were A, B, C, D, and F—A being the highest and F denoting failure, the lowest.

Numerical and letter grades

The A–F（A–F）quality index is typically quantified by correlation to a five-point numerical scale as follows：

A=4.0　　B=3.0　　C=2.0　D=1.0　　F=0.0

Grade	Percentage/%
A	90–100
B	80–89
C	70–79
D	60–69
F	59 and below

Grade point average

Grade point average（GPA）is a number that represents the average of a student's grades during his/her time at an institution. Usually it is weighted by the number of credits given for the enrolled courses.

Most high schools and nearly all colleges in the United States use a four-point system. The universities in Hong Kong and Canada, as well as some schools in Singapore, also use this system. Under the GPA system, the maximum grade is 4.0 which is equivalent to 100 on a 100-point grading scale.

Numerical values are applied to grades as follows：

A=4　　B=3　　C=2　　D=1　　F=0

This allows grades to be easily averaged. Additionally, many schools add 0.33 for A+grade and subtract 0.33 for A−grade. Therefore, a B+yields a 3.33 whereas an A−yields a 3.67. A+, if given, is usually assigned a value of 4.0（equivalent to an A）due to the common assumption that a 4.00 is the best possible grade-point average, although 4.33 is awarded at some institutions. In some places, 0.25 or 0.3 instead of 0.33 is added for A+ grade and subtracted for A−grade. Other institutions maintain a mid-grade and award 0.5 for the grade. For example, an AB would receive a 3.5 grade point and a BC would receive a 2.5 grade point.

Questions：

1. What's the popular academic grading policy in the U. S.?
2. What is GPA? Explain it in details.
3. Based on the last paragraph, what is the Arabic numeral for C+?

Notes：

➢ college：专科大学（区别于 university，即综合大学，主要为本科生提供教育的四年制大学。）

➢ university：综合大学（除大部分州设立的州立大学之外，私立大学较多。）

➢ community college：社区学院（两年制学院，学生学习一项技能或大学预科课程。）

Topic Nine

Sports

A. Common sports

Swimming 游泳	Artistic gymnastics 竞技体操	Gymnastics trampoline 蹦床
Freestyle 自由泳	Hockey 曲棍球	Balance beam 平衡木
Backstroke 仰泳	Floor exercise 自由体操	Wrestling 摔跤
Breaststroke 蛙泳	Pommel horse 鞍马	Rowing 赛艇
Butterfly 蝶泳	Rings 吊环	Boxing 拳击
Water polo 水球	Vault 跳马	Canoeing 皮划艇
Diving 跳水	Parallel bars 双杠	Judo 柔道
High jump 跳高	Horizontal bar 单杠	Taekwondo 跆拳道

B. Equipment—what you use in different sports

golf——golf clubs

cricket/table-tennis/baseball——bat

hockey——stick

canoeing——paddle

darts——dart

fishing——rod/line

squash/tennis/badminton——racket

boxing——boxing gloves

snooker/pool/billiards——cue

rowing——oar

archery——bow

C. Athletics—some field events

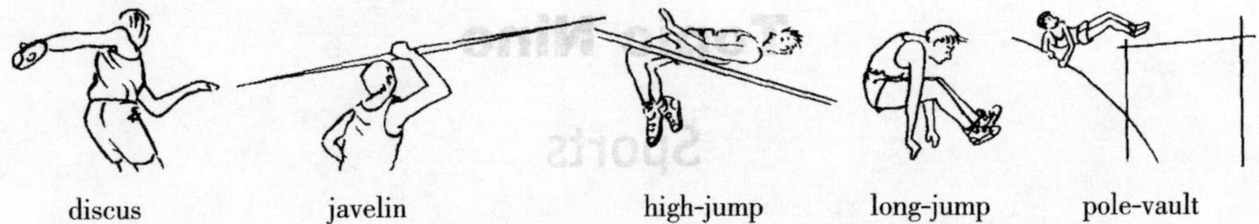

The young track and field athlete could already hurl the **discus** 60 yards.

The **high jumper** took off at a bad angle.

The great-grandmother is also a keen **hammer and javelin thrower** and believes other pensioners should follow her example.

If you **vault** something or vault over it, you jump quickly onto or over it.

The **sprinter** himself thinks he can run the race at 9. 4 seconds. [fast over short distances]

D. Useful expressions in the context of sport

Our team **won/lost by** three goals/points.

She **broke the** Olympic **record** last year.

He **holds the record** for the 100 metres breast-stroke.

Liverpool **beat** Hamburg 4–2 yesterday.

The team have never been **defeated**. [more formal than beat]

How many **goals/points** have you scored this season?

I think I'll **take up** bowls next spring and give up golf.

E. People who do particular sports

-er can be used for many sports, e. g. footballer, swimmer, windsurfer, high jumper, cricketer, golfer, etc.

Players are often necessary, e. g. the tennis player, snooker player, and darts player; we can also say football player, cricket player.

Some names must be learnt separately, e. g. the canoeist, cyclist, mountaineer, jockey, archer, and gymnast.

Exercises

I. Based on the key words, guess what sports are probably talked about.

1. throw, pitcher, runner, catcher, home plate
2. hole, grassland, water hazard, backswing, fairway

3. net, baseline, serve, linesman, tramlines
4. dunk, pass, score, forward, dodge
5. goal, goalpost, referee, goalkeeper, penalty spot

II. Discuss with your partner and talk about the functions of the following equipment in gym.

1. step machine 2. cross-trainer 3. weights 4. barbell 5. treadmill
6. multigym 7. rowing machine 8. bench 9. exercise bike 10. mats

III. Make sure you know which sports these places are associated with, as in the cxample. Use a dictionary if necessary.

1. court *tennis, squash, etc.*
2. course
3. ring
4. pitch
5. rink
6. alley
7. piste

IV. Read the following passages and pay special attention to the underlined words.

Passage A

The Origin of Sports

When did sport begin? If sport is, in essence, play, the claim might be made that sport is much older than humankind, for, as we all have observed, the beasts play. Dogs and cats wrestle (摔跤) and play ball games. Fishes and birds dance. The apes have simple and pleasurable games. Frolicking (嬉戏) infants, school children playing tag, and adult arm wrestlers are demonstrating strong, transgenerational and transspecies bonds with the universe of animals — past, present, and future. Young animals, particularly, tumble (翻筋斗), chase, run wrestle, mock, imitate, and laugh (or so it seems) to the point of delighted exhaustion. Their play and ours appear to serve no other purpose than to give pleasure to the players, and apparently, to remove us temporarily from the anguish (苦恼) of life in earnest.

Some philosophers have claimed that our playfulness is the most noble part of our basic nature. In their generous conceptions, play harmlessly and experimentally permits us to put our creative forces, fantasy, and imagination into action. Play is release from the tedious battles against scarcity and decline which are the incessant (不断的), and inevitable tragedies of life. This is a grand conception that excites and provokes. The holders of this view claim that the origins of our highest accomplishments—liturgy (礼拜仪式), literature, and law — can be traced to a play impulse which, paradoxically (自相矛盾地), we see most purely enjoyed by young beasts and children. Our sports, in this rather happy view of human nature, are more splendid creations of the nondatable, transspecies play impulse.

Passage B

If You Want to Win in Sports, Wear Red

If winning is everything, British anthropologists（人类学家）have some advice: Wear red. Their survey of four sports at the 2004 Olympic Games in Athens shows competitors were more likely to win their contests if they wore red uniforms or red body armor.

"Across a range of sports, we find that wearing red is consistently associated with a higher probability of winning," report Russell A. Hill and Robert A. Barton of the University of Durham in England. Their findings are in Thursday's issue of the journal *Nature*.

Red coloration（着色）is associated with aggression in many animals. Often it is sexually selected so that scarlet markings signal male dominance.

Just think of the red stripes on the scowling（闷闷不乐的）face of the male Mandrill, Africa's largest monkey species. But red is not exclusively a male trait. It's the female black widow spider that is venomous（有毒的）and displays a menacing red dot on her abdomen.

Similarly, the color's effect also may subconsciously intimidate opponents in athletic contests, especially when the athletes are equal in skill and strength, the researchers suggest.

In their survey, the anthropologists analyzed the results of four combat sports at the summer games: boxing, tae kwon do（跆拳道）, Greco-Roman wrestling（古典式摔跤）and freestyle wrestling.

In those events, the athletes were randomly assigned red protective gear and other sportswear. The athletes wearing red gear won more often in 16 of 21 rounds of competition in all four events.

The effect was the same regardless of weight classes, too: 19 of 29 classes had more red winners, and only four rounds had more blue winners.

Keys to Exercises

Part I

Lexicology

Chapter 1

I. 1. A 2. C 3. A 4. D 5. C 6. D 7. A 8. C 9. D 10. B

II. 1. core 2. conventional 3. meaning 4. minimal

Chapter 2

I. 1. C 2. B 3. A 4. B 5. B 6. A 7. C 8. C 9. B 10. D

II. 1. Old English 2. 1500 3. French 4. Latin, Greek

Chapter 3

I. 1. B 2. C 3. C 4. B 5. B 6. B 7. B 8. B 9. B 10. A

11. C 12. A 13. C 14. B 15. B 16. A 17. A 18. D 19. A 20. A

II. 1. inflectional 2. affixes 3. prefixes 4. prefixation 5. root 6. back formation

III.

1. Prefixation is the formation of new words by adding prefixes to roots. Prefixes do not generally change the word class but only modify its meaning, e. g. unsafe.
   Suffixation is the formation of new words by adding suffixes to roots. They mainly change the word class, e. g. safety.
2. Initialisms are pronounced letter by letter. e. g. VIP.
   Acronyms are pronounced as a normal word, e. g. NATO.
3. Suffixation is the formation of new words by adding suffixes to roots, such as creation. Back formation is the opposite process of suffixation, the method of creating words by removing the supposed suffixes, such as edit from editor.

Chapter 4

I. 1. C 2. D 3. B 4. D 5. C

II.

1. The collocative meaning refers to that part of the word meaning suggested by the words before or after the word in discussion. For example *pretty* and *handsome* share the conceptual meaning of "good-looking," but collocate with different nouns.
2. The conceptual meaning is the meaning given in the dictionary and forms the core of word meaning, so it is constant and relatively stable, which forms the basis for communication.
   The associative meaning is the secondary meaning supplemented to the conceptual meaning. It is open-ended and indeterminate.

3. The grammatical meaning refers to that part of the meaning of the word which indicates grammatical relationships such as part of speech of words, the singular and plural meaning of nouns, the tense meaning of verbs and their inflectional forms, e. g. forget, forgets, forgot, forgotten, and forgetting.

Chapter 5

I. 1. B 2. D 3. D 4. D 5. B 6. B 7. C 8. B 9. B 10. C

II. 1. concatenation 2. identical 3. contradictory 4. Homographs

III.

1. Polysemy refers to the condition in which a word has two meanings or more. For example "neck": *n.* (1) the part of your body that joins your head to your shoulders; (2) the part of a piece of clothing that goes around your neck…
2. Radiation refers to the semantic process in which the primary meaning stands at the center and the secondary meanings proceed out of it in every direction like rays. The meanings are independent of one another, but can all be traced back to the central meaning, such as "neck." While concatenation means the semantic process in which the meaning of a word moves gradually away from its first sense until the original meaning is totally lost, such as "treacle."
3. There are four sources of synonyms: (1) Borrowing—fire (En) & flame (Fr); (2) Dialects and regional English—railway (BrE) & railroad (AmE); (3) Figurative and euphemistic use of words—occupation & walk of life (fig.); (4) Coincidence with idiomatic expressions—win & gain the upper hand.
4. The differences between synonyms boil down to three areas: denotation, connotation, and application.
   (1) Difference in denotation: Synonyms differ in the range and intensity of meaning. The verb "understand" is used in a much more extended sense than "comprehend."
   (2) Difference in connotation: Synonyms differ in the stylistic appropriateness and affective values. "Wood" is native and not style-specific, whereas "forest" is borrowed and is more formal.
   (3) Difference in application: Synonyms differ in usage and collocation. For example, we say an "empty" box, but a "vacant" seat.
5.

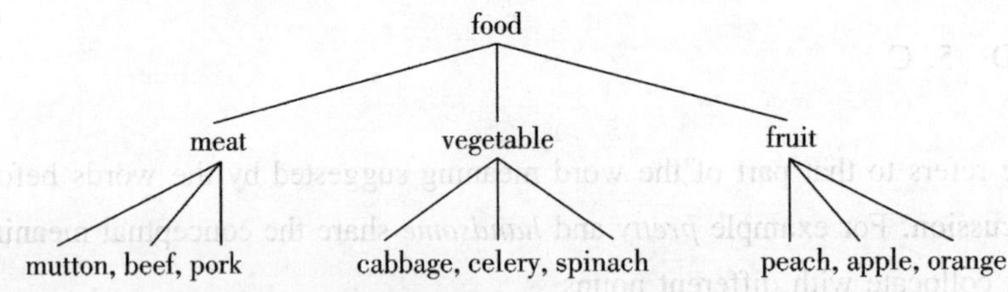

6. *Long time no see* is usually said as a form of greeting between two friends when they meet after a long time. Here the customer cleverly employed the structure of the idiom to his advantage to criticize in a humorous way the bad quality of the food served at the restaurant. *Long time no sea* implies that "sea food kept for a long time is not fit for eating."

7. In the two sentences, [b] is better than [a]. In [b], the writer uses subordinates/hyponyms, which are concrete and precise, presenting a vivid verbal picture; in [a], the superordinates only convey a general and vague idea.

Chapter 6

I. 1. A 2. A 3. C 4. A 5. A 6. B 7. B

II. 1. degradation 2. transfer 3. minister 4. extension/generalization 5. degradation

III. That's true. The vocabulary is the most unstable element of a language. It has been undergoing constant changes both in form and content. Many of Shakespearean words were used in different senses from what they have now in contemporary dictionaries.

Chapter 7

I. 1. D 2. B 3. C 4. A 5. C 6. C 7. C 8. A 9. D 10. B 11. D 12. C

II. 1. ambiguity 2. polysemy 3. word 4. antonymy

III.

1. Contextual clues are the hints given by the author which might help readers to grasp the concept or understand the idea, when a new word appears for the first time.
   (a) Definition—kinesics（体势学，身体语言学）
   (b) Explanation—microprocessors（微处理器）
2. We can work out the meaning of the word "avocado" to be a kind of fruit through the following contextual clues of relevant details: ① smack lips (something eatable); ② glance up at the branches (something people get from the tree); ③ ripe (fruit).
3. These two sentences are ambiguous due to the structure. The first sentence may mean "The fish is cooked or served, so ready for people to eat" or "The fish is ready to eat things." Its meaning can be pinned down if we change it into "What a nice smell! The fish is ready to eat." The second sentence can be interpreted as "I like Mary better than I like Jean" or "I like Mary better than Jean like Mary." To achieve clarity, we can either say "I like Mary better than Jean does" or "I like Mary better than I do Jean" or "I like Mary better as Jean is untidy," etc.

Chapter 8

Part A

I.

make	**get**	**take**
a contribution	a diploma	*risks*
a breakthrough	a promotion	the temperature
a profit	experience	the lead
arrangements	qualifications	the initiative
endeavors	the sack	responsibility
judgments	training	possession

II. 1. resolve 2. exerting 3. obtained 4. decline 5. poses
6. commit 7. imposed 8. aroused 9. way
10. builds lays seals disturbed hatch

III.

DCBFJ GHAIE

IV. 1. correspond with 2. derive... from 3. delighted in
4. insure... against 5. account for 6. elaborate on
7. deprived of 8. resort to

Part B

I. 1. narrowly 2. vaguely 3. softly 4. reluctantly 5. miserably
6. honestly 7. harshly 8. heavily 9. bitterly 10. high and low

II. 1. heatedly 2. brutally 3. markedly 4. sincerely 5. frankly
6. frantically 7. completely 8. steadily

III. CEDGAFB

Part C

I. 1. C 2. J 3. I 4. H 5. B 6. D 7. G 8. F 9. A 10. E

II. 1. coverage 2. booster 3. force 4. rate 5. services
6. base 7. building 8. stories

IV. 1. J 2. A 3. H 4. I 5. G 6. B 7. D 8. C 9. F 10. E

Part D

I 1. e 2. a 3. c 4. d 5. f 6. b 7. g 8. h 9. j 10. i

1. delicately balanced 2. enthusiastically received
3. highly qualified 4. ideally situated
5. badly mistaken 6. dangerously overcrowded
7. carefully chosen 8. closely associated with
9. strictly limited 10. lavishly illustrated

II. 1. express 2. heavy 3. strong 4. critical 5. domestic
6. Toxic 7. legitimate 8. empirical 9. recurrent 10. verbal
11. Civil 12. close 13. core 14. severe 15. financial
16. heavy 17. Firm 18. full 19. Careful 20. Blurred

Part E

I.

1. D 2. G 3. B 4. F 5. A 6. C 7. L 8. J 9. I 10. H 11. K 12. E

II.

1. C 2. H 3. E 4. I 5. F 6. B 7. G 8. K 9. J 10. L 11. D 12. A

III.

1. L 2. B 3. G 4. D 5. I 6. H 7. C 8. A 9. K 10. F 11. J 12. E

IV.

1. B 2. G 3. D 4. I 5. C 6. H 7. A 8. F 9. E 10. J

V.

1. G 2. E 3. D 4. J 5. L 6. M 7. B 8. C 9. I 10. H 11. K 12. A 13. F

VI.

1. C 2. H 3. D 4. I 5. B 6. G 7. A 8. F 9. J 10. E

VII.

1. L 2. B 3. K 4. J 5. G 6. C 7. F 8. D 9. E 10. I 11. H 12. A

VIII.

1. G 2. F 3. C 4. A 5. B 6. J 7. E 8. L 9. O 10. D 11. H 12. I 13. K 14. M 15. N

IX.

1. G 2. C 3. I 4. J 5. A 6. F 7. B 8. D 9. E 10. H

X.

1. A 2. K 3. I 4. G 5. F 6. D 7. J 8. E 9. H 10. B 11. L 12. C

XI.

1. G 2. B 3. A 4. F 5. C 6. H 7. D 8. J 9. E 10. I

XII.

1. L 2. B 3. C 4. A 5. H 6. J 7. G 8. K 9. F 10. D 11. I 12. E

Part II

Basic Roots and Words

Theme 1

I. 1. K 2. G 3. J 4. A 5. C 6. I 7. B 8. D 9. E 10. H 11. L 12. F 13. M 14. O 15. N

II. 1. inspire 2. perspire 3. conspired 4. aspired 5. expire 6. respire

III. 1. peddle 2. expedite 3. patriot 4. incorporate 5. immortal 6. pediatrician 7. manuscript 8. expedition 9. manipulate 10. nourish

IV. 1. feminine 2. humble 3. malignant 4. epidemic 5. indigenous 6. populous 7. congenial 8. mortgage 9. republican 10. vitalize

Theme 2−1

I. 1. C 2. F 3. H 4. B 5. G 6. I 7. D 8. A 9. E 10. K 11. J 12. O 13. M 14. N 15. L

II. 1. infected 2. activated 3. agitate 4. detained 5. affection 6. sustain 7. abstained 8. actualize 9. repulsive 10. capture/captured

III. 1. retain 2. enact 3. dismiss 4. replenish 5. habitual 6. propose 7. tenable 8. counteract 9. benefactor 10. facilitate

IV. 1. B 2. D 3. D 4. C 5. A 6. D 7. B 8. B 9. C 10. A

Theme 2−2

II. 1. occur 2. invaded 3. mobilize 4. immigrant 5. fertility 6. indifferent 7. recede 8. belligerent 9. motivate 10. intervene

III. 1. wade 2. automobile 3. extravagant 4. proceed 5. antecedent 6. precedent 7. infer 8. fertile 9. exaggerate 10. locomotive

IV. 1. emigrated 2. immigrated 3. migrate 4. transmigrate 5. egress 6. regress 7. ingress 8. transgress 9. digressed 10. aggress 11. progress 12. congress

Theme 2−3

I. 1. C 2. F 3. H 4. J 5. E 6. I 7. B 8. G 9. A 10. D

II. 1. revolt 2. tendency 3. reversion 4. laundry 5. constitution 6. Intensive 7. diplomat 8. subside 9. duplication 10. explicit

III. 1. anniversary 2. diversify 3. corruption 4. bankruptcy 5. controversial 6. fragile 7. subsequent 8. refuge 9. persecute 10. fragment

IV. 1. A 2. B 3. D 4. A 5. C 6. B 7. C 8. C 9. A 10. B

Theme 2-4

I. 1. C 2. B 3. A 4. I 5. E 6. F 7. D 8. G 9. K 10. H
11. J 12. M 13. L

II. 1. torture 2. paramount 3. probation 4. indispensable 5. escalate
6. contagious 7. casualties 8. distinguished 9. compensate 10. prompt

III. 1. sponsor 2. expenditure 3. correspond 4. suspend 5. stimulate
6. instinct 7. exemplary 8. capture 9. apprehensible 10. coincident

IV. 1. tortured 2. distorted 3. contorted 4. retort 5. extorting

V. 1. intangible 2. dismount 3. misapprehend 4. occident 5. descend

Theme 2-5

I. 1. F 2. K 3. E 4. I 5. C 6. J 7. D 8. H 9. B 10. G 11. A

II. 1. deduce 2. concise 3. intellectual 4. conform 5. fluctuate
6. affluent 7. neglect 8. distribute 9. acquisition 10. diffuse

III. 1. exclusive 2. origin 3. condone 4. pesticide 5. donate
6. questionnaire 7. competence 8. endowment 9. oriental 10. transform

IV. 1. A 2. C 3. A 4. C 5. B 6. C 7. B 8. B 9. A 10. C

Theme 3-1

I. 1. cite 2. audience 3. audio 4. resonate 5. apology
6. contradict 7. recite 8. monotonic 9. vocal (across)
9. vacation (down) 10. linguist 11. infantry 12. infant
13. advocate (across) 13. adore (down)
14. eulogy 15. microphone 16. neology

II. 1. verdict 2. dictating 3. edict 4. contradiction 5. predicting
6. contradictory 7. predictable 8. abdicated 9. jurisdiction 10. indicted

III. 1. eulogy 2. neologism 3. eulogistic 4. eulogizing 5. interlocution
6. obloquy 7. analogy 8. epilogue 9. catalogue 10. monologue
11. loquacious 12. elocution 13. prologue 14. eloquence 15. colloquial

IV. 1. B 2. A 3. C 4. D 5. A 6. B 7. C 8. D

Theme 3-2

I. 1. G 2. J 3. F 4. L 5. D 6. A 7. C 8. I 9. H 10. E 11. K 12. B

II. 1. conspicuous 2. verbal 3. respective 4. optional 5. Legendary
6. improvise 7. notified 8. scribble 9. testimony 10. spectacular

III. 1. bibliography 2. monograph 3. phonograph 4. calligraphy
5. autography 6. biography 7. epigram 8. polygraph

IV. 1. describe 2. inscribed 3. postscript 4. subscribe 5. prescribed
6. retrospect 7. prospects 8. inspected 9. introspect 10. despise
11. circumspect 12. respect 13. expecting 14. speculate 15. suspect (ed)

V. 1. C 2. A 3. D 4. D 5. B 6. D 7. B

Theme 4

I. 1. F 2. G 3. A 4. H 5. E 6. I 7. C 8. B 9. J 10. D

II. 1. deter 2. timid 3. deride 4. dole 5. amateur
6. explode 7. enamor 8. amiable 9. horizon 10. neophilia
11. implore (across) 11. intimidate (down) 12. philanthropy
13. adhor 14. complaint 15. tremble 16. amorist 17. grace
18. phobia 19. gratitude

III. 1. disgrace 2. rejoice 3. amateur 4. agreeable 5. plausible
6. condole 7. terrific 8. reverence 9. plaintive 10. derision
11. indolence 12. exhilarated

IV. 1. B 2. D 3. A 4. C 5. C 6. B

Theme 5

I. 1. D 2. B 3. E 4. F 5. G 6. C 7. A 8. H 9. I 10. J

II. 1. reassure 2. fidelity 3. mirage 4. sentimental 5. commemorate
6. diagnose 7. certificate 8. confederate 9. conscience 10. amnesia

III. 1. mentor 2. commentary 3. discredit 4. psychology 5. philosopher
6. sympathy 7. sophomore 8. pathetic 9. prosperous 10. confidential

IV. 1. impute 2. compute 3. dispute 4. repute 5. deputed/deputes
6. sensitive 7. sensual 8. sensational 9. sensible 10. sentimental

Theme 6

I. Group 1
1. E 2. H 3. A 4. F 5. G 6. C 7. I 8. J 9. D 10. B
Group 2
1. D 2. B 3. E 4. A 5. C
Group 3
1. C 2. D 3. A 4. E 5. B

II. 1. desolate 2. sole 3. candid 4. lunatic 5. coeval
6. lucent 7. illustrious 8. luxuriant 9. deluxe 10. opaque

III. 1. synchronize 2. solicit 3. dehydrated 4. temporized
5. isolated 6. flagrant 7. inflame 8. adjourned
9. illustrate 10. console

IV. 1. B 2. D 3. A 4. C 5. B

Theme 7

1. H 2. G 3. J 4. A 5. F 6. E 7. D 8. I 9. C 10. B

II. 1. embellish 2. armistice 3. potent 4. military 5. combat
6. sociable 7. gregarious 8. conjunction 9. stringent 10. indemnity

III. 1. obligates 2. inherit 3. abate 4. revenge 5. infesting
6. inflict 7. conflicts 8. annexed 9. adhere 10. fixated
11. marred 12. convict 13. vanquish 14. impugn 15. offend

IV. 1. strain 2. constrained 3. distrain 4. restrain 5. constricted
6. discerned 7. decree 8. concerned 9. discreet 10. discretion

V. 1. C 2. D 3. B 4. C 5. D

Theme 8

I. 1. G 2. F 3. H 4. C 5. A 6. E 7. B 8. D

II. 1. repent 2. lax 3. penal 4. legist 5. legal
6. regime (across) 6. resolve (down) 7. mandatory 8. unjust
9. monarch 10. jury 11. dominate 12. privilege 13. predominant
14. equivalent 15. archaic 16. dome 17. penitent 18. archetype
19. prejudice 20. perjury 21. autocrat

III. 1. salvage 2. impair 3. legislate 4. alleged 5. absolves/absolved
6. dominate 7. disparage 8. coordinate 9. liberate 10. paralyzed

IV. 1. prejudice 2. reign 3. legalize 4. subordinate 5. unequalled
6. justify 7. appease 8. irresolute 9. domestic 10. judicious

Part III

Vocabulary in Context

Topic 1: Weather

I. 1. drizzle—downpour, gale—breeze, damp—dry, overcast—sunny, scorching—freezing

II. 1. heavy 2. fast 3. high 4. long 5. low

III. Possible answers:

1. smog 2. stifling 3. Hurricane 4. snow 5. torrential
6. humid 7. drizzling 8. showers 9. floods 10. gale

IV. 1. bad: too dry, a drought, or frost; good: mild weather just after rain

2. bad: cold weather or windy weather or wet weather; good: warm, mild, or even cool (if it has been a terribly hot day) and preferably dry

3. bad: gales, high winds, hurricanes, storms, wet weather, mist/fog; good: clear, sunny dry, breezy weather

4. bad: cold, wet and windy weather or humid, muggy weather; good: fine, dry, but not too hot

5. bad: wet, windy, snowy weather; good: dry, no wind, warm nights

6. bad: fog, mist, rain; good: clear, dry, sunny weather

V. Passage A: 1. B 2. C 3. C

Passage B: 1. It's to provide information for weather forecasts and to study the weather and climate.

2. No.

3. At least once daily.

Passage C: 1. Storms could lead to negative impacts to lives and properties, such as storm surge, heavy rain or snow, lightning, wildfires, and vertical wind shear.

2. Storms could alleviate natural disasters such as drought or allow special recreational activities.

Topic 2: Health

I. Open for discussion.

II. 1. E 2. D 3. F 4. C 5. A 6. B

III. 1. For measuring temperature. 2. For injection.

3. For anesthetizing people (使人认识模糊). 4. For doing operations.

IV. Open for discussion.

V. Passage A: organism 有机体; infectious disease 传染性疾病; autoimmune diseases 自身免疫性疾病; dysfunction 机能障碍; deficiency diseases 营养缺乏性疾病; hereditary diseases 遗传性疾病

Passage B: 1. D 2. D 3. D

Passage C: 1. B 2. A 3. D

Topic 3: Character

I. 1. F 2. A 3. C 4. E 5. B 6. D

II. 1. likes 2. likes 3. likes 4. dislikes 5. dislikes

6. dislikes 7. dislikes 8. likes

III. 1. Wang's very stingy.
2. Lisa's usually brusque.
3. Andy's quite unprincipled.
4. Sam can be assertive.
5. Mark's quite assertive.
6. I find Kate self-assured.
7. Don't you think Tim's inquiring?
8. Jimmy is peculiar.

IV. Open for discussion.

V. Open for discussion.

VI. Passage A: 1. T 2. T 3. F

Passage B: 1. The answer may vary.

2. Type A: calm, composed, very level-headed and serious.

Type B: curious about and interested in everything.

Type O: peaceful, carefree. On the one hand, stubborn and strong-willed. On the other hand, flexible and adaptable.

Type AB: delicate, sensitive, strict.

3. The person with Type O Blood.

Topic 4: Crime

I.

Crime	Criminal	Verb	Definition
shoplifting	shoplifter	shoplift	stealing something from a shop
blackmail	blackmailer	blackmail	threatening to make a dark secret public in order to get money
drug-trafficking	drug-trafficker	traffic in drugs, to peddle drugs, to deal in drugs	buying and selling drugs
assault	attacker assailant	assault	physical attack on another person
pickpocketing	pickpocket	pickpocket	stealing from someone's pocket or handbag

II.（1）accused；（2）lawyer；（3）jury；（4）judge；（5）was acquitted

III. Type：offence against the person，sexual offence，violent offence，offence against property

Seriousness of the offence：felony or misdemeanour（轻罪，小罪），treason（叛国罪）

Mode of trial：indictable（可起诉的）offence，indictable-only offence，hybrid offence，summary offence（无须履行正常法律程序的轻微的罪行）

IV. Criminal：suspect，outlaw，ex-convict，accessory，principal

Crime：rape，sexual harassment，blackmail，robbery，fraud

V. Passage A：1. Opposing.　2. Witnesses.　3. The judge.

Passage B：1&2 Open for discussion.

3. Traffic cases.

Topic 5：At home

I. Kitchen：tea towel，coffee machine，food processor，kettle，microwave

Study room：notepad，filing cabinet，printer，wastepaper basket，paper clip

II. 1. attic or loft；in this picture it looks more like a loft，where things are stored.

2. landing　3. the hall　4. utility room　5. pantry or larder

Topic 6：Money

II. Open for discussion.

III. Passage A：1. Money is a medium of exchange，a unit of account and a store of value.

2. 法定货币或不兑现货币。

3. Bank money.

Passage B：1. 活期存款，即随时可提取的存款。

2. Commercial bank money is non-physical and risky.

3. The total amount of currency in circulation，checking and savings.

Passage C：1. C　2. C　3. C

Topic 7：Arts

I. 1. Movie　2. Sculpture　3. Dance　4. A play/stage performance

5. Painting　6. Drama texts/plays in written form

7. Architecture　8. Novel/book　9. Poetry

II. Open for discussion.

III. 1. "I wandered lonely as a cloud" is my favorite **line** of English poetry.

2. What's the name of the **publisher** of that book you recommended?

3. Most of the **stories** in this collection are only five or six pages long.

4. He's a very famous **sculptor**.

5. The **sets** are excellent in that new production of *Macbeth*，so dark and mysterious.

6. There's an **exhibition** of ceramics at the museum next week.

7. **What's on** at the Opera House next week?

IV. Passage A：1. B　2. D　3. C

Topic 8：Education

I. Open for discussion.

II. (1) preschool (2) Primary (3) secondary (4) Higher education
(5) secondary

III. Students: freshman, sophomore, junior, repeater, graduate, undergraduate, senior
Academic affairs management: credit, syllabus, term paper, grade, GPA, curriculum, diploma
Educational institution: college, university, school

IV. Passage A: 1. Around six 2. No. 3. By giving scholarships and financial aids.
Passage B: 1. Letter grades.
2. GPA, grade point average, is a number that represents the average of a student's grades.
3. 2. 33

Topic 9: Sports

I. 1. Baseball. 2. Golf. 3. Tennis, badminton, etc. 4. Basketball. 5. Football.

II. Open for discussion. Please look at the following picture for reference.

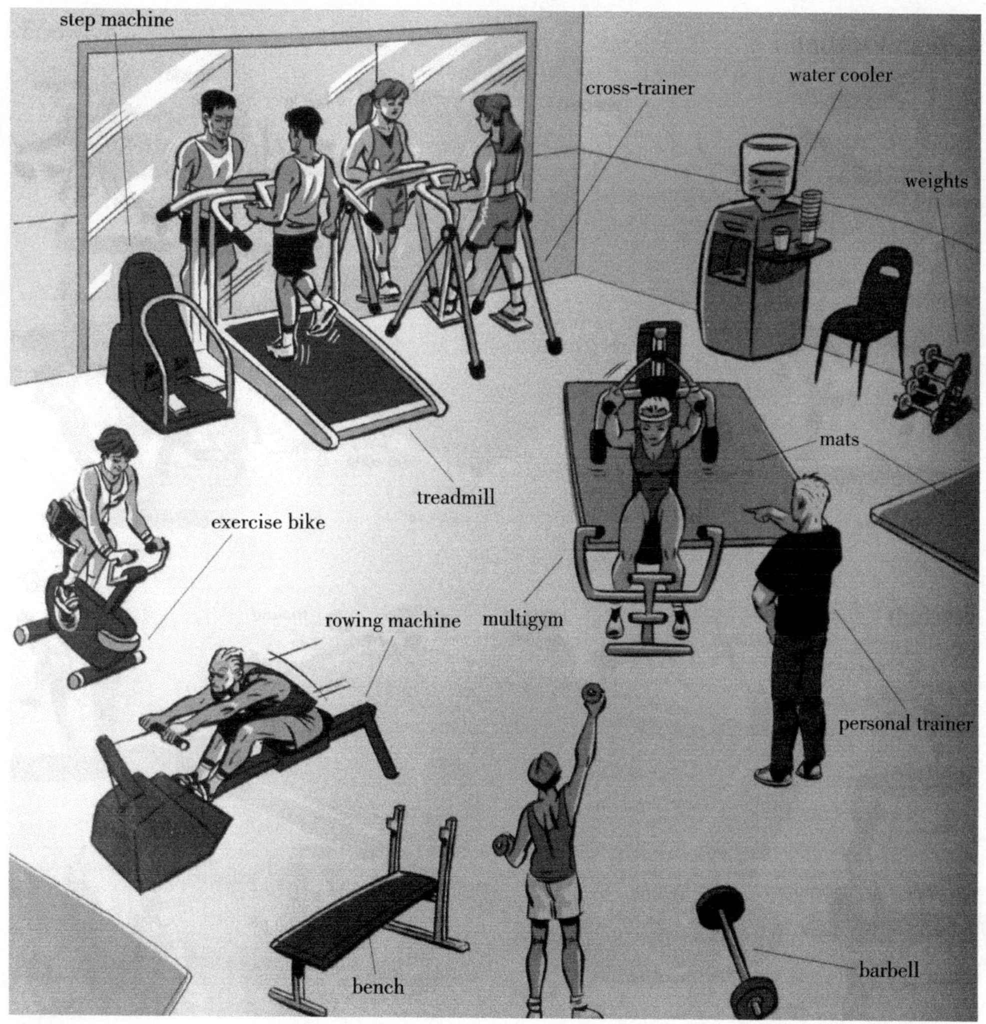

From *Macmillan English Dictionary*

III. 1. Tennis, squash, etc. 2. Golf or horse-racing. 3. Usually boxing or wrestling.
4. Used for football, rugby and cricket. 5. Ice-skating.
6. Ten-pin bowling or skittles. 7. A track where you ski.

Appendixes

Appendix One

Indo-European Language Family

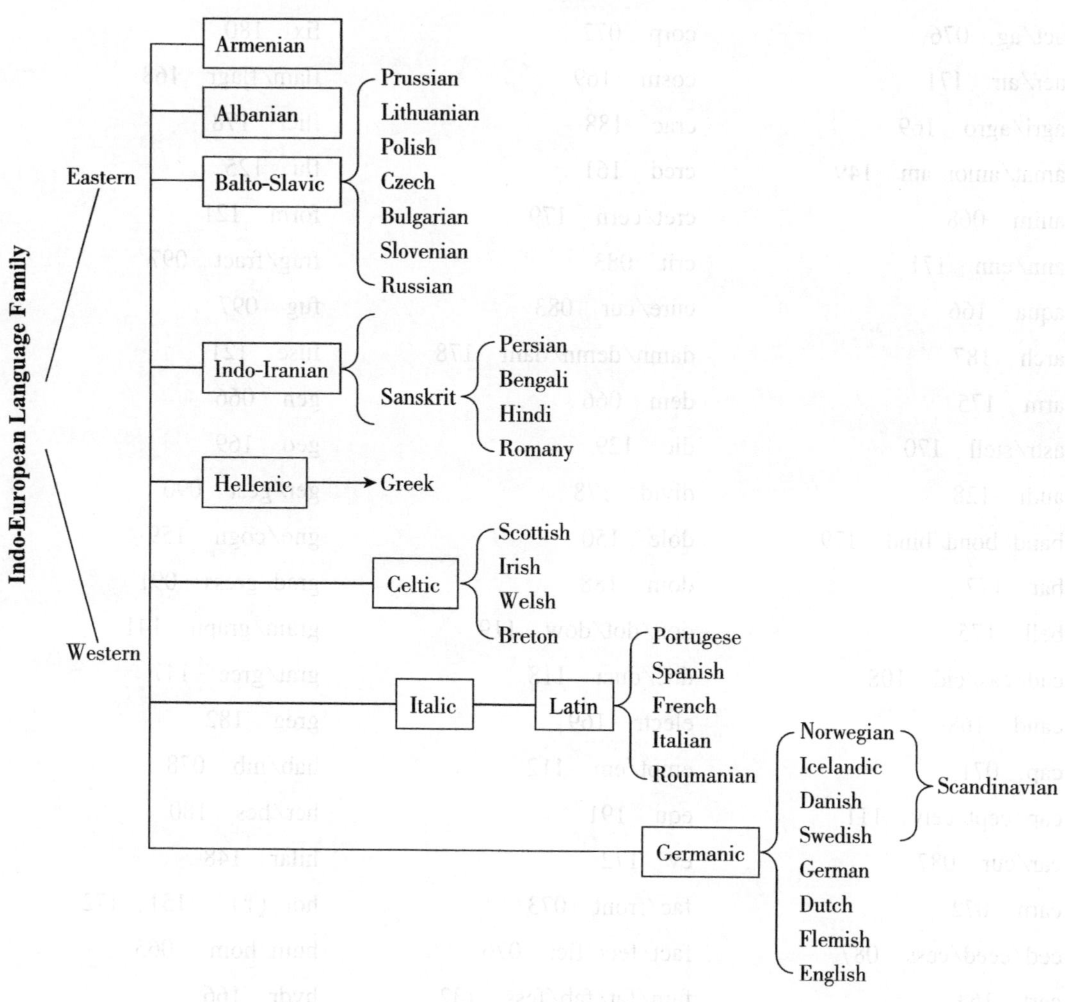

Appendix Two

Index of Roots

Appendix Three
List of Common Prefixes

Prefix	Meaning	Example
a-, ac-, ad-, af-, ag-, al-, an-, ap-, as-, at-	to, toward, near, in addition to, by	aside, accompany, adjust, affix, aggression, allocate, annotate, appoint, associate, attend
a-, an-	not, without	apolitical, anarchy, apathy, anonymous, anoxia
ab-, abs-	away from, off	abrupt, absent, abstain, abstract
ambi-, amphi-	both	ambiguous, amphibian (两栖动物)
ante-	before	anteroom (前厅), antebellum (战前的), antedate, antecedent, antique
anti-, ant-	against, opposite	antisocial, antibiotic, antibody (抗体), antithesis (对偶), antipathy (反感), antonym
auto-	self	automobile, autobiography, automotive, autograph
be-	make, cause	befriend, belittle, beware
bene-	good, well, gentle	benefit, beneficial, benevolent, benediction, benefactor
bi-	two	bilateral, bilingual, biped (两足动物), biweekly
cata-, cat-	down, by, completely	catastrophe, catalogue, category, catholic
cent-	hundred	centennial, century, centigrade
circum-	around	circumstance, circumference (圆周), circumspect (慎重), circumscribe (设定界限)
com-, con-, co-, col-, cor-	with, together, fully	compel, contemporary, coincide, collaborate, correlate
contra-, contro-, counter-	against, opposite	contradict, contrary, controversial, counteract, counterclockwise
de-	from, down, away, to do the opposite	decrease, detract, deodorize, deflate

Continued

Prefix	Meaning	Example
deca-, dec-,	ten, ten times	decade, decimal（十进制的）, decathlon（十项全能运动）
di-	two, twice, double	dilemma, dioxide
dia-	through, across, between	diameter, diagonal（对角线）, dialogue, diagnosis, diachronic
dis-, di-, dif-	not; apart, away	disallow, dishonesty, disconnect, dispel, disrupt, divert, digression, differ, diffuse（扩散）
dys-	bad, abnormal, impaired, unfavorable	dysfunctional, dyslexia（阅读障碍）
ex-, e-, ec-, ef-	out of	extract, excavate, emit, eject, eccentric, efface（擦掉）
en-, em-	put into, make, provide with, surround with	enslave, enchant, empower, embody
epi-	upon, close to, over, after	epicenter（震中）, epilogue（后记）
extra-, exter-, extro-	outside of, beyond	extraordinary, extraneous, extravagant, external, extrinsic, extrovert
fore-	before	forecast, foresee
hetero-	other, different	heterogeneous（不同种类的）, heterosexual
hex-, sex-	six	hexagon, hexameter（六步格的诗）, sextet（六重唱曲）, sextuplets（六胎）
homo-	same	homogeneous, homosexual, homophone（同音异义词）
hyper-	over, above, excessive	hyperactive, hypersensitive, hypercritical（吹毛求疵的）
hypo-	under, less	hypodermic（皮下的）, hypothesis
in-, im-, il-, ir-, i-	in, on, towards; not	induce, import; inhumane, imbalance, illegible, irresistible, ignore
infra-	beneath	infrared（红外线）, infrastructure
inter-, intel-	between, among	international, intercept（拦截）, interrupt, intellectual
intra-	within, during, between layers, underneath	intrastate（州内的）, intranet
intro-	into, within, inward	introvert, introspection, introduce

Continued

Prefix	Meaning	Example
mal-, male-, mali-	ill, bad	malnutrition, malevolent (恶意的), malediction (诅咒), malignant (恶性的)
mega-	great; million	megaphone (扩音器), megastar; megabyte, megawatt
meta-	beyond, change	metaphor, metabolism
micro-	small	microscope, microfilm, microwave, micrometer (千分尺)
mill-, milli-,	thousand, thousandth	millennium, millipede (千足虫), millisecond, milligram
mini-	little, small	miniature, miniskirt
mis-	wrong, bad, badly	misconduct, misinform, misinterpret, mispronounce
mono-	one	monopoly, monograph (专著), monologue (独白), monorail
multi-	many, much	multifold, multilingual, multiped, multipurpose, multinational
neo-	new	Neolithic (新石器时代的), neologism (新词), neonatal (新生儿的)
non-	not	nonsense, nondescript (不可名状的)
ob-, oc-, of-, op-	against; toward, in the way	obstruct, offensive, oppose; obtain, occur, offer
octo-, oct-	eight	octopus, octagon (八角形), octave (八度)
omni-	all, every	omnipotent, omniscient (博识的), omnipresent, omnivorous (杂食的)
over-	above, across; excessive	overhead, overland, overweight, overpopulation
paleo-	old	paleolithic (旧石器时代的), paleobiology (古生物学) paleography (古文书学)
pan-	all	pan-American, panacea (万能药), panorama (全景)
para-	beside; beyond	paradox (悖论), parasite (寄生物), parallel, paranormal
per-	through, intensive	permit, perspire, perspective
peri-	around	periscope (潜望镜), perimeter (周长), peripheral (周围的)

Continued

Prefix	Meaning	Example
poly-	many	polytheist（多神论），polygon（多边形），polyglot（通晓多语言的人）
post-	after，behind	postpone，postscript（后记）
pre-	before	precede，precaution，prescribe
pro-	forward，for	propose，propel，provoke
proto-	first	prototype，protocol（协议），protagonist（主人公）
psych-	mind，soul	psychology，psyche（灵魂），psychiatrist（精神科医生）
quadr-，quart-	four	quadrangle（四边形），quadruplets（四胞胎），quartet（四重奏）
quint-，penta-	five	quintuplets（五胞胎），quintet（五重奏），pentagon，pentameter（五步格诗）
re-	back，again	recede，revoke，revise，renovate
retro-	backwards	retrospect，retrogression（后退）
se-	apart，move away from	secede（脱离），seclude（使隔离）
semi-	half，partial	semifinal，semiconscious，semiannual，semicircle
sept-，hept-	seven	septet（七重奏），septennial（七年一次的）heptathlon
sub-，suc-，suf-，sup-，sus-	under，below，secondary，instead of	submarine，substandard，succeed，suffocate，heptathlon，suppress，sustain
super-，supr-，sur-	over，above	supersede（取而代之），superscript（上标），supernatural，survive，surmount（越过）
syn-，sym-	together，at the same time	synchronous，synthesis，sympathy，symmetry
tele-	distance，far，from afar	telephone，telegraph，telegram，telescope，television，telepathy（心灵感应）
trans-	across，beyond，change	transform，transoceanic，transmit，transportation
tri-	three	tripod，triangle，trinity，trilateral
un-	not，against，opposite	unceasing，unequal
uni-	one	uniform，unilateral，unity，unanimous（一致的），unite，unicorn

Appendix Four

List of Common Suffixes

Suffix	Meaning	Example
-able, -ible	Adjective: capable or worthy of	solvable, incredible, edible, invincible
-ade	Noun: act, product, sweet drink	blockade, cannonade, arcade, lemonade
-age	Noun: condition, act or result	storage, marriage, pupilage, breakage
-al	Noun: action, result of action	criminal, denial, disposal, trial
-al, -ial	Adjective: quality, relation	herbal, territorial, beneficial, colonial
-an, -ian	Noun: person	artisan, Arabian, pedestrian, comedian
-ance, -ence	Noun: action, state, quality or process	endurance, tolerance, obedience, diligence
-ancy, -ency	Noun: state, quality or capacity	vacancy, redundancy, agency, frequency
-ant, -ent	Noun: an agent, something that performs the action	applicant, occupant, component, resident
-ant, -ent, -ient	Adjective: having the quality of	dominant, prevalent, convenient, obedient
-ar,	Adjective: resembling, related to	spectacular, polar, solar, rectangular
-ary, -ory	Adjective: relating to	legendary, arbitrary, sedentary, mandatory
-ate	Noun: a group of people with particular duties; the job, rank, or degree of a particular type of person	candidate, electorate, delegate, graduate
-ate	Verb: cause to be	complicate, differentiate, formulate, mediate
-ate	Adjective: full of or with a particular quality	considerate, moderate, innate, legitimate
-cy	Noun: state or quality	democracy, infancy, intimacy, accuracy
-dom	Noun: place or state of being	stardom, boredom, wisdom, martyrdom
-ed	Adjective: having the quality or characteristics of	winged, aged, dogged, ashamed

Continued

Suffix	Meaning	Example
-ee	Noun: recipient of an action	employee, trainee, examinee, refugee
-eer	Noun: person that does something	engineer, pioneer, mountaineer, volunteer
-el	Noun: person or thing that does something	personnel, colonel, funnel, hostel
-en	Verb: to cause to become	fasten, moisten, sharpen, thicken
-en	Adjective: made of; material	golden, woolen, silken, waxen
-er, -or	Noun: person or thing that does something	flyer, fryer, collaborator, inventor
-ery, -ry	Noun: quality, act, practice, trade, collection, state, condition	snobbery, bakery, gallery, machinery
-esque, -ique	Adjective: in a manner of or resembling	antique, picturesque, unique
-ess	Noun: female	actress, goddess, princess
-etic	Adjective: having the quality or characteristics of	theoretic, sympathetic, genetic, energetic
-fold	Adjective/Adverb: of a particular number	fourfold, tenfold, manifold
-ful	Noun: an amount or quantity that fills	handful, mouthful, armful, spoonful
-ful	Adjective: having, giving, marked by	fanciful, shameful, grateful
-fy, -ify	Verb: make, form into	falsify, identify, magnify, justify
-hood	Noun: relation, state or condition of being	neighborhood, brotherhood, bachelorhood, likelihood
-ia	Noun: name; disease; territory, country	academia, utopia, phobia, insomnia, Australia
-ic, -ical	Adjective: quality, relation	cosmic, chaotic, psychological, methodical
-ic, -ics	Noun: related to the arts and sciences	arithmetic, critic, athletics, economics
-ice	Noun: action, condition	prejudice, malice, novice, cowardice
-id	Adjective: belonging to, connected with	humid, florid, fluid, invalid
-ile	Adjective: having the qualities of (relating to, or capable of)	mobile, fragile, hostile, juvenile
-ine	Adjective: like, relating to quality	genuine, divine, feminine, masculine
-ine	Noun: something or somebody	cuisine, doctrine, nicotine, heroine
-ing	Noun: material made for, activity, result of an activity	clothing, accounting, filling, footing

Continued

Suffix	Meaning	Example
-ing	Adjective: causing	fascinating, underlying, agonizing
-ior	Adjective: comparative	interior, senior, superior, inferior
-ise, -ize	Verb: become	advertise, criticise, sympathize, jeopardize
-ish	Adjective: having the character of	childish, reddish, snobbish, sluggish
-ism	Noun: doctrine, belief, action or conduct	optimism, modernism, plagiarism
-ist	Noun: person or member	communist, feminist, sexist, botanist
-itude	Noun: state or quality	longitude, latitude, solitude, magnitude
-ity, -ty	Noun: state or quality	loyalty, novelty, equality, absurdity
-ive	Noun: someone or something that does something or can do something	native, detective, fugitive, representative
-ive, -ative, -itive	Adjective: having the quality of	abusive, cooperative, sensitive, pervasive
-less	Adjective: without, missing	motiveless, flawless, boundless, effortless
-let	Noun: small	booklet, streamlet, piglet, starlet
-ling	Noun: small, connected with	duckling, gosling, seedling, sapling
-logy	Noun: study of	biology, geology, archaeology, etymology
-ly	Adverb: related to or having quality	oddly, definitely, exceedingly, gloriously
-ly	Adjective: related to or having quality	elderly, timely, costly worldly
-ment	Noun: condition, result, something	argument, enchantment, commencement, pavement
-ness	Noun: state, condition, quality	goodness, emptiness, progressiveness, promptness
-nomy, -onomy	Noun: study of (A system of laws governing or a body of knowledge about a specified field)	economy, astronomy, taxonomy
-oon	Noun: thing, person	balloon, saloon, bassoon, tycoon
-ory	Noun: place for	factory, dormitory, observatory, territory
-ous, -eous, -ious	Adjective: having the quality of, relating to	adventurous, courteous, tedious
-ship	Noun: status, condition	hardship, internship, partnership, dictatorship

Continued

Suffix	Meaning	Example
-sion, -tion	Noun: state of being	aggression, comprehension, promotion, inflation
-ster	Noun: person	mobster, monster, youngster, gangster
-th	Noun: action, state, quality	birth, truth, stealth, filth
-ure	Noun: act, condition, process, function	exposure, failure, expenditure, sculpture
-ward, -wards	Adjective/ Adverb: in a direction or manner of	homeward, inward, afterwards, backwards
-wise	Adverb: in the manner of, with regard to	likewise, clockwise, coastwise, otherwise
-y	Noun: state, condition, result of an activity; action or process of	jealousy, victory, delivery, discovery, inquiry
-y	Adjective: marked by, having the quality of	handy, homey, tardy, bumpy, icy

References

[1] Jackson, Howard. Words and Their Meaning [M]. London: Longman, 1988.

[2] Jespersen, Otto. Growth and Structure of the English Language [M]. 9th ed. Garden City: Doubleday & Company, Inc., 1948.

[3] Joos, Martin. The Five Clocks [M]. The Hague: Mouton, 1962.

[4] Michael, M. & Felicity, O. English Vocabulary in Use [M]. Cambridge: Cambridge University Press, 2001.

[5] Michael, R. Macmilian English Dictionary [M]. London: Macmillan Publishers Limited, 2002.

[6] Nida, Eugene A. Language, Culture, and Translation [M]. Shanghai: Shanghai Foreign Language Education Press, 1993.

[7] Webster's Third New International Dictionary of the American Language [M]. 2nd ed. William Collins Publishers, Inc., 1980.

[8] Wikipedia [EB/OL]. [2013-05-06]. http://en. wikipedia. org/wiki/Education.

[9] 方振宇. 英语词汇的奥秘 [M]. 北京：海豚出版社，2011.

[10] 金正基. 英语词根词典 [M]. 李先汉，南燕，译. 北京：群言出版社，2009.

[11] [美] 刘易斯（Lewis, Norman). 英语词汇纵横谈 [M]. 张嘤嘤，译. 北京：清华大学出版社，1998.

[12] [美] 尼斯特（Nist, S. L.)，[美] 莫尔（Mohr, C.). 英语词汇扩展 [M]. 上海：上海外语教育出版社，2005.

[13] 徐西坤，王鑫. 新说文解字——细说英语词根词源 [M]. 北京：中国水利水电出版社，2011.

[14] 杨信彰. 英语词汇学教程 [M]. 北京：高等教育出版社，2009.

[15] 张维友. 英语词汇学 [M]. 北京：外语教学与研究出版社，1999.

[16] 张维友. 英语词汇学教程 [M]. 武汉：华中师范大学出版社，2004.